Not Without My Sister

Not Without My Sister

Celeste Jones, Kristina Jones,
and Juliana Buhring

HARPER
element

HarperElement
An Imprint of HarperCollins*Publishers*
77–85 Fulham Palace Road,
Hammersmith, London W6 8JB

and *HarperElement* are trademarks of
HarperCollins*Publishers* Ltd

ISBN-13 978-0-00-724807-0
ISBN-10 0-00-724807-5

Printed in the U.S.A.

To our sister, Davida

To my sister in sorrow:
Too well did I understand
The look in your haunted eyes;
Pain and disillusionment.
You fought a losing battle,
And lost.
And died.
I will shed for you the tears
Of a lifetime you will never live.
The tears you will never more shed.
Madonna of suffering,
Wrapped in the cold shroud of death.
I wept with you.
I weep for you.
For I still can.
The tide of tears has turned.
Sleep, my sister,
And weep no more.

(Written on Davida's tombstone, Juliana 2005)

Lies written in ink cannot disguise
facts written in blood.
– Lu Xun (1881–1936)

prologue

In January 2005, our sister Davida died from a drug over-
dose. She was twenty-three. The shock of Davida's death
affected us deeply though we understood her pain and
despair. Each of us in our own way has struggled with painful
memories of abandonment, neglect, and abuse as children
born and raised under the malign influence of a religious cult,
the Children of God.

We were systematically abused, physically, mentally, emotionally, and sexually, from the earliest age. We were separated
from each other and our parents and raised communally in this
organization, which was also known as the "Family."

Unlike our parents who had burned their bridges and
left their former lives, we were never given a choice over the
paths our lives would follow. Isolated from society, we were
controlled by fear—fear of the government, police, doctors,
and social workers, and the even greater fear of God's wrath
if we ever left the protection of the Family.

Our childhood was dominated by one man: David
Berg—a man we never met, but who was like an invisible

ghost that was with us at all times. He was the warped and manipulative force behind the Children of God. David Berg liked to see himself as a benevolent parental figure, and called us, his followers, the "Children of David." He saw himself as the successor of King David and the Prophet Moses—calling himself Moses David, or Mo for short. The children were taught to call him "Grandpa." He was the head of our family, the prophet, the leader, our "light in the midst of darkness." The rules we followed were dictated by his words. We read about every detail of his life, his dreams, his likes and dislikes, and the women he slept with and the children he abused. From a very young age we memorized his words and hours of every day were dedicated to studying his writings, called Mo Letters. "Word Time"—which was the time spent reading these letters and studying the Bible—was an important part of daily life. It would be difficult if not impossible to write about our life without acknowledging the dominating influence of David Berg on our lives.

From birth, we were conditioned to obey and follow the way of the cult. We had no choice, and knew no other way. We never heard our father express an opinion that was his own; it was always, "Grandpa said..." If we were punished it was because we had disobeyed Mo's rules; if we were rewarded it was because we were "faithful followers." Our father's devotion to Berg and faith in his prophecies and predictions was unwavering. If he questioned if any of it was real, or if it was a chimera—smoke and mirrors—he never showed it, not even behind closed doors.

Berg taught that birth control was rebellion against God, so within a few years there were thousands of children born into the group. He boasted that we were the "hope of the future"—a pure second generation untainted by the outside world. We were told it was the highest privilege to be born and raised in the Family, free from the shackles of the "System," as the outside world was called. It was our destiny to become God's Endtime soldiers, and to give our lives for the cause. Berg predicted the world would end in 1993, and we would become the leaders of the New Millennium. As our lives on earth would be short, we were never allowed to just be children. Our individuality was suppressed, and we were simply commodities used to further the collective goals of the group.

The belief that damaged us the most was Berg's "Law of Love." God was love, and love equaled sex. Sharing your body with someone else was considered the highest expression of love. Age was not a barrier in Berg's Law of Love and Family children were made to participate in his warped, pedophilic philosophy. His own children and grandchildren suffered from his incestuous predilections.

In this book we describe the emotional journey we undertook from our earliest years, through to our teens when we secretly, then more openly questioned it—and finally, when we struggled to break free, like butterflies caught in a spider's sticky web. This is a story of darkness and light, of imprisonment of the soul, of redemption and freedom. We survived—many didn't. Thousands of the Family's second generation have had to deal with the devastating consequences of their parents' blind faith in a leader who claimed he was the voice of God on earth. Those who have bravely spoken out about their suffering have been vilifiedslandered by their former abusers. Our hope is that in telling our story, you will hear the voices of the children they tried to silence.

Celeste Jones, Kristina Jones, Juliana Buhring
England 2007

Introduction

The Children of God started in Southern California in the late 1960s, among the hippiesdropouts of Huntington Beach. The founder, David Berg, was born in 1919, in Oakland, California. His mother, Virginia Lee Brandt Berg, was a celebrated evangelist with the Christian Missionary Alliance. In 1944 Berg married Jane Miller, a young Baptist youth worker. After the birth of their second child, Berg became the pastor of a Christian Missionary Alliance Church in Arizona. However, after only three years he was expelled, reputedly for a sex scandal. His expulsion began his life-long bitterness and disillusionment with organized religion.

In December 1967, Berg moved his family—his wife Jane (later known as Mother Eve) and their four children, Deborah, Faithy, Aaron and Hosea—to Huntington Beach, California, where they stayed with his eighty-year-old mother. She had started a small ministry from a coffee shop called the Light Club, distributing sandwiches to the hippies, surfers, and dropouts who congregated on the pier. But when the Light Club's clean-cut image failed to attract the longhaired hippies,

Mrs. Berg saw the opportunity for her son and grandchildren to minister to the youngsters with the music and fervour of their own generation. In a short time, David Berg and his family began attracting the youth in droves with the free food and anti-system, anti-war message they endorsed.

The group traveled across the United States gathering more young disciples as they went, and soon opened communities across the country. They attracted a substantial amount of media coverage, and in some articles the writers referred to them as the "Children of God," a name that the fledgling group subsequently adopted.

After a string of illicit affairs with some of his young female members, Berg found a devoted companion in his young and ambitious secretary, Karen Zerby, aka "Maria." Publicly branding his estranged wife Jane and late mother the "Old Church," Berg endorsed Maria and the Children of God as the "New Church," and himself the last prophet of the Endtime. He also started using the pseudonym "Moses David," identifying himself with King David of the Bible and the prophet Moses, who had led the Children of Israel out of captivity in Egypt (the "System") to the Promised Land. Berg decided to start a royal dynasty. His series of residences were designated "The King's House" and he crowned himself and Maria, the King and the Queen.

For many years a council of ministers ran the cult, mostly members of Berg's extended family, referred to as the Royal Family. He expected Family members to obey him and the other leaders without question. The only contact between Berg and his members came through his many writings, detailing policies, beliefs, and instruction on how the communes were to be run, as well as prophecies and revelations he claimed proceeded directly from God.

In the early 1970s, the Children of God fell under the close scrutiny of the media and law-enforcement agencies, as parents of recruited children witnessed complete personality changes in their offspring after they joined the cult. More worrying was the fact that all contact between them was severed, some of their children disappearing in the night not to be seen again for years.

Evading negative publicity and a court summons, Berg fled to Europe, advising his followers to get out of America. The group left the USA in 1972 in a mass exodus to evangelize and recruit in other countries, beginning with Europe. Berg and Maria arrived in England in 1972.

Increasingly paranoid for his personal safety, he gradually withdrew from his followers, keeping his whereabouts secret. While in seclusion, Berg and Maria experimented with a new controversial method of using sex to win converts and supporters, infamously known as "Flirty Fishing." Berg gradually introduced the idea of Flirty Fishing to his members through a series of letters documenting their own encounters. He also promulgated a new revelation called the "Law of Love." Berg told his followers that the Ten Commandments were now obsolete. Everything done in love (including sex) was sanctioned in the eyes of God. Adultery, incest, extramarital, and adult–child sex were no longer sins, as long as they were done "in love." He demanded loyalty to his radical message of the Law of Love and Flirty Fishing and every member was required to actively put them into practice or leave. Consequently, two-thirds of the group left, marking the end of the Children of God era and the beginning of the Family of Love.

In 1979 Berg wrote a letter called "My Childhood Sex" in which he revealed that a nanny had performed oral sex on him as a young toddler, which he said he had enjoyed. He said that it was normal, natural, and healthy and that there was nothing wrong with it, which gave anyone so inclined carte blanche to follow suit. In the following years other Mo Letters and Family publications reinforced the idea that children should be allowed to enjoy sexual contact among themselves as well as with adults—and many adults in the Family embraced and carried out these suggestions.

*   *   *

Christopher Jones was born in December 1951 in a town near Hamelin, Germany, to Glen, a British military officer and Krystyna, a young Polish woman he had met while stationed in Palestine. He was educated at a public school in Cheltenham, and studied drama at Rose Bruford College. He dropped out after the second year and joined the Children of God in 1973. He has fathered fifteen children, including Celeste, Kristina and Juliana, by seven different women and remains a member of the cult.

Rebecca Jones was born in March 1957 and had a secure middle-class upbringing in the south of England. Her father, Bill, was a civil engineer and her mother, Margaret, a devoted housewife. Her parents were not religious, but they sent her to the local Sunday school at the age of five. She became a

Sunday-school teacher when she was twelve and two years later she was baptized. Rebecca was recruited from her school by the Children of God at the young age of sixteen, and met and married our father in 1974. They had three children together, including Celeste and Kristina, before they were separated. Rebecca left the cult in 1987.

Serena Buhring was born near Hanover, Germany in October 1956. Her father was an architect and her mother an accomplished musician, playing the piano, violin, and the cello. Serena traveled as a hippie in India where she joined the Children of God. She met our father after he separated from Rebecca and had three children by him, including Juliana. Serena is still an associate member of the cult.

Part One

Celeste's Story

CHAPTER ONE

Daddy's Little Girl

I was playing alone in the front garden of a white house near the small fishing village of Rafina, in Greece. Our garden had three olive trees, as well as an apricot, fig, and peach, all ripe with fruit. I sat under a large, old pine tree that cast deep pools of shade. The ground was bleached and bone dry from the sun, and I amused myself by drawing pictures on the parched earth with a white rock. I was five years old.

I had little recollection of my mother, only a brief memory of her playing guitar and singing, "Jesus loves me, this I know, for the Bible tells me so," as I played with my little sister Kristina on a bunk bed in a small room in another land. But I was fiercely loyal to Mum and talked about her every day, even though I had not seen her for two years. I still missed her and my sister, and barely remembered my baby brother David. I clung desperately to the hope that Mum would come back. Like a record that never stopped spinning, I'd repeatedly ask my dad, "Why did she leave us?"

Dad would hug me and explain. "Mum decided to be with someone else, and I couldn't let you go. You were the oldest, and we've always been close, haven't we?"

I nodded. I loved Dad just as much as my mum, but I thought it was unfair to have to make a choice between them.

"What about Kristina and David?" I asked.

"They were too young. They still needed to be with their mother."

Dad worked long hours in a makeshift recording studio set up in the basement of our house, producing and acting as DJ on a radio show, *Music with Meaning*. Because of this I had a nanny, Serena, a young German woman. I resented her, and made life as difficult as I could for her by not cooperating or even acknowledging her. Serena had long, straight dark hair and brown eyes magnified by a pair of thick glasses. Poor Serena. Whatever she did to try to win me round, I was determined not to like her. I thought her German accent sounded funny, and she was constantly trying to give me wheatgerm with unsweetened yoghurt and spoonfuls of cod liver oil, which I hated the smell and taste of.

We belonged to the Children of God, a deeply secretive and religious organization with tentacles that spread across the world. The leader and prophet was named David Berg. We knew him as Moses David; my Dad called him Mo, and I knew him as our "Grandpa." He ordained everything we said, did, thought, and even dreamed. Everything in our lives, even the smallest and most insignificant detail—including the food we ate—was regulated by Mo. He had said that our diet should consist of healthy food and no white sugar, and Serena enthusiastically embraced Mo's healthy eating policy. "It will give you strong bones and teeth," she would tell me—but it didn't make it taste any better. She was never cruel, but she was strict, and I saw her as an unwelcome intrusion into my life. Originally, Dad had told me she would be staying for three months, and I had been counting the days until she left.

That sunny day as I played under the pine tree, I glanced up to see Dad and Serena walk out on to the front veranda. They were standing very close together and, instantly, I sensed a kind of electricity between them.

"Honey, I have something exciting to tell you," my father called to me. As he spoke, my tall, handsome Dad, whom I adored more than anybody in the world, turned and embraced Serena.

As I walked towards them, I noticed their faces were lit up with beaming smiles. *Oh no*, I groaned. This did not look good.

"We've decided to get together, sweetheart," Dad pronounced, in a far too happy tone of voice for my liking. "Serena is going to be your new mother."

"Not her!" I shouted. "I hate her!" I could not even bear to speak her name. "I want my mother. Why can't she come back to live with us? It's not fair!" I sobbed. I turned and ran off to a corner of the garden and stood with my back to them.

Dad followed me and bent towards me, concerned. He put his hand on my shoulder. "Sweetie, you know your mother has gone for good. She's not coming back."

"But I want my sister and brother here. It's not fair." I stuck out my bottom lip in a pout.

"But you have so many brothers and sisters here you can play with," Dad said.

"It's not the same," I complained.

"Honey, we're all one family. Now watch that lower lip…or you'll trip over it if you're not careful."

I half smiled, if only to make Dad feel better.

Mo said that we weren't supposed to have individual families. Our brothers and sisters in the Children of God were our true family. We even referred to ourselves as the "Family." But I refused to forget my mother or Kristina and baby David, though I was scared I was beginning to forget what they looked like.

The only photograph Dad had of Mum was of her standing behind a double buggy, with me sitting in one side and my baby sister next to me. I studied the photograph carefully. Mum had long, sandy blonde hair down to her waist, blue eyes and a wide smile.

"She's beautiful," I said. "And that's my sister?" I couldn't see her face clearly because of the picture's poor quality. Kristina was just a toddler, aged about a year old, with two little pigtails. I was eighteen months older and very like her. We were both dressed in pretty cotton frocks and had sun hats on. As hard as I stared, I couldn't summon up the slightest memory of them and mourned, feeling a gaping hole in my being.

Dad described how he and Mum used to take us with them when they went out witnessing in the streets. "I'd manoeuvre the pushchair in the way of someone walking the opposite direction and then hand them a leaflet and witness to them, telling them about Jesus and how they could be saved. Indian people love children and you were so cute and pretty. They'd pinch your cheeks and chat to you. They felt they couldn't be rude with you two sitting there gazing up at them like two little angels."

"Do you have a picture of David?" I asked.

"This is when he was just three months old," Dad replied, producing a small black and white photograph.

"He's so cute. Look at those cheeks!" I said proudly. He was lying on his tummy lifting up his head with his chubby arms, and had a big grin on his face.

My own early memories were brief, seen in a series of quick little snapshots, like windows opening in my mind's eye. Much of what I gleaned, Dad told me in our rare quiet times alone. I'd cuddle up on his lap and he'd tell me selective vignettes that gradually built into a bigger picture. But it was always half a picture; he never told me much about Mum.

Perhaps as a way of keeping her alive, and forlornly holding on to the remnants of a family life, I often asked Dad to tell me the story of how he and Mum had first met and then married, and my birth. He didn't tell me a lot about it; it wasn't until I had grown up that I heard the full story.

"Your mum was young and beautiful—just seventeen years old when we married. I was twenty-two."

I was always full of questions. "And what about your dad?"

Dad told me his father was a lawyer and military judge in the British army. He had no recollection of his mother, as she had died when he was four and his father had remarried soon after. He and his half-brother were sent to a boarding school in Cheltenham.

"I was a rebel at school. I was even expelled after I led a protest where a group of us locked ourselves in the main hall."

"Why—what did you protest about?" I asked.

"The school prefects used to beat us for almost anything, no matter what. They'd come in at night with their flashlights and shine them in our faces to wake us up. We got fed up with the injustice and stood up against it."

Thrown out, he enrolled at a drama school in London and in his holidays traveled throughout Europe. "I was searching for the meaning to life," he explained.

I listened earnestly as he described how, in pursuit of life's meaning, he read many spiritual books and dabbled in the occult and meditation.

I shivered. It had been relentlessly drummed into us by Mo that drugs and Ouija boards were dangerous, because they could open the door of your mind to the Devil.

When he was telling me about those years, Dad said, "I ended up deeply depressed and disillusioned with life."

"Wasn't drama school what you wanted?"

"It was empty. Without the Lord, it's meaningless. Just husks, sweetie."

It was at this low point that one day he received a call from one of his mates who had just returned from Istanbul. This friend had planned to walk on foot to India, but instead had been converted by the Children of God en route, and had returned to England to spread the word.

Dad was taken aback by the dramatic change in his previously disturbed and doped-up friend. He now seemed confident, with purpose and direction. "He told me it was all thanks to the Children of God. I was curious."

In the hippie era of peace and love, the message proclaimed by the Children of God seemed exciting: find a new life in Christ, drop out, live communally, forsake materialism, and share all things, just like the early disciples. But this was not just another zealous evangelical group from America— it was God's Endtime Army, the elite, who would lead a lost world in need of salvation during its darkest hour.

The Children of God believed that with the end of the world looming near, pursuing anything else in life seemed pointless. Dad was convinced. He gave away most of his possessions and turned up at the doorstep of a commune in Hollingbourne in Kent with just a small suitcase, ready for his new life as a disciple.

His eyes lighting up at the memory, Dad told me, "It was amazing. Everyone lived under the same roof and shared all things just like the Early Christians in the Book of Acts. It was the family I had been searching for."

New members were told to choose a Bible name to reflect their new life. Dad chose Simon Peter. His full-time job was now to go out on to the streets and witness—the name they used for trying to win converts. Handing out literature for a donation was called "litnessing."

Always full of new ideas, Dad came up with a novel way to litness. He laughed as he described it. "I dressed up as a clown, with a bright red nose and a funny hat that had a bouncing little plastic birdie on top."

He wiggled his fingers on top of his head and made a face. I giggled. "I bet you looked silly!"

"Oh, I did—but I was a clown. Clowns are allowed to look silly. I'd jump in front of passers-by and make them laugh before handing them a tract and asking for a donation. I became a star litnesser and fundraiser—I made hundreds of pounds a week for the Family."

I laughed as I tried to imagine my dad clowning it up in London, a city I didn't remember, although I'd been born there. Street solicitation was against the law, however, and Dad had run-ins with the police. Of course, he didn't see anything wrong in what he was doing. He was obeying God.

Dad told me he met my mum in Hollingbourne, as they both joined the same commune as new disciples on the same day. She was just sixteen and had been recruited straight from school. Young and idealistic, she thought the Children of God was a bona fide missionary society. My parents were "married" by the group, before being legally married in church. After a three-day honeymoon in the Lake District, they squatted in a large house in Hampstead that the Children of God had taken over.

Dad used his training as an actor to do stage performances, dramatically reciting whole portions of the Mo Letters —missives from the prophet that were mailed regularly to every commune as a guide for us disciples to follow and live by. He loved the thrill of acting, and his talent soon set him apart as a sort of celebrity within the group. Spurred on by his success, he recorded more of these Mo Letters in a series of cassette tapes called *Wild Wind*, which were distributed across the communes for disciples to listen to. While Dad was busy and fulfilled, Mum, who was pregnant, was terribly ill, and it must have been a great relief when, on January 29, 1975, after three days of difficult labor, I was born in the small attic room on the third floor of the Hampstead Home.

Becoming new parents did not stop Mum and Dad from pursuing their new-found mission to save the world. Missionary teams were being set out and my parents received a "prophecy" to go to India. A disciple was not supposed to have a will of his own, but had to follow God's will by praying and hearing from Him in a prophecy. These prophecies gave the stamp of Divine approval on any plans or decisions that needed to be made.

In reality, the British authorities had begun to investigate the Family's activities, especially their aggressive proselytizing and soliciting of donations, and Mo told everyone to move from the UK and go on to greener pastures, such as India, South America, and the Far East—places where the authorities would be far less likely to care about what a group of Western dropouts did.

When our little family first arrived in India we went to an apartment in a block in Bombay designed for the middle classes, although it was about the size of an English council flat. It had three bedrooms, which we shared with two other couples and two single brothers. After a few weeks my parents found a two-bedroom ground floor flat in Khar, a subdivision of Bombay. There were so many people staying there, disciples coming and going from other parts of India, it was always crowded. They had very little furniture except two single beds and a table and chairs in the living room.

Mum was heavily pregnant again, but right up to the birth she and Dad slept on a sheet on the floor of our small communal apartment, because the mattresses were infested with bedbugs. There were often up to twenty people in the flat, and Mum would try to hide them from the landlord. My baby sister was born in June 1976 in a private nursing home nearby and named Kristina after Dad's mother. I was only eighteen months old, but I adored her from the moment I saw her. I would lie next to her on Mum's sheet on the floor and put an arm around her, smothering her with damp kisses. I became the doting older sister, and loved to hug her and watch Mum change her nappies and nurse her. We were so close in age our bond was unbreakable. I called her Nina.

To Dad, many things about India were a huge culture shock. Despite the fact that he had been a hippie and had traveled to Cyprus and Israel and throughout Europe, he hated the heat, the dirt, and the disease he found in Bombay. He also contracted a bad case of hepatitis and was in hospital for a few weeks after Kristina was born.

"The water and the food made me ill, I had diarrhea so badly I lost tons of weight. And I felt humiliated as a foreigner having to sell tracts on the street, like a beggar, when there were so many beggars around me and children without a roof over their heads or food to eat," he said.

Dad's diet and that of the commune was a constant source of distress. They had little money at first since everything they earned had to come from selling tracts in the street for minuscule sums. At times, they could only afford to buy rice and lentils day after day.

Stoically soldiering on in the steaming heat of Bombay, Dad struggled to make more sense of his personal role. He was intelligent and had been well educated and got a job at the local radio station writing jingles. According to Mo the Final Battle of Armageddon was only a short time away, and Dad tried to come to terms with the teeming masses in just India alone that wouldn't be saved.

He suddenly remembered the old *Wild Wind* cassettes that had won him so much praise in London. There had also been talk of the potential of radio as a medium to spread the message. He came up with the idea of recording a series of half-hour programs that he would call *Music with Meaning*. This show could be played on local radio stations. He could do it all practically on his own, scripting it, acting as host, and DJ.

From the very beginning, the Children of God used music as bait to attract interest and attention. Group singing to worship Jesus was called "inspirations" and was a daily part of the disciple's life. The Family attracted many talented artists and musicians, including ex-Fleetwood Mac guitarist Jeremy Spencer—who literally had been converted in the street one day and walked out on a concert tour to join a local commune in San Francisco. Instead of rock and roll, they wrote songs based on the Bible and Mo Letters. Dad decided that he would use this talent on his show to help spread the word. Working on something that fulfilled him gave him the impetus to remain in India.

Proudly, Dad described his enterprise to me. "We offered *Music with Meaning* free of charge to radio stations. I knew that a lively music show would spread the message in a cool format and attract young listeners. At a fell swoop, instead of struggling in the heat to witness to a handful of people a day, and perhaps winning only one or two souls a week, I could reach *millions!*"

"That was so brilliant, Dad," I exclaimed, thinking that he was wonderful.

When Mo heard about the show, he commended Dad for his pioneer spirit, and helped to finance the project. Dad hadn't met our prophet—very few of his followers had—but his instructions and messages were dictated in Mo Letters and passed down via leaders who were known as shepherds. Dad worked all hours of the day and night on the show, while Mum was left to care for my baby sister and me. By this time, Mum was pregnant for the third time, and fell terribly sick again. But, sick or not, she still had to earn money by going out selling tracts in the heat, walking miles every day, wheeling us in a pushchair.

Many of Mo's followers—like my parents—had been faithful to each other and lived as a family unit, albeit in crowded communes with very little privacy. In 1978 "one wife," which was writen in 1974, reached down to the communes, making it crystal clear that family women should be providing for the sexual needs of the men, especially the single ones. We were all married to each other and there was no such thing as adultery in God's Family. Sex was the highest expression of love and giving and was called "sharing." The Children of God was now a Family of Love, in every sense of the word.

Some disciples found it hard to adjust to the new freedoms, while others jumped at the chance to have sex with multiple partners. Both my parents started sharing with others— though I think Dad was keener on it than Mum. With two children close together and another on the way, sex was not high on her agenda. But Mum was a sincere believer and faithfully obeyed the prophet even though she struggled with feelings of jealousy at having to share Dad. However, she felt alone and unloved and fell further into depression after the birth of my brother David in April 1978. The district shepherdess noticed that Mum was quiet and sad-looking and asked what was wrong out of concern. Mum confided in her that she was becoming unhappy with the marriage. Without her knowledge the shepherdess reported the conversation to a higher up and was told to send Mum away for a break and to think about whether she wanted to continue in the marriage. One moment Mum was there, and the next, she had gone, taking David with her to a commune in Madras.

When Mum returned from her break in Madras six weeks later, a young man came with her. His name was Joshua, a brother from Australia, and he was infatuated with her. This only led to further complications in my parents' relationship and to their eventual separation.

Then, unexpectedly one morning, the Bombay police showed up at the door of the commune and told all the foreigners they had to leave the country immediately. It seemed that some of the nationals who had been won to the cause had been shocked and alarmed by the promiscuity they had witnessed. Some of the new converts were beautiful Indian women and this was simply not in their culture and their families reported it. Interpol was also involved, at the behest of parents in the West who were trying to trace their missing children. There was a frenzy of packing as our shepherds closed down the commune.

Mum and Joshua decided to return to England with Kristina and David. "But I insisted on keeping you," Dad said. "You're my girl."

My young dad was so handsome I couldn't imagine anyone leaving him. But even though he had chosen me, I was devastated that I had lost my mum.

Dad hugged me and said, "You were such a miserable, sad little thing. You pined so hard that nothing would make you happy. In the end, I promised you that I'd wait before taking a new partner just in case Mum changed her mind."

I believed his assurances whether they were true or not, and his words gave me hope that our broken family was only temporary, a poignant hope I carried in my heart for the next two years, over two continents.

Two weeks later, Dad and I and flew out to Dubai. Dad was devastated because he had learned to love India and the future before him was uncertain. In Dubai, Dad received an unexpected phone call from Faithy, Mo's youngest daughter. She had been scouting in Greece, looking for a new location in which to begin a new project. Faithy had flair and charisma and a way with words that could convince just about anybody. She set out to gather together the most talented musicians, singers, songwriters, and artists to use them as an attraction to advance the cause to the outside world and gain them more followers.

"Simon Peter," she started, "Mo is very pleased with all that you have achieved. He has decided to support the production and distribution of the *Music with Meaning* show worldwide."

The show was to be bigger and far more commercial than before. It would be a hook to catch listeners, who would write in. They would be invited to come along to local *Music with Meaning* "clubs" in their area. There would be regular mailings, a magazine, and friendly conventions. Being telephoned personally by Faithy was a great honor. Dad was thrilled that he was receiving full support and backing for his program. His goal was always to win souls and he was very passionate about it. Not being a very practical person, he was happy to allow the leadership to take over all the organization of it so he could just concentrate on the show.

That was how we arrived in Athens in late 1979. The scenic view of high, pale mountains, soaring into a bright blue sky was breathtaking, as we crossed the ancient peninsular to reach the coast on the opposite side, a couple of hours away. As we drove down, between stands of dark pine trees, I could see the sparkle on the sea and fishing boats bobbing in the harbor of the old port in Rafina.

Our house was a typical modern Greek villa, painted white, and with a red tiled roof. The surrounding garden contained fruit trees, some scratchy lawn grass, yellow mimosa, and olive trees. We were within walking distance of a large campsite by the sea called Coco Camp. Half was for regular holidaymakers; the other half was block booked for us, the Family. Families began arriving in their caravans and trailers until about two hundred new people had joined us. All of them were either musicians or technicians who had been specially chosen to work on Dad's show.

During the day I would run free, playing with the children within the camp's grounds and along the beach. There were big colored pebbles to collect, and dead starfish, shells, and sea urchins. There was so much to see and do I never stopped playing from dawn to dusk. My hair would go unbrushed for days. I remember an American woman called Windy, a singer/songwriter for the show, sitting me down with a comb and laboriously untangling my thick mop of curls.

Sometimes in the evening I would lie on my bed for hours, bored while Dad recorded late into the night in the studio with Faithy Berg and Jeremy Spencer, whose fame had followed him here. Faithy had decided to use him as a selling point to pitch the show to broadcasters.

To solve the problem of the little wild mustang I was becoming, Faithy sent a succession of nannies to take care of me. First it was a married woman named Rosa. Then Crystal, a hot-tempered American woman, replaced her. Crystal was a petite woman with pursed lips and a mane of shoulder-length light-brown hair. She didn't have a motherly bone in her body and cussed like a trooper, not the sort of language that good Christians should use, and was always getting into trouble for drinking too much. Crystal often referred to me as the "girl with the curl in the middle of her forehead. When she was good, she was very good, but when she was bad, she was horrid." I admit I did have a stubborn streak, especially with her. I hated her because I knew she had set her sights on snatching up Dad for a husband and I was determined to do all I could to scotch any romance between them. I wasn't successful. Dad did have a fling with her, but their love affair was to be short-lived.

The only one I would listen to was Dad. I loved him more than anybody in the world and did my best to please him. I took no notice of anyone else, expecting my mother to come back at any time, even though we had said goodbye and she had been gone for what seemed aeons of time.

But why, why, couldn't I remember her? Why couldn't I even remember that dreadful final moment of our parting in Bombay?

I pined so much that finally Dad arranged for me to speak with Mum on the phone, long distance to London.

I felt weak with shock and took the phone, hardly able to believe that I was hearing her voice again. "When are you coming, Mummy?" I asked anxiously, the years of yearning filling my voice.

"I love you, Celeste. I'll try to come soon." I heard a voice I didn't recognize say on the other end of the line. "Your sister Kristina and brother David love you and want to see you too."

She had said that she was going to come back to live with us again! I was so excited.

"It's all worked out," Dad told me after the phone call. "The tickets are booked and everything. It won't be long now, darling."

I looked over at Crystal, who was sitting nearby, and pronounced triumphantly, "You don't need to be here anymore. My mummy's coming back."

Crystal glowered. A few weeks later the leaders—who had the final say in everything, even love—broke up their relationship, thinking she was not good enough for my father, their new media star. I certainly didn't think so. All I knew was that my mum would be there soon and I would be reunited with her and my sister and brother. I longed to have her there, cuddling me, brushing my hair, and being my mum again. But time passed and I heard nothing. I waited in a frenzy of impatience. Every day I talked—and thought—about my mother. When, when, when?

One day, when I asked Dad for the umpteenth time, "When's Mummy coming back?" he could not put off telling me any longer what he knew would shatter my world. "She's changed her mind. She decided to stay with Joshua."

I stared at him, shocked, feeling my heart jump and beat in panic like a fluttering bird. I did not understand. Why had she changed her mind? Who was this man Joshua, who had taken her away from us? It did not make sense to me and I could not accept that it was final. My memories of her had faded by this time, and I did not even remember what she looked like anymore—but she was my mother and it was the idea that I had clung to for half my life. I remained fiercely determined that no matter what, no one would take her place.

CHAPTER TWO

Loveville

We had a little beat-up car that barely puttered along. The back seats had been taken out by the previous owners (which is why we got it cheap) so you had to sit on the floor. I was in the back with my playmate, Nicki, and we were giggling as we experimented with what we imagined sex to be, like we'd seen the adults do it, undies down, on top of each other and humping away. We were both only five years old. Obviously, things didn't work properly and it was just a game.

"You're tickling!"

"No I'm not—"

"Yes you are. Ouch. My leg's stuck."

I heard muffled laughter, and glancing up, saw Nicki's mum, Patience, peering in through the car window at us, her face alight with amusement. Like a shot, I sat up and shoved Nicki away.

He saw his mum and went bright red.

"It's okay, you guys can carry on," she said.

But I felt very embarrassed and silly. What a moment ago had seemed like fun no longer did. One thing I didn't feel was guilt. Of all the sins we had to avoid, sex wasn't one of them. Mo said God intended everyone, even newborn babes, to enjoy the full sexual experience.

If anyone turned on the radio and heard one of my dad's *Music with Meaning* shows the message would seem idyllic: love was the answer to all of the world's problems—sharing love, living in love, and making love. Mo instructed Dad not to use the word "Jesus" on the show. This strategy was an important one, because many listeners had no idea what they were tuning in to, or that the show had any religious affiliation, let alone a notorious one. But some of the songs on the show were hardly subtle. Jeremy Spencer sang a song entitled "Too Young for Love," based on the Mo Letter "Child Brides," where Mo set out his belief that children as young as eleven and twelve were ready for marriage, sex, and children.

Part of Mo's plan was to produce a second generation of children, like me, who were born into the Family of Love and who had never known the outside Systemite world. They would be untarnished by the sins of a former life. To show what faith he was putting into this earthly paradise he called "Loveville," Berg sent members of his own family to live with us.

There was Faithy of course, his youngest and most loyal daughter, who was such a zealot her blue eyes shone fiercely. Mo also sent his granddaughter, nine-year-old Mene, who became a star of the show. When I first saw her I thought she looked like an angel, with her bright blue eyes, milky white skin, and blonde, wispy hair. She had a soft, sweet voice and a dreamy look in her eyes. She behaved like the perfect Family child, always obedient and smiling, reading and quoting the Word.

We rarely spent time together anywhere except in the recording studio or at practice rehearsals. I never played outside with Mene in a normal childish way—I don't think she was ever allowed to play.

Everyone had something to contribute to the *Music with Meaning* radio and video shows. It was fun and, like any child, I loved to show off my talents. There were musicians, artists, technicians, seamstresses, and secretaries. Some of the more famous characters were Peter Pioneer and Rachel, a married couple and singing duo from Denmark, and Joan and Windy, a singer/songwriter team who were openly bisexual. Zack Lightman, from Norway, was the lighting man and cameraman, and his wife Lydia designed the costumes and backdrops. Sue, a softly spoken American with brown eyes and a charming smile, was the "club secretary." Jeremy Spencer's wife Fiona was the "Queen Mother" of the camp, and the chef was a fiery Italian named Antonio. They lived as a threesome and Fiona had seven children by these two men.

In the center of the camp a large canvas army tent was used as a gathering place for meetings and a dining hall in the winter months, when nights were cold. Two big gas fires heated the arena and we used kerosene lamps for light. To feed so many people, there was a whole team of people whose job was to "provision" free food from the markets and local companies.

When the weather was warm, we ate on rows of benches and tables under the trees. Our food was fresh and, on the whole, delicious. Our breakfast consisted of semolina, sweetened with brown sugar, honey or molasses. Antonio tended to cook Italian food, the kind that could be quickly prepared for some two hundred hungry people. Big bowls of pasta with rich tomato sauce, or stews with beef chucks, potatoes, and carrots.

Children were regimented and expected to behave. Even the very youngest had to sit still on the hard wooden benches lined up in the big tent and listen during the long meetings we had in the evenings. These sessions were incredibly boring and I would end up retreating into my thoughts and a make-believe world as a way of escape. I also found it incredibly difficult to keep my eyes closed during the long prayers, and I would cover my eyes with my hands and peek through my fingers so no one would catch me.

Once Faithy had established the running of the camp, she turned over the leadership of Loveville to a married couple, Paul Peloquin—a French Canadian from Quebec—and his wife Marianne, and departed on her next mission, to set up a Spanish version of the show, *Musica Con Vida*, in Puerto Rico.

Paul and Marianne took their task seriously—too seriously. They were a childless couple and had been desperately praying for a son for many years. Paul had jet-black hair and brown eyes and spoke English with a heavy French accent. He was a real charmer, but also had a fierce temper that could flare up unexpectedly. Marianne was French—a well-built woman, big boned, nearly six feet tall with deep-set eyes and a pronounced nose. Part of their responsibility was to draw up the daily schedule and assign everyone their jobs for the following day.

Reveille was at 7.30 a.m., and after breakfast, I'd go to a nearby house which we named the Blue House because it was a pretty shade of faded blue—the same color as many of the fishermen's boats. This was our communal school, where we had Word Time and Scholastics, taught by our regular teachers, Johnny Appleseed, Fiona—Jeremy Spencer's wife—and Patience, Nicki's mother. We were shown flannelgraphs and read True Komix—illustrated Mo Letters for kids. An endless river of these Letters and books from Mo and Maria would come in the post, usually once every two weeks. Every Home had to open a mail box and the leader in each Home was the only one who knew that address and had the key. It was run like a military espionage service, with secrecy the code word.

On sunny days Word Time would take place under the shady umbrella pines in the campsite. Sunday-school teachers in the outside world would have swooned if they'd opened up a True Komix. Many of them showed scenes of explicit sex, nudity, or gruesome demons and bizarre dreams that Mo believed always had some meaning—they were God's messages. "Mo is God's prophet for today, His mouthpiece to give us His new Word," our teachers would tell us. "System Christians don't have the Spirit; they are 'old bottles' who can't receive the new wine."

God, Jesus, the angels, and the Devil were real and part of our everyday lives. Jesus would reward us when we were good, or the Devil would punish us when were bad. Our indoctrination was constant, and questioning anything opened our minds up to the Devil's doubts. A picture from one of the True Komix sticks in my mind. There's a little table with a tea set, and the Devil is depicted as a little elf with horns and a pitchfork. A little girl is sitting in the chair next to him and four little "doubtlets," and the Devil is pouring her a cup of tea. The next scene shows her trapped in quicksand, sinking back into the System, because the Devil and his doubtlets had got to her. "It's dangerous to have a tea party with the Devil and his doubts," the comic said.

Some of the True Komix stories we read were based on the Royal Family's children, Davidito, Davida, and Techi. We already knew them from the "Davidito Letters" as examples of how to raise "revolutionary" children in God's way. Mo's secretary and second "wife," Maria, had two children, Davidito and Techi. Davidito was born in 1975 from a Flirty Fishing encounter with a hotel waiter in Tenerife. He was only three days older than me, and I was very proud of that fact. Maria's lover and Mo's right-hand man, Timothy, was Techi's father. Mo wrote that Timothy was "just hired for his seed" and that Techi was his. He claimed that he'd received Techi's unusual name in a vision, when a spirit of a little girl had come to him when he was sick (and just before she was born, in 1979). He decided that Techi was a reincarnation and tried to fit this Buddhist doctrine in alongside Christian doctrines.

Davida was the daughter of Sarah Kelley, Davidito's full-time nanny. She called herself Sarah Davidito. All three children were part of the Royal Family and lived in seclusion in Mo's Home. The Royal Family children were to have a lot of influence in my life. They were our idols we looked up to, and we followed their lives in the Mo letters we read with great interest and curiosity.

After siesta, we would be allowed out to play. My regular playmates were two sisters, Renee and Daniella. I liked their mother, Endureth, and took to her as my second mother. I still did not accept Serena as my stepmother and often ignored her. I suppose my childish mind figured that if I blanked her out, she didn't exist. Serena also had her hands full caring for her six-month-old daughter, Mariana, and was now heavily pregnant by my father. To ease the situation, I ended up staying indefinitely with Endureth and her husband Silas, My sister Kristina would have been the same age as Daniella, and I would always talk about her as if I knew her, only she was in "India with my mother and baby David." Being with my friends in their family atmosphere helped me to pretend that I had lots of sisters. During the day we would play together, and at night we slept in a large double bed in the back of the caravan.

My other friend was Armi. We could not have looked more different. She had dark, straight black hair and brown eyes just like her mother, who was half Native American. She was one of the first children to be born into the Children of God, in February 1972. Her father, Jeremiah Russell, was one of the first disciples to join Mo's team in Huntington Beach when there were only fifteen members. He was a musician and wrote songs that were played on the *Music with Meaning* show. Armi inherited her father's musical talents and was a star performer and I wanted to be just like her, sing like her, and hang around with her and her group of friends. We laughed at the same jokes, told each other our secrets, and she would help me and teach me things, like how to draw a body in proportion, instead of just a triangle for a neck and a circle for a hand. And she was also the one who helped me lose my clipped English accent and speak "American" like most of the other children.

Armi and Mene, Mo's granddaughter, bonded together as sisters of misfortune. Their parents had been asked by Mo to send their daughters to Loveville with the assurance that they would be returned in six months. This never happened. Instead, Paul Peloquin and Marianne became their guardians.

No one dared to go against Mo's requests, which were obeyed as orders. After all, he was the prophet. We were conditioned to believe that carrying out Mo's directives was following God's will. It's clear looking back on it now that we were simply his playthings, his followers, used to fulfil his ambitions, lusts and fantasies. When Mo requested the women to dance naked for him on video, Paul got us all together, even the three-year-old girls, for a special meeting to read us the Mo Letters "Glorify God in the Dance" and "Nudes Can Be Beautiful."

"Thank the Lord! Isn't it a special privilege to be able to dance for the King?"

Excited, the adult women responded with many "Praise the Lords" and "Amens" to Paul's question.

Paul continued, "He's given us detailed tips in these letters of how to do it. Praise the Lord."

I watched as the women picked their music and see-through veils and then performed their strip dances. When it was the girls' turn, Paul said, "Now this is for Davidito—so smile for him."

Armi, Mene, Renee, and Daniella did their dances for the little prince—and then it was my turn. Paul chose two songs for me and tied a white veil around my neck that I was supposed to take off during the dance. He gave me directions from behind the camera.

"Wiggle!" He pantomimed it. "Wiggle nicely and rub your bottom, honey."

I simply copied the motions I had seen the adult women perform earlier.

"Good, very good! Now blow kisses to Davidito so he'll know you really love him."

I tried hard to smile and at the same time listen to what he was telling me to do behind the camera. This video still exists and the adult I have grown to be looks back in time at that sweetly smiling six-year-old child who was me. I am gazing into the camera, seducing it; and what is stunning is the knowing-innocent look in my eyes. What makes it worse in retrospect is at the time Davidito was only six years old—so this request was Mo's sick idea that his namesake should be groomed like him, while the dirty old man enjoyed these dances for his own pleasure.

From then on, nude pictures were taken of us girls on a regular basis and sent to Mo. He told us that he would post them around his room for his daily inspiration—a euphemism for masturbation. It is quite obvious to me now that Mo got his jollies off on voyeurism. However, we didn't realize that he was getting closer to the stage where he would select his favourite girls to be brought to him for his personal gratification. Their parents believed naively that they were in "good hands," even though they were unaware of their children's whereabouts and unable to communicate with them. But all that was in the future and, happily for me, I didn't yet know where some of my friends were destined to go.

*   *   *

Sex was completely open and transparent in our world. The adults had no inhibitions about making love in front of us and actively encouraged us to masturbate and explore our bodies. As a result, our childish curiosity was exploited, although we were always told to never, never do it in front of strangers, or discuss it where they would hear. "The System hates sex," we were cautioned. "They think it's dirty and sinful." When the weather was very hot, everyone walked around in bathing suits or shorts. I didn't have any problem with running around in only my knickers, like all the children. By the age of five or six I was highly sexualized and extrovert.

My father never did anything to me in a sexual way, nor did I see him do anything improper at this time with my peers, but I assumed he knew what was going on. His best mate was a drummer, Solomon Touchstone, who would often go into town with us on Sundays for lunch at a little taverna overlooking the harbor. Like Dad, Solomon came from London and they'd speak together in fake cockney accents, joking about. Solomon was short—about five and a half feet—handsome, and all the women liked him. I liked him too, because he was fun, and would pay attention to me.

Sexual grooming was normal to us and happened everywhere. Everyone was always hugging and kissing and being affectionate with one another. To me it was just a game. But my openness and eagerness to gain attention, love, and approval was horribly exploited. Playful, friendly Solomon, my dad's best friend, was just one of the many men who exploited my natural, puppyish affection for him. When we were alone in his bedroom he would ask me to dance for him naked while he masturbated on the bed.

"You're so sexy!" he would moan.

Little wonder that in that video specially shot for Mo I have such a knowing-innocent look. I was innocent—but I was learning what turned men on. The only positive attention we received from the adults was when we did what they wanted, acted flirtatiously or were sexy. Children crave acceptance, and I was no different. We would be rewarded for being "yielded" and showing God's love. Being stubborn, saying no or being prudish was of the Devil and bad, and would get us in trouble. I learned quickly to act in a flirtatious manner to get attention, and didn't know how to act otherwise around men.

Another man who pursued us young girls was Peruvian Manuel. He and his German wife, Maria, taught us our dance routines. They were another childless couple. He had dark eyes and an intense, almost piercing gaze that made me feel uncomfortable. He always paid us girls special attention, especially Mene and Armi. Maria enjoyed performing lesbian acts with the women, and they both taught the girls to mimic their actions for the enjoyment of the men who would watch. Because I was younger, I was not included in many of the sexual acts that my friends were roped in for. I always counted myself lucky compared with them. But I did not escape completely.

One afternoon Peruvian Manuel came into Silas and Endureth's caravan, where Renee, Daniella, and I slept together in the back. I knew the caravan well and treated it as my second home. The red curtains were drawn. He told me to lie down, then pulled my panties down and spent some time kissing me—"This is how the adult women do it," he explained as he knelt over me and proceeded to rub himself on me, complete in all respects without full penetration, until he had an orgasm.

When I felt the sticky white stuff come over me, I was repulsed. I had never seen semen before. It felt disgusting and was messy. He took some tissues and wiped it off me then went into the small toilet closet of the caravan and cleaned himself up. I remained on the bed, dazed and confused. It was the same feeling as when you are in a nightmare: you want to scream or say something and nothing comes out. I had so many thoughts, questions and feelings but was unable express them. Even when adults asked me directly what I was thinking, I always froze, my tongue rooted to the top of my mouth.

When I watched the adults having sex they seemed to enjoy it, so why didn't I? These men were trying to instil in me the knowledge that a little girl like myself would provoke the same sexual attention and arousal from a man that a woman would. My self-perception was distorted, and I had no concept of my own vulnerability or that I was different from the adult women.

Though in many ways we were expected to act like adults, we were still just little kids. At least once a week, Loveville would gather for a dance night, which would end up as an orgy. As usual, we were left to do our own thing while the adults—all those over the age of twelve—paired off for sex.

One night in particular, Renee, Daniella and I watched as the adults danced naked, groping each other. We decided to pull a prank, and took turns sneaking up behind a busy couple and pinching them on the bum. We thought it was hilarious when they gave a startled jump. By the time they turned around to try and catch whoever did it, we'd be long gone and giggling in the corner.

We weren't supposed to tell anyone outside the Family about our sexual freedom, as the adults called it. I was told that Systemites would not understand the truth and liberty we had, and I learned to lead a double life.

I remember singing at an orphanage one morning, and then having siesta time in our camper van before going to the TV studio in Athens to perform a Christmas song on a local TV show. We parked on the street, closed the flimsy curtains of the van and had what the adults called Love Up, or Cuddle Time.

My teacher Johnny Appleseed lay down beside me and stroked me while kissing me on the mouth. He opened his clothing and guided my hand to his penis and helped me to masturbate him. In the end, he finished himself off while I lay next to him. I was conscious of the others having sex around us. His eyes were closed, his mouth open while he panted and gasped. When he was finished he said a prayer.

"Thank you Lord, that we can share with one another your love," he prayed, and then he rolled over for a short nap.

The whole time, I was scared—he was my teacher—and also because there were gaps in the curtains. I could hear the footsteps of people passing by, and I thought that at any minute someone could look in and see us.

When it was time for our appointment, as if none of the afternoon sex had happened, the adults made up our hair and gave us a little pep talk. "When we get in there, remember to smile and show God's love. Don't worry about the cameras, like Grandpa said, just sing from your heart and think of the lost souls who will be watching."

We piled out of the van and into the studio. The TV presenter thought we were great and we pulled off a well-rehearsed performance. Of course, no one watching us would have had a clue what had gone on just an hour before behind the red curtains in the van.

When visitors came to the camp to stay with us, everyone dressed up a little more conservatively and I soon learned there were subjects we didn't talk about with "outsiders"—such as sex and our prophet Mo—and Mo Letters and Family publications such as the Davidito Letters would be tucked away from sight.

"Sweetheart, my parents, your grandpa and grandma, are coming to visit us from England," Dad said one morning, after receiving a letter from them.

"But we call Mo Grandpa," I said. "Is this another Grandpa?"

"Yes, his name is Glen, and he's my Dad."

"Oh. I might get confused if I call him Grandpa too," I said. After a moment I had figured out how to solve the problem. "Maybe I'll call him Granddad, that way I won't get confused. Did I meet them before?" I asked.

"Yes, they met you when you were a baby when we were in London," Dad replied. "I've been wanting to witness to them. My father hasn't been saved yet, he's been stubborn, but maybe he'll pray this time."

Dad always talked about saving souls. He sincerely believed that without Jesus in their hearts, they were doomed to hell. Dad didn't want his parents to suffer such a fate in the afterlife.

When I met them, I noticed the difference in their appearance and manner immediately—how reserved they were, and the way Penny, Dad's stepmother, dressed was different from Family women. Her hair was cropped short and permed and she wore a long-sleeved blouse and trousers. Penny gave me a kiss on the cheek, but there were no hugs, though they seemed happy to see me.

"My, you've grown since we last saw you when you were just a baby," Penny said.

The evening they arrived Antonio prepared a delicious pasta dish and we sat together on one of the tables under the trees. Faithy Berg had come for a visit, and introduced herself to them and spoke glowingly of the radio show. Windy and Peter and Rachel played guitar and sang songs from the show. Dad sat beaming with pride, like he was a little boy again, at being able to show his parents what he had achieved.

The next day we accompanied them on a tour of the town, but what I remember most from their visit was the stories Granddad told of when he was a young man. He told stories about his escapades in Palestine during the war as a British army officer. "One time I woke up in the morning to find my bed had been stolen right out from under me," he chuckled.

My grandparents' visit and hearing Dad talk about his real mother made me feel special. I was excited that I had another family, my own flesh and blood that was separate from the Family. After Granddad Glen and Grandma Penny left, I wrote letters and sent them drawings and gifts of little things I had made, telling them that I hoped that I would get to see them again.

Perhaps all these family stories struck a chord with Dad. He wanted to know more about his mother and he received permission from Mo to make a trip to Poland to find his mother's relatives. He was able to track down a surviving relative in Krakow and came back with stories and pictures of my grandmother, Krystina. She looked so young and beautiful in her wedding photo with brown eyes and fine dark hair. Dad told me proudly that I got my singing voice from her. The sad ending to her story was that she got a degenerative illness like mad cow disease and died within months when she was just twenty-four years old. Dad was a little boy of three and a half and had no memory of her, but he idolized her just like I did my mum.

I knew then that Dad and I had a deep link—and understood why he never forced me to have a relationship with my stepmother Serena. I still talked about wanting to visit my mum in India, but Dad told me it was too expensive and he was needed for the radio show. He suggested instead I make a tape for them. I sang my favourite *Music with Meaning* songs and jingles while shaking a tambourine. When I forgot the words, Solomon Touchstone was there to coach me. I also quoted Mo Quotes and Bible verses. At the end I told Kristina and David that I loved them and to be "good witnesses for Jesus."

Before saying goodbye I said, "If I don't see you here, then I'll see you in the Millennium."

This was Dad's favourite line when I would talk about missing my family. He always said, "You'll see them again soon, if not here on earth, then in the Millennium."

The end of the world was going to happen any day and it would not be long before we would all be together forever. Whatever my dad said was true. He knew everything. He was also very important, as I discovered one evening we all gathered together for a big celebration. It was the anniversary of *Music with Meaning* and I was beaming with pride when I learned that we were going to honor Simon Peter—my dad!—as the founder of the show. Mo had declared it "Simon Peter's Day." I don't think my father could believe that this was happening and that he and his work was being recognized by the prophet himself. In a glowing letter Mo had even called him Saint Simon Peter.

Adoringly, I stayed by Dad's side the entire evening. When the "birthday" cake was brought out, Paul passed an envelope to Dad with a large sum of money. "Simon, this is for you, to spend in any way you like, along with a full week's holiday. It's your just reward for your hard work in the Lord's service. As you sow, so shall you reap. Praise the Lord."

There was a further reward to mark that auspicious event. Everyone got a three-day holiday. Of course they were all delighted with Dad and crowded around congratulating him and thanking him. He glowed in their praise and I glowed in his reflected glory as I stood beside him, hanging on to him and gazing up at him—my dad.

After our three-day family holiday Dad took Serena, who was eight months pregnant, to the island of Patmos for his special week's holiday while I stayed back with Silas and Endureth and my friends Renee and Daniella. When Dad returned, he showed me the pictures they took on their trip.

"We rode on a donkey. It was really bumpy, and I was sore after that for a few days." He chuckled.

"What else did you do?" I asked, wanting to know every detail of what he had done without me.

"Well, we went into the cave where the Apostle John received the Book of Revelations. Just think, it was the very place where he received in visions the final events before the End of the World!"

A few weeks later, on June 2, 1981, my half-sister, Juliana, was born in a little Greek hospital in Rafina. I couldn't wait to see her. Solomon Touchstone drove up to the house, with Dad and Serena in the back of the car. The door opened and there was a cute little baby girl in Serena's arms, with her eyes shut tight.

Excited, I asked, "Can I hold her?"

"Sure," Serena replied. "Be careful."

She placed the baby in my arms gently. I thought she was like a little doll as I lifted her up. But as I did, her head hit the car door and the poor thing let out a mad cry.

"Oops," I said, upset. Serena quickly took her from my arms and comforted her. She didn't tell me off though, which was reassuring.

Dad gave me a hug and we all went into the house. "What's her name?" I asked.

"We're calling her Juliana Faithful," Dad said. I was so happy to have a baby sister. I watched as Serena changed the baby's nappies and nursed her. I even tried to nurse her myself—and got a few purple hickeys as a result. But because of the age gap between us, after the initial excitement of having a new baby sister, I saw her and Mariana rarely, except for Sundays. I preferred to spend time playing with Renee and Daniella. I was never jealous of our new addition to our family. I was Dad's first, and he assured me that no one would ever take my place.

Sundays were our Free Days and the only time I spent with Dad and our little family. I looked forward to Freeday, but dreaded the traditional afternoon Sunday fellowship. On one of these fellowships, everyone filed in to the big communal tent and sat down on rows of benches lined up in front of a television set.

Paul led everyone in a prayer and then announced excitedly, "This is a very special privilege. I have here in my hands a series called the *Garden of Eden.* Mo has allowed us here in Loveville to view these tapes, but no one must talk about it with anyone else or discuss what he looks like."

There was complete shock and silence, and then an excited buzz of conversation while the first tape was turned on. Except for a few trusted leaders, no one knew what David Berg looked like. His last name was never mentioned in internal publications and pictures of Moses David showed his face covered by an artist's drawing of a lion's head. This was done to protect his identity and whereabouts, as he was already a fugitive from the law. The media regularly printed articles about him—all of them negative—that raised public awareness and alerted government authorities around the world. All these cumulative reasons had led to David Berg—Grandpa Mo—living a shadowy life, guarded by his inner circle, who slipped from country to country with forged passports.

I was curious to find out what Grandpa really looked like and stared hard at the screen as his image came up. He had deep-set eyes, a balding head and a long, pale blond beard. He was dressed in a dark-brown robe, and around his neck he wore a great big yoke—the kind of wooden thing worn by oxen—hanging from a chain. He fit the perfect image of what I imagined a prophet would look like.

It was as if Jesus had appeared on earth. Everyone drew a breath, as they oohed and aahed.

"It's such a privilege—"

"What an honor—"

"Praise the Lord!"

The room went quiet immediately Mo began to speak. When he talked "in tongues," everyone joined in. They raised their hands in the air when he did and followed his every move. I looked from one person to another, wondering what on earth was going on. I didn't understand what they were saying. I didn't know how to speak in tongues. When they started weeping and crying, I wondered what I was missing out on. Sometimes, during united singing the atmosphere became emotionally charged and I felt a slight shiver, like goosebumps—had Jesus touched me? People said that was what it felt like. Everyone seemed as if they had been touched by Jesus watching those videos, and I wished that something would happen to me too—but it never did.

For the next few weeks, we spent many hours watching those videos. Mo preached on the Endtime, interpreting passages from the Book of Daniel and Revelations and explaining to us that a one-world dictator called the Antichrist would soon arise and usher in the last seven years on earth.

According to his calculations, Christ would return to earth in 1993.

Everyone praised the Lord. No one seemed worried or terrified that the End of the World was about to occur. Mo said that meant the Antichrist would have to appear in mid-1986—only five years away. I was almost seven years old. To me, five years seemed like a long time.

The *Garden of Eden* series marked a great exodus from Europe. Mo told us to move to the Southern Hemisphere, to escape the nuclear fallout that would soon engulf the West. Paul Peloquin announced that Loveville would soon be packing up camp and moving wholesale to Sri Lanka. We were not told this at the time, but I found out later that Mo and his team had moved from France, where the *Garden of Eden* series had been filmed, to South Africa, and then to Sri Lanka. We would simply be following in our prophet's footsteps.

A few days later, Dad told me that he had been asked to go on a scouting team ahead of the rest of us to find a suitable place to re-establish Loveville.

"I don't want you to go, Dad," I pleaded. "I'll miss you."

"Don't worry, honey. It will only be a few months." He tried to encourage me.

I clung on tight like a baby when he said goodbye and Serena had to prise me away.

CHAPTER THREE

Come Union

"Where are we going to live in Sri Lanka?" I asked.

'You'll see. It's a surprise," Dad said with a twinkle in his eye. "Did you know that it was a Sri Lankan radio station that was the first to play *Music with Meaning*? It's a beautiful country, and the people are receptive to the Lord's message."

When we stopped over at Karachi International Airport, I knew Pakistan was near India, and I gazed avidly out of the airport windows, through the heat haze across the Arabian Sea. The air smelled vaguely familiar, a mixture of exotic spices and gasoline, as were the intense heat and humidity. I was close but so far from the place where I had last seen my mother. I thought about my sister Kristina. *If only we could have stopped off in Bombay to see them.* Then it was time to board another plane to Colombo, Sri Lanka's capital city and I was caught up with the excitement of arriving on an island in the Indian Ocean.

After the long trip, we stayed in the capital at a hotel resort for the first two days to rest up before continuing our journey. The air was hot and humid, filled with the fragrance of frangipani, the sacred temple flowers that were used in Buddhist ceremonies. You could see these trees everywhere, their brightly colored flowers hanging down in bunches, the ground beneath them littered with fragrant carpets of yolk yellow, white, purple pink, and red. My first day in this beautiful, exotic land was unforgettable. The first thing I noticed were black birds crowing loudly. They seemed to be everywhere. As I walked under one of the banana palms in the grounds of the resort, I felt something warm hit my head. To my horror, I discovered a crow had shat on me.

The journey to our new home was exciting. Dad kept saying, "Just wait, you'll see." The anticipation was killing me. We crammed all our belongings into the air-conditioned bus we'd hired to take the three-hour drive into the mountains. It was all so different after the barren rocks and scant vegetation of Greece. Here, palm trees and the rich red soil of fields where black-skinned buffaloes toiled gave way to rounded slopes covered with tea plantations. With so much rain—the island is in the path of tropical monsoons and hundreds of inches of rain fall each year—we saw many tranquil lakes, which reflected the sky and the encircling high mountains. Everything seemed so peaceful, yet rich. I gazed at it all avidly, absorbing the sights and sounds.

Finally we arrived at the new home that Dad had found for us. It had been a farm, with a large colonial farmhouse and a few other smaller houses nearby. Dad took me round and showed me the large sugarcane field at the far end of the property, and rows of strawberries and green and red chilli bushes.

The main house was large, with a huge, vaulted living room with a white marble floor. Our little family got one of the best rooms, a big, airy bedroom with an en suite bathroom that the five of us shared. In the back garden of the main house we built a swimming pool, and within a few months I learned how to swim the breaststroke and the crawl. Dad established his studio as quickly as possible so his work could continue without interruption.

On our Freeday Dad and I would always do something fun together. Sometimes we walked down the mountain to the local town, which was twenty minutes away by foot. It was easy going down, but quite a haul going back up. All the women dressed in colorful saris and the men in lungis, a kind of long cotton skirt, tied in a knot at the waist. Their chests were bare, and gleamed in the heat and humidity. I tried not to stare, but I was put off by the sight of the women's earlobes, which hung down almost to their shoulders. I whispered to Dad, "What's wrong with their ears?"

"Oh, they're used to wearing really heavy gold earrings for special occasions," he explained. "The weight stretches their lobes. It's quite common in many parts of the world."

I liked being with Dad when we were just alone, because he acted different; he was relaxed and there were no rules to follow. We'd head out on our own to "seek adventure" he would say playfully. We'd pack a little picnic lunch and set off on the mountain trails around us. The sights were breathtaking, with waterfalls tumbling down from sheer cliffs, rocky little rivers, thick undergrowth filled with birds and huge butterflies, and the most incredible ancient trees hundreds of feet high.

The leeches were the only things I dreaded. They would burrow their way into my socks and I would find at least three or four on each leg, sucking my blood. Dad showed me how to get rid of them by putting salt on them and they would melt away. I hated having to come home, because it meant going back to our commune routine. After a shower, we would join everyone in the main living room for Sunday fellowship, led by Paul Peloquin and Marianne. We always ended our fellow-ships with the Christian tradition of Communion.

One Sunday, Paul read to us a new Mo Letter, called "Come Union." Mo had received a revelation that our fellow-ship ceremony had a sexual meaning. We were all one, and part of each other, body as well as spirit.

> Do we have complete full communion? Come-union? Com-mon-union? All things common Communion in the flesh as well as the spirit? How long has it been since you've given your body to someone, a brother or sister—or even a fish? Jesus gave his body even for the unsaved! Have you? Maybe you need to get liberated from your selfishness and fears—fear of love, fear of sex, fear of pregnancy, fear of disease, fear of commitment, fear of the future, fear of the unknown, fear of flesh!

Paul stopped reading and stripped off his clothes. Everyone, including the children, obediently followed. He broke out into tongues, "*Haddeda, Shedebeda, Hadaraba, Shadbrada.* Praise the Lord. Thank you Jesus—" and the whole room suddenly erupted into loud chants and babbling, praising the Lord with their arms raised in the air.

I looked around in amazement, baffled at the sight of the adults with tears streaming down their faces. I could not understand the sudden outburst of emotion and euphoria.

I was young, but I had a seeking mind. None of it made any sense to me. What had stripping naked to do with showing dedication to Jesus our Savior? Everyone sat together naked, arms around each other, while Paul finished reading the "Come Union" Mo Letter. But worse was to come when Paul went on to demonstrate a new way to pass the wine.

"'Now we have signified we're all one body,'" he read, "'the bread, and one in spirit, the wine. That's why I like to drink from one cup, which is what they did. These Protestant churches that have a bunch of little tiny cups, they never get the point. And they've got the bread all broken up beforehand, so they don't get the point of that either, that you've got to be one body. Boy, there's a hot one for our Family! One in the flesh, one body, one spirit! Sexually as well, really one Bride of Christ, One wife, One Body!'"

Everyone partnered up, and the men were instructed to take a sip from the communal cup and pass it on to the mouth of their female partner. When the wine came round, my adult partner took a gulp and then fixed his mouth on mine. The warm, red wine mixed with his saliva tasted awful. For a seven-year-old this was as yuck as yuck gets, and I swallowed as little as possible.

Because Jesus had turned the water into wine in the Book of John, Mo had always said that it was permissible to drink alcohol, and in Greece wine was always served with food or enjoyed in the evenings. Now Mo admitted in a Letter of Confession that he was an alcoholic and had ruined his oesophagus and stomach through heavy drinking. But he blamed his drinking binges on those who had deserted and betrayed him.

"See, I'm not like other preachers who hide their sins," he would write in his confessions. "I'm a terrible sinner, but God has chosen me to lead you. God still called King David of Israel 'a man after his own heart' even after he had Uriah murdered so he could marry his wife. I'm just a man with many faults, but when I'm in the spirit, I'm God's prophet and King."

This show of openness and false humility was swallowed hook, line, and sinker. Dad would tell me, "He's so humble, if only we could be more like him." But slowly I began to see the glaring double standard, and that the adults seemed to readily excuse his indiscretions because he was "God's anointed."

Maria was constantly sending out prayer requests for his health and would blame us for our lack of fervency in prayer when he became seriously sick and unable to eat solid foods. We had to fast and pray for our prophet's healing on many occasions. During these three-day fasts, no solid food, sex, or alcohol was allowed. Children like me who were under twelve were given minimal food, usually liquid soup, and the hunger pangs were just as difficult to endure as the long prayer and prophecy sessions.

Up until this time, our cook, Antonio, made wine by fermenting grapes in large containers. This meant that alcohol was free flowing. Some apparently could not hold their drink. One morning, on the day after an orgy, I could see that the adults were on edge as we were all summoned to the living room. Paul Peloquin rolled in, his face like thunder.

"There is sin in the camp! The Devil has been allowed to get in!" he roared.

I knew something must have happened to get him going like this and listened carefully. From his ranting, I pieced together that one of the men, Paul Michael, had done some "perversion" in the bedroom with Endureth, the mother of Renee and Daniella. I tried to imagine what it might be. As his ranting escalated to the frothing at the mouth and arms waving level, I sat there terrified at what he would do next. I wondered why the children were in trouble too. I did not drink wine. I had been in bed asleep.

"There has been too much partying and drinking, damn it!" Paul shouted. "Antonio, I want you to bring all the wine containers here right now and line them up on this table," he ordered.

Antonio scuttled back and forth as he brought out every last wine bottle and container from the storage room. There were at least fifteen of them.

"Is that everything?" Paul yelled.

"Yes, sir," Antonio replied, and sat down.

Paul picked up the first of the large containers. He could barely lift it off the table. "There will be no more drinking. Period! If this is what is causing the poison in the camp, then it's going to go. And if you think I don't mean it, then…"

In what seemed like slow motion, I watched him throw his arms back and hurl one container after another out on to the patio. The sound of crashing glass continued for ten minutes, as he chucked every last bottle out.

I looked in horror at the shattered glass and pools of wine that had seeped out into the garden. I wondered if Paul had thought about who would have to clean up the mess afterwards and how dangerous broken glass was.

"We're going to have desperate prayer and fasting," he shouted, "and no alcohol for the next three months."

Fervently, everyone got down on their hands and knees, and took turns praying for forgiveness for the next two hours. The floor was hard, cold marble, and my knees began to ache and my legs tingled with pins and needles. I was relieved when the tongues and weeping finally died down, thinking that maybe we could get up and sit down again. But then the prophecies started. I tried to move into different positions to get comfortable, but I was scared that Paul might notice and single me out for punishment.

I had good reason to be scared. Paul thought I had disobeyed him during another public correction. Armi had been found with a note under her pillow that she had written as a prank, forging someone else's name to the letter. It was supposed to be for a laugh, but jokes like this were taken seriously. All of us children were called into the living room for a correction. Paul told us to close our eyes while he prayed and to keep them closed as he read a Mo Letter. When he said "Amen" at the end of the prayer, I immediately opened my eyes.

"Celeste, how dare you disobey! You're rebellious, and disobedient," he shouted. I did not know what I had done wrong at first, but then I remembered he had said to keep our eyes closed not just for the prayer but for the entire length of the letter. I tried to explain.

"Stop talking back! Now go outside and stand against the wall NOW!" Paul shouted.

Shaking like a leaf I went out of the room and stood next to Renee, who had been sent out earlier for not sitting still.

After half an hour, he called us back and told me to stand and listen, or else.

Trying my best to obey, I stood upright, but, as the time wore on, my legs became uncomfortable and tired. I leaned the back of my leg on the couch that was behind me.

"There you go again! Disobeying orders!" The man had eyes in the back of his head. "You asked for it, Celeste. Let this be a lesson to all of you." He told me to hold out my hand and rained down blow after blow on it. The pain was so excruciating I could barely move my wrist for a week. That night I sobbed quietly as I fell asleep exhausted, hurting and angry at my unjust punishment and humiliation in front of my peers.

I hated unfairness and injustice, and like Paul, my teacher Patience had a terrible temper; she had very little of the virtue she named herself after. She would cuss and swear at us when we made mistakes or slap us across the face if we tried to explain ourselves. "Stop talking back," she would snap.

One time when she was teaching us to write in cursive, I struggled to follow her instructions. She slammed my book closed and shouted, "Are you bloody stupid or something? Stand in the corner now if you won't obey and do it right."

My mother would never treat me like this, I fumed as I stood against the wall for the next half hour. I often thought about my Mum…

I knew Sri Lanka was an island south of India, and I hoped that we could go to visit her and Kristina and David, or maybe they could come and visit us. Somehow it made me feel closer to them, living in a similar culture. I always imagined Mum would be just like my dad. He was never unpredictable, bad tempered or violent. This made me love him all the more. I never wanted to hurt or disappoint him and would do my best to obey him. On the rare occasions he did spank me, it was usually because he was expected to by another parent because of something I had done—like when I raised a tent peg in anger at another girl during an argument, or when I snuck my friend Koa some marbles when his mother had forbidden him to play with them. Dad never gave more than six swats with his bare hand or a slipper.

"Sweetheart, it hurts me more than it hurts you to have to spank you," he'd say and he'd sigh. The way he said it, his face and tone of voice made me believe him.

"Honey, you know Jesus died for your sins on the cross," he said. "He saved you, now you don't want to disappoint him, do you?"

I shook my head as I imagined Jesus hanging from the wooden cross, nails making his hands bleed. I had watched *Jesus of Nazareth*, and the death scene was frightening. But the fact that I had disappointed my dad hurt more. After the talk he put me over his knee and counted out the swats. "One … two … three … four … five … six."

I tried not to cry. Usually, I just braced myself and closed my eyes because I had my pride and did not want him to see me in tears. Dad never nursed a grudge. As soon as it was over, it would be as if it never happened. *If only all adults could be like him*, I thought to myself. He was my hero. No one and nothing could touch him. But that made it hard for me to acknowledge anyone else's authority.

The monsoon season in the central hill country where we lived falls from September to November, so to escape the wet and cold, we packed up and moved to the Northeast coast of the island where the weather was warmer. The holiday resort we moved to was a collection of bungalows and a swimming pool five minutes away from the beach. Our little family stayed in our own small bungalow. Juliana—who by now was two years old—did not react well to the hot weather and suffered terrible heat rash. She was constantly itching and scratching at herself and making herself bleed. Serena covered her in pink calamine lotion to soothe her. I felt so sorry for her as she also had a bad case of cradle cap on her head. It was no wonder the she learned to swim early.

Three-year-old Mariana had a fear of water and refused to go in, but Juliana loved it. I often joked that she was like a fish, bobbing up and down in the water.

Every day was like a holiday—even school was fun as we sat round on Patience's bungalow's balcony and she showed us the shells she had collected and made into a collage. But we never had a chance to settle in our new hideaway. A few months earlier, the story had spread around that a Family member had spotted Mo sitting by the swimming pool of a hotel in Colombo. His cover had been blown, and immediately, Mo and his personal entourage left the island. In the endless reams of rambling letters he wrote to us, he always said that the Family was his biggest security risk, as they could not keep quiet. He was supposed to be our shepherd, our prophet who loved us and yet he showed such mistrust of his own followers and ran away from them. I wondered why.

Mo also frequently changed his views and opinions and yet we were supposed to obey his every word. We had fled the West to escape an atomic war and then, hardly a year later, Mo said his interpretation of scripture was wrong. An atomic war would not come before the Antichrist's rise to power. Instead, Jesus would return first to rescue the saved to heaven. I was still worried, though, about what we might have to suffer in the Great Tribulation.

"I don't want to die as a martyr, Dad, or be tortured."

He sought to reassure me. "It's okay, honey, God will give us powers to defeat the Enemy."

As if it were a state secret, he winked at me, then quietly opened his dresser drawer, pulling out a sock. "Look—this is our Flee Money to use to get us out of danger," he said, as he showed me two gold coins he'd hidden in the sock. Every family had been given a stash of gold to hold on to, under strict orders that it was not to be spent under any circumstance other than an emergency.

Just after my eighth birthday, in January 1983, civil war broke out between the Tamil Tigers, who were fighting for independence, and the Singhalese. Our resort was right in the middle of the fighting zone and we had to pack up the camp within days and evacuate. Over one hundred of us were divided into small traveling teams and flown out in an eight-seater military plane to the airport and tickets were bought for everyone. Our gold coins were cashed in to get out of the country to safety. Those who were crucial to *Music with Meaning*, were to go to the Philippines. The others went to India and other neighbouring countries. I had no idea where I was headed to—I had never heard of the Philippines—but I was happy that I didn't have to say goodbye to any of my friends: Armi and Mene, and Renee and Daniella. Whatever happened, we would be in it together and that made the journey into the unknown just a little less scary for me.

CHAPTER FOUR

Behind Four Walls

Our new house was not unusual for a well-to-do neighbourhood in Manila, with twelve bedrooms, a swimming pool and basketball and tennis court. Eight-foot walls surrounded the rented property with jagged glass on top to keep out robbers; but the walls also kept me in, shut away from the outside world, like a convent.

I had been used to playing in open spaces—the campsite, the farm, and the beach. But here, on the outskirts of a polluted city, I felt caged with nowhere to escape from the constant noise and so many people living closely together.

When we first moved into the big house, our family of five stayed in one room on the second floor. Dad and Serena slept on a double bed, and the girls and I had a triple-bunk bed. As soon as we had settled in, our shepherds Paul and Marianne told us, "We're now officially a World Services Home, and that means tighter security. Everyone is going to need to change their names."

Later I asked Dad why. I couldn't imagine being called anything but Celeste.

"It's a security measure," he explained. "The Family might recognize us on the street. New names will throw off anyone if they happen to see us or hear us talking when we're outside. We have important work to do and if our enemies find out where we are, it would hurt God's work."

Now we had to hide just like Mo did, even from the Family that we were supposed to be servicing.

"What about Rebecca, my middle name?" I suggested.

Dad was pleased. "My parents chose the name Rebecca."

"And what about you? What's your new name?"

"I've chosen the name Happy."

I thought Dad's choice of name was very odd; but worse, he grew a handlebar moustache. I told him he looked awful, and to my relief he shaved it off soon after.

As a World Services Home, we were directly under Mo and Maria's control. These operational homes helped to oversee and produce the Mo Letters, videos, and publications for the Family. They stayed apart from normal communes and were financed by the tithes of the common Family members. Mo had introduced a 10 per cent tithe in the early 1970s on all income from litnessing, inheritances, and Flirty Fishing. The percentage had slowly increased, and by this time an additional 3 per cent was levied for additional administration costs. If a commune failed to pay their monthly tithe on time, the penalty was excommunication until the debt was cleared.

The rules in World Services were tighter and there were more restrictions on our freedom. We were not allowed to tell anyone our phone number, address, or even the country we lived in. All personal correspondence had to be read by the leaders before being mailed, and all letters from the outside

were opened before being handed to us. I was never told our
address and the only phone in the house was in Paul and Marianne's room.

Even though I had little contact with my mother, she
knew I was in Greece and then Sri Lanka because of the
videos we made that were distributed to all Homes worldwide. Now, I was not allowed to tell her anything. We could-
n't talk about the weather or what we ate in case it would give
our location away. I wrote her a letter—another one of those
sad little missives sent out into the unknown—but all I could
say was that I was doing fine and learning lots of lessons.
With my note, I sent her and my sister and brother some
hand-made gifts that I had labored long and lovingly over
during school time. To my delight, a few months later I
received a letter back from my sister. It didn't have much
detail but it contained a photograph of Kristina, aged about
seven, standing on a porch with banana trees in the background.

It is impossible to express how I felt as I gazed at that
photograph. The last photo of her I'd seen had been the snapshot Dad had shown me in Greece, of Kristina and me in a
pushchair. This was of a grown-up girl with dark-brown hair
down to her shoulders and beautiful blue eyes.

I treasured that picture and kept it with my other keep-
sakes in a little box. But why hadn't Mum sent me a photograph of herself or written a letter? It was all very
mysterious—but almost everything in my life seemed to be
tinged with secrets.

Manila sweltered in the tropical sun and everyone
walked around in their underwear or a sarong tied around

their waist, even in the garden. Despite our attempts to keep a low profile, word spread round the neighbourhood that a group of foreigners had moved in. Our property was near a coconut grove and a local man climbed up one of the trees to peek into the "foreigners' garden." He was treated to the sight of topless women in sexy underwear. Next thing we knew, every man who could climb a tree did so to see for himself. This exposure was terrible for our security. Instead of putting on clothes, someone had the bright idea to make signs saying "Peeping Tom." When a man was spotted up a coconut tree, the warning signs would be posted at every outside door. If a sign went up it meant that no one was allowed to go outside. When the all clear was given, the signs came down and everything went back to normal—or what was normal for us: adults having sex in the swimming pool, hanging up the laundry and playing badminton in our underwear.

Music with Meaning had been the Family's ministry for five years, but when the media and government officials discovered that the show was a front for the Children of God, the radio stations dropped it. The Family had to adapt in order to survive. It was sad the day Dad completed his last and final *Music with Meaning* show. He took me down to the studio as he packed up his master tapes. I knew he was very disappointed to have to end *Music with Meaning* and like me, he disliked being confined to the house, but he told me he resigned himself to it as part of his sacrifice for the Lord.

"I've been given a new project," Dad explained to me. "Grandpa's asked me to write stories for children about life in his house, and about Davidito, Davida, and Techi. The series is going to be called *Life with Grandpa*. I've never written children's stories before, but I'll give it a try." He always tried to remain upbeat, but he admitted that he would miss recording.

"How will you write about them unless you get to meet Grandpa and the children?" I asked.

"They'll send me all the information I need, and there's a lot in the Mo Letters as well, some that haven't been published."

Ultimately, *Life with Grandpa* became a series of comics compiled in seven books.

With the *Music with Meaning* era officially over, our Home was also given another new project—to record a series of music tapes that we could sell to the public under the name of *Heaven's Magic*. I spent hours with Windy learning harmonies and recording with Armi and Mene in the studio room. I looked forward to recording because it broke up the monotony of my day.

At the same time the Home was also given the project of producing color posters that could be distributed to the public and we received new members from other World Services homes to work on this. One of them was Eman Artist. He was commissioned by Mo to illustrate the posters and a series of comics called *Heaven's Girl*. Mo wrote of a dream he had of a young teen girl, "Heaven's Girl," who had superpowers to defeat the Enemies of God, the Antichrist police forces, in the Endtime. She was also an expert Flirty Fisher. Mo said Heaven's Girl would be our role model, and like her we would become superheroes for God and that we would be able to call on God's zap rays to destroy our enemies by blinding them. On the other hand, some of us would have to die as martyrs for the faith. I had no doubt that it would happen— and soon.

Eman needed a model that fit Mo's description of Heaven's Girl. All the females in the house took turns posing semi-nude for him and photographs were sent to Mo for his approval. In the end, Mo chose his own granddaughter, Mene. He even said that she could be the one to fulfil the vision and lead us in to the Endtime. In one picture, Eman Artist drew Mene—Heaven's Girl—standing with her arm outstretched with a rod in her hand, while the earth swallowed up Antichrist soldiers and army tanks.

Mene was now twelve years old, and a month later she disappeared. No one was told where she went. If someone "disappeared," it usually meant they had gone somewhere secret, such as to another World Services Home or to Grandpa's House.

One evening, I asked Armi, "Do you know where Mene went?"

She nodded. "She went to live with Grandpa."

At this time too, the larger families of our Home were asked to move to other regular communes. Fiona and Antonio left to set up a commune in Manila with all their children. I also had to say goodbye to my friends Renee and Daniella who left with their parents, Silas and Endureth. Even though they remained in the same city it was as if they had moved to the other end of the earth. No contact was allowed between the World Services elite and the rank and file Family members. There were only four children in my age group now—

Armi and myself, and Michael and Patience's sons, Patrick and Nicki.

Although I was only nine, I was often entrusted with the care of the younger children on my own or with Armi while the adults had meetings, or during their Saturday-night movie—the one film they were allowed to watch a week. One evening, I was reading True Komix to my little sisters Mariana and Juliana before putting them to bed. For fun, I decided to play a trick on them. I slammed the book shut and sternly said, "Line up against the wall. You've both been very naughty and need a spanking."

They were good little girls and, obediently, they did as I had said. Taking four-year-old Mariana into the bathroom, I put her over my knee, put my right hand on her bottom, and then spanked my hand. Immediately, she caught on to the joke that I was not really giving her a beating after all and began to laugh. I had a chuckle with her and told her not to tell her sister outside. "Okay," she whispered.

When I came out to call Juliana in, she was already sobbing. I expected her to get the joke too, although she was only three. I brought her into the bathroom. "Right, now it's your turn," I said in my strictest voice.

"No, no, please no—" She started to get hysterical and broke out into a sweat.

I bent her over my knee and did the same as before. Only she did not get it. She screamed and begged me to stop. Immediately I stood her up and told her I was only hitting my hand and not her bottom. She kept crying and her heat rash became inflamed and her whole body slippery with sweat. I had seen her break out in the same sweat and hysterics before, when she got spankings, but for the first time I saw the panic and helplessness in her eyes. She was terrified at even the thought of another beating.

Ashamed of myself, I cooled her under the shower and then did my best to distract her and calm her down. Mariana told her that she did not get a spanking either, and finally she settled down. I felt terrible for what I had done and that night I made a resolution that I would never be physically violent towards children when I grew up, no matter what. For the first time, I understood that even children had a right to dignity and respect and saw how depraved and abusive the treatment the leaders meted out to us was. Hitting did nothing but damage a child's fragile trust in those they looked to for love and care. I hated when I was hit across the face, knuckled on the head, or spanked, and I vowed that I would never forget.

Not long after this incident, our little family was split up. After Serena gave birth to her son, Victor, she was moved with the two girls to another World Services Home in a nearby subdivision of Manila. Victor was only three months old but he did not go with her. He was adopted by a childless couple in our Home.

I was never told the reason why Victor was given away or why Dad and Serena allowed their son to taken from them. We weren't supposed to ask questions, but it was terribly confusing. It seemed to me that Dad and Serena were in trouble for something and this was some form of punishment. I thought that maybe after Serena left it would be just Dad and me again together, but instead Marianne told me,

"You'll be staying with Michael and Patience in their room."

"But why can't I stay with Dad?" I pleaded.

"You'd be better off with Patience, who can take care of you properly."

I resented this change. Patience was the last person I wanted to live with and I was frightened of being separated from my father, who was my only protection. But we were kept apart and I only saw him once a week, when we went to visit Serena and the girls for our Freeday.

On one Freeday, Dad and I watched a video compilation of the *Benny Hill Show*. In one scene Benny Hill was a news presenter and he did a play on the phrase, "Fish and chips."

"Ummm, fish and chips!" Dad moaned, licking his lips. "Fish and chips wrapped in newspaper with vinegar. It's the only thing I miss from England."

"Yuck!" I exclaimed. "Dad, newspaper is dirty. All that ink comes off on your hands."

He smiled and shook his head. "It adds to the flavour. One day, we'll go to England and I'll buy you English fish and chips," he promised.

It was the first time I heard Dad reminisce—or say anything positive about England. Mo often ranted against America and the West as "cesspools of iniquity" and Dad believed that God would soon judge England for their "rejection of God's children."

Every word Mo said was taken so seriously, even down to his likes and dislikes. One of my jobs was to set the table for dinner, and one day I was instructed to lay spoons instead of forks and knives. After the meal, I asked Dad why.

"Well, Grandpa said that all you need is a spoon." He went on to demonstrate. "You can scoop things up with it, and use the edge to cut. You really don't need forks. The food just falls through anyway."

"But I like forks," I replied.

I thought it was ridiculous. We could not use black pepper, women could not wear jeans, and men replaced their briefs for boxer shorts, just because Mo expressed his dislike for them. Fruits and vegetables had to be soaked in salt water for twenty minutes—which made them taste awful; salt was supposed to kill the germs. Mo always boasted how frugal he was—his childhood in the Great Depression of the 1930s had left a mark on him. He could take a shower in a bowl of water, he saved stamps, and always made the most of a napkin, by first using it to wipe his mouth, then clean his glasses, then blow his nose, then finally to wipe his bottom.

Ewww, I thought when I read that. *How gross.*

He also declared that three sheets of toilet paper were all that you needed for a bowel movement. This became a Family rule. We were always threatened with the Scripture, "The eyes of the Lord are in every place, beholding the evil and the good," and I did my hardest to fold carefully those three sheets to maximize their use. I was convinced that Jesus was there in the toilet with me, watching to make sure I didn't use more than I was allowed. At this time I started to suspect that Mo lived nearby. His location was supposed to be top secret but I noticed that Paul Peloquin and Marianne often disappeared for a few days only to return with new rules, projects and "news from Grandpa." Paul talked often about Mo's household and would introduce new rules that he had picked up from his visits to their Home.

One evening, he announced during a meeting, "I want everyone to write down in order of preference who you would like to be on the date schedule with. You won't be guaranteed that you'll get the person you asked for, so put down your first, second, and third choices." While the adults were given a choice, Paul arbitrarily decided my and Armi's date schedule. We had to have a date—sex in other words—with both Patrick and Nicki, twelve and nine years old, once a week.

When Nicki and I were five years old at the campsite, I remember fooling around with him and mimicking sex like we had seen the adults do, and it was fun. I liked him. But being forced on to a schedule where I had to perform whether I wanted to or not quickly turned it into a duty. I resented being parcelled out without any consideration for how I felt or what I wanted.

Besides our dates with the boys, Armi and I were also scheduled with the adult men. Paul Peloquin would ask me to masturbate as he got off. He said it turned him on to watch me. I hated it, especially since I was afraid of him. I would imitate the motions as I had been taught, but felt nothing but fear that if I didn't please him he would lash out in anger.

I had been taught that black was white until my normality was upside down and backwards—but there was some kind of inner spark of morality deep-seated in me that told me what was really right and what was wrong. Sex with men old enough to be my father—with anyone I didn't choose—was wrong. Their touches were uncomfortable and awkward. It was an assault on my body that I had to grin and bear; I was powerless to stop it. I was trapped. Dad should have saved me, but he didn't.

Jeremy Spencer worked with Dad on *Life with Grandpa* as the artist. He lived in the small, detached room in the courtyard that was built for the maid. On our dates he would play a tape of saxophone music. The routine was by now familiar—undress, pray, kiss, and then give him a hand job. Jeremy would try to masturbate me but it just ended up feeling raw and hurting. I would move position so that he would rub a different spot, but I never understood why he—and the other men—kept on rubbing and rubbing. If I said I did not enjoy it they would accuse me of being prudish or proud. I just pretended to have an orgasm to get them to stop.

Because we were supposed to "be loving and share," my protests were seen as rebellion which was the spirit of the Devil. Eman Artist worked directly with Mo he was treated as special and had the pick of any woman or girl he wanted. He was a short man, overweight, wore glasses, and had already lost most of his hair even though he was only in his early thirties. I had just started to develop breasts and they were tender. Eman liked to come up behind me and feel me up, or wrap his arms around my chest and squeeze me tight. It felt like he was suffocating me.

"You're hurting me," I would say, as I pushed him away.

"You're just little Miss Queeny, aren't you?" he'd snap back. "So proud, *Queeny*," he would mock, emphasizing the word "Queeny." I hated that name.

I managed to avoid him for a while, but then the dreaded evening came when he asked me to come to his room for a date. I could not bear the thought of being alone with him. In desperation, I went to my teacher, Sally, and said I could not do it.

"He's horrible, pushy, and disgusting," I told her.

"Sweetie, sometimes it can be difficult to share but God gives us the strength to do it. Why don't we pray together?"

She laid her hand on my shoulder.

I listened dejectedly to her prayer, feeling betrayed and helpless. If she was not going to stop it then no one would. She handed me her tape recorder and suggested I play some music and do a dance for the loathsome man. She even escorted me to Eman Artist's room. I hated her. I hated the fact that I was being forced to suck the dick of a perverted, fat man who persisted on pushing himself on me when he knew I hated it. The worst part was the way he gloated. He had power over me and there was nothing I could do about it.

He smirked as he exposed himself. "Suck me off," he ordered. Forcefully he pushed my face down on to his penis until I gagged. But although he puffed and groaned, nothing happened. So he asked me to dance for him, directing me to wiggle and rub my bottom in a suggestive way, as he tried to get it on himself. He failed to climax and his impotence made him agitated and more demanding. After what seemed like hours, I stumbled out of his room and cried myself to sleep on my own bed. The assault was over, but the nightmare continued to haunt me for years.

I never thought of telling Dad how I felt about the incident, especially after one evening when I walked in on him lying on the bed half-dressed with Armi. Upset and dreadfully embarrassed, I left the room quickly. The thought of my dad having a date with my best friend deeply disturbed me. He did it too, just like all of them. Of course he wouldn't rescue me. We never talked about any of my sexual experiences, nor did he ask me. In fact, I rarely saw him. He was completely stripped of all his parental responsibilities—he was my father in name only. I spent most of my time with Michael and Patience, who acted as my foster parents.

But to Michael, I was more than a daughter. Like all the girls, I walked around in little panties during the day. After a game of badminton with him, he came up to me and flicked my panties playfully.

"You've been a good girl recently. As a reward we should have a date," he said.

I gave a weak smile, but inside I was screaming, *Why? What sort of a reward is that? Your penis down my throat is no reward for me.* That was the last thing I wanted. I finally reached my boiling point. I was tired of anything do to with sex. I was fed up of what seemed to be a never-ending hell. I decided to risk it—I figured I had nothing to lose—and I went to Paul Peloquin. "I don't want to have dates anymore. It's not fun, I'm sick of it," I said.

His face turned bright red. "That is the spirit of rebellion speaking in you," he shouted. "Go to my room and wait there."

My stomach churned. I was in trouble. When he entered the room an hour later, Paul told me he had a letter to read me, called "The Girl Who Wouldn't." It was a stern Letter of Correction from Mo to a woman who had refused to have lesbian sex with Keda, one of his leaders.

Afterwards, Paul applied what the letter said to me. "You know that's your problem. So full of pride and self-righteousness, thinking you know better than everyone else. Do you think you know better than God?" He fumed. "It's the woman's place to yield to the man and given them what they need. It's not about *you*. You'd better be willing to sacrifice and show a little more love, damn it. You're yielding to the Devil, you know? Rebellion is witchcraft."

I had to write a Letter of Confession and repentance, but inside I hated Paul. I hated being forced to have sex, with no way to escape from it. I started to have violent thoughts about him and wished he would die. I felt I was going crazy with so many bottled up feelings that I couldn't express. Sometimes I would go outside in the early evening just to be alone for a few moments and daydream. One evening after a game of badminton, as the sun was setting I heard haunting music from over the high wall. I lingered and as moths fluttered, attracted by the lamplight that illuminated the court, I listened to the words.

"Flashback warm nights...suitcases of memories...time after time..."

I was mesmerized. All our songs had to be inspirational, about witnessing, Jesus, the Bible—the words of this song captivated me. They were poignant and filled my head with dreams of love and romance and pain.

"You're calling to me...I can't hear what you've said..."

I wanted to cry with the pain that the song drew out of me.

"If you're lost you can look and you will find me...time after time..."

I felt as if all my dreams and hopes and aspirations for the future were in the words of the song—and a sense of loss, of being lost in a world I longed to find my way out of.

"If you fall I will catch you… I'll be waiting… time after time…"

Night after night, I would wait outside in the dusk for that record to be played again. Whoever was playing it could have had no idea that, just the other side of the wall, I was listening and dreaming. Restricted behind four walls, with few changes of scene, us kids came up with ways to entertain ourselves and have fun. Armi and I taught ourselves to do the splits, cartwheels, and backflips. We even put together a half-hour circus show with the boys that we proudly performed for the Home.

Through the good times and the bad, Armi and I were inseparable; she was my best friend and my closest confidante, so when I found out that she was leaving for Teen Training at the King's House—Grandpa's Home—I was devastated. It was the greatest privilege and honor to be invited to his house, and I wondered what I had done wrong that I had not been considered worthy enough to go too. I had no idea at that time that teen training at the King's House would be no honor, but purgatory.

"We're going through some changes of personnel," Marianne told me, after summoning me to her room. "And it seems it would be best if you joined Serena. There won't be anyone your age here." Michael and Patience and the boys were also leaving for another commune in Manila.

"What about my dad?" I asked.

"He's needed to write *Life with Grandpa* here," she said, not even trying to soften the blow when she saw my crumpled face.

I burst into tears. My dad and my best friend were being taken from me in one fell swoop. I had nothing left. Perhaps in an attempt to cajole me to obey, Marianne explained that little Victor needed to go back to his mother, and since it had been six months and he would have forgotten her, I was needed to accompany him. "He knows you and it will make it easier for him," she said.

Victor was a darling, with chubby cheeks and big, brown eyes. I could not understand why he had been taken away from Serena in the first place. Nothing at this point made any sense. But I cared about him and, knowing that I had no choice, agreed to go.

The night before I left, Armi and I made a pact. It was not long before the Great Tribulation, and no matter where we were in the world we would meet at the edge of the jungle outside Manila. I was an avid reader of the "Survival Sam" Comix series that described how to set traps, live off the land and get clean water in the wild. We drew up a list of essentials we would need, like rope, matches, water-purification tablets and a Swiss army knife.

"I'll be there, waiting for you," I said. "No matter what happens, do you promise to be there?"

"I promise," Armi assured me.

It might have been a fanciful dream, but I believed it with all my heart, and somehow it made me feel better.

CHAPTER FIVE

Indoctrination

I arrived late in the evening at my new destination—Dan and Tina's Home—with baby Victor in my arms. I was uncertain of my future; my stomach tied in knots.

Serena came flying into the living room with Mariana and Juliana, beside herself with joy. "Victor! He's grown so big!" she exclaimed. I handed him to her but he didn't recognize his own mother and screamed and his chubby arms flailed at her face.

He continued to struggle and turned to me, his little face red and blotched and held out his arms. I took him and rocked him, while Serena looked on distressed. I was the one familiar face he knew, but still he cried and cried late into the night. I tried my best to comfort him, but he wanted the only mother he knew—Claire.

Eventually I was shown to my bed, the top of a triple-bunk bed in the enclosed porch that had been turned into a children's bedroom. Emotionally worn out, I lay in the dark with the other children, wondering why I was being punished by being sent into exile. It was total banishment. No contact, no telephone calls, no visits.

Dan and Tina had four children: Peter, who was ten like me, two younger brothers and a little sister. The house had four bedrooms, and in addition to Serena and my sisters, two other couples lived there—Peter Pioneer and Rachel, whom I knew from *Music with Meaning*, and Joseph and Talitha, a German couple who spoke English with a heavy accent. Juliana had made friends with their four-year-old daughter Vera and they spent most of the day with Talitha.

I found it hard to adjust to being with Serena again after so many months of being apart. She felt a virtual stranger to me and I spent most of my time at first caring for Victor. It took two weeks for him to stop crying, and by six weeks he showed no signs of missing his former foster family.

For the first time I began to sympathize with Serena, who had struggled for many years with a debilitating condition that made it very painful for her to walk, especially when she was pregnant, which she was at the time with her third child by Dad. Her knees swelled up to twice their normal size and this crippled her ability to help in the Home. Then Victor contracted tuberculosis, which was endemic in many parts of the East. Medical care was expensive. Finally, it was decided that they both had to go to Germany to get proper medical attention. Being sent back to the West was a mark of dishonor, and to have to resort to doctors meant she was weak in faith and had spiritual problems. Everything was hush, hush, and Serena never said goodbye. The day she left, Tina asked me to distract Juliana.

"She's not going with them?" I asked.

"No. It would be too much for Serena. She's eight months pregnant, and Victor is sick. Mariana is the oldest so she'll be able to help with Victor." Mariana was only five.

I felt terrible for Juliana, the middle child, who was now left without a mother just like me, only Dad wasn't here either. Immediately I felt I had to try and protect her and be a "mother" to her. Dan and Tina were appointed our legal guardians. I was ten and Juliana was four. I didn't mind Tina, but I was afraid of Dan and tried my best to stay out of his way. He beat his boys with a metal flyswatter, sometimes a hundred swats at a time. Their shrieks made my blood run cold. After a beating, their bottoms would be bloody and swollen for days.

There was always the fear hanging over me that one day he would beat me too, but I was lucky he never did. It was his two younger boys that were beaten the most, and they often behaved violently themselves, attacking me as if passing on their pain. Once they even tried to strangle me. That scared me even more and I began to withdraw into myself. Juliana moved in with Joseph and Talitha, but, unlike me, she did not escape Dan's violent outbursts. There was little I could do to prevent the beatings he inflicted on her every day, mostly for wetting her bed, something I thought was completely unfair. When anyone would get a beating, the screams would resound through the house and a terrible feeling in the pit of my stomach would grip me until it was finally over.

I'd close my eyes and grit my teeth and mentally beg, *Dad—please come, please come.* The hope that he would some-how hear my silent prayers and come to take us away soon kept me going through the days.

*   *   *

It was one long year later, when I was eleven, that without warning, Dad arrived suddenly at the doorstep of our home with Jeremy Spencer. Now I knew how Serena had felt when she'd seen baby Victor again. I screamed, "Dad!" and flung my arms tightly about him.

He gave me a big hug. "How's my girl?"

"Oh Dad—I missed you."

"Well, we're together now. We're going to live on a farm!" he said.

"A farm? Where?"

"In Macau."

"Where's Macau, Dad?"

"It's a Portuguese colony near Hong Kong. We're going to live on Hosea's farm. You know who Hosea is, don't you?" He didn't wait for me to say that I did. Everyone knew who the entire Royal Family was by heart.

There was a part of me that was curious to meet Hosea— Mo's youngest son. I had read about him in the Mo Letters, but even more, I didn't care where we were as long as I stayed with Dad.

Hosea's farm was located in a little Chinese village called Hac Sa. The property included a fifteen-room cottage, two smaller cottages, stables, and farmland, where some forty-five members lived. Hosea had two wives, Esther and Ruth, with seven children—two girls and five boys—between them. The evening we arrived, I was unwell and had been throwing up all day. The temperature was 10 degrees—and that was cold compared to the Philippines where it is hot all year round. Esther immediately wrapped me up warm and soaked my feet in a bucket of warm water.

"You might have a fever," she said, concerned, and took my temperature, which was just slightly higher than normal. "Just have a good rest tomorrow," she cooed.

I hadn't been made such a fuss over in a long time, and Esther was the warm, motherly type, the way I had dreamed my mother would be.

Dad, Juliana, and I were shown to our room in one of the smaller cottages. It was cosy, and I liked the idea of staying in a smaller house apart from the main commune.

The next morning I had a better look around. There were no walls around the houses like the Homes in the Philippines. Chinese families lived next door to us and I would see them playing table tennis or cards outside. Because of the language barrier I was unable to talk with them. I also met Crystal and her husband, Michael. This woman was the same Crystal who had been my nanny in Greece many years earlier.

"Welcome," she said, smiling at my father. "And I remember you," she said, giving me a wink.

It didn't seem ten minutes before he started a full-blown affair with her. Her husband didn't seem to mind.

While Esther was the kindest person I had ever met, I discovered quickly that Hosea was a violent and explosive man. I saw him beat his boys and he would grab them by the back of the neck, nearly choking them. David, Hosea's second oldest son, was fifteen and I was shocked when I found out he couldn't read. The boys never had good schooling. David and his older brother Nehemiah shouldered most of the responsibility of the farm and animals. They were expert farmers, but lacked the basic 3Rs. David was very self-conscious about this and it contributed to his low self-esteem. I had learned to read before I was three, and so too had Juliana. I couldn't understand why boys that age had never been properly educated.

We had to get up at five in the morning. Waking up before dawn took some adjusting to. Hosea's boys would milk the cows, collect the eggs from the chickens, feed the goats and horses, and clean out the stables. In the meantime, I was given the job of making breakfast, and soon lunch and dinner for up to forty-five people. I was often on my own in the kitchen and struggled to lift the pots and pans, which were industrial size. I also received a few cuts and burns, though thankfully nothing too serious. I followed recipe books and experimented on my own. I made pasta salads, stews, and roasted heart and beef in the oven.

Apart from Hosea's two daughters, I was the only other pre-teen girl. I found out that the boys had regular dates with the adult women there, but I was not prepared for when I walked in on Aaron, who was thirteen, having sex with Crystal, their teen shepherdess, on her bed. Embarrassed and disturbed, I quickly closed the door. The boys rivalled for my attention, and constantly teased and badgered me for sex. I was appalled by their behaviour. They made holes in the bathroom walls so they could spy on me. They called me prudish and stuck up. I didn't care. What little natural curiosity I had about sex had turned to disgust, and I made it clear that I was not interested.

I'll never forget one morning when David came into the kitchen while I was preparing lunch and asked me, "Do girls get horny?"

"How dare you ask me that," I snapped. "Of course they don't." I had no idea that girls could want sex or that it could be a pleasurable experience. I stormed off in a huff, while he just laughed.

Everything we read still emphasized sex. A new book was published for teens and pre-teens, called *The Basic Training Handbook*. In it I read about my friend Armi and the teens in Grandpa's Home, who had gone through a training program led by Sarah Davidito and Maria. The strict discipline, corrections, date schedules and confessions I read about made me glad that I had not been invited.

During the week, Dad worked with Jeremy Spencer on *Life with Grandpa*. But on Freeday, we would go out together for walks by the beach. He also taught me to ride a bicycle by holding on to the back of my bike and running alongside me. I fell and cut my leg and knee quite badly—I still have the scars—but he pushed me on even when I got discouraged and almost gave up. It took two days of determination on both our parts, but soon I could pedal off without wobbling. I was beginning to enjoy living with my father for the first time in two years. But after only three months he was unexpectedly summoned back to World Services. When he told me the news, I felt hollow.

"Oh no! But Dad—why?"

"I'm going on my own with Jeremy," he said, despondently. "You and Julie have to stay here—but it won't be for long, I promise sweetie."

"Dad, you know you can't promise anything," I said despondently.

We spent our last day together at a hotel in town. Macau was a strange mixture of brash excitement—like Hong Kong, which lay a few miles away across the gulf—and antiquity—its old brick buildings reflecting its history as a Portuguese colony dating back to the early seventeenth century. I was happy for the moment, but sad that we were to be parted so soon.

Eating lunch at a small café table in a cobbled square, I told Dad what was on my mind. "I don't want to stay here without you. I hate Hosea," I burst out. "He scares me."

"Oh sweetie—" he broke off and looked down, despondent. "I'll see what I can do."

After lunch, we had a siesta in the hotel room. When I woke up, Dad was not in the room. I heard noises coming from the bathroom, and opened the door a crack. Dad's head was buried in his arms and he was sobbing. I had never seen him cry so hard. I did not want to embarrass him so I crept back to the room and lay back down on the bed. Somehow it made me feel better to see him cry. At least I knew that leaving us hurt him too.

I don't know if it was Dad's doing, but a month later, Juliana and I were escorted back to the Philippines to what was now called Marianne's Home. A lot had happened during the time I had been away. Paul and Marianne had separated, and Paul had been given a new job as national area shepherd for the Philippines. Marianne's Home had a new mission to Flirty Fish and convert the officers in the Filipino military. No task seemed too big or too outrageous; after all, Jesus was on their side. Mo was adept at using women and sex to influence men in position of power and government.

The best part of moving back to Marianne's Home was finding Armi there. I had missed her, and being with her again gave me a sense of familiarity. I was also eager to hear about what it was like at the King's House, but she had been sworn to secrecy and could not tell me much. I did notice, however, that she had a gold ring on her finger.

"Where did you get that?" I asked, curious. She twisted the ring nervously as she shared her secret with me.

"Grandpa gave it to me. It's a wedding ring."

"He made you his wife?" I asked, completely shocked.

She glanced up into my eyes briefly and I saw so much pain and unhappiness there I could weep with rage.

She told me the ceremony took place in Grandpa's bed as Maria sat and watched. I shuddered. She was just thirteen when the mock wedding took place.

"All the girls who went for teen training got a wedding ring."

"Even Mene?" I whispered.

"Yes," Armi replied.

But she's his granddaughter. The thought disgusted me.

I could tell that there was more she wished she could say, but it was treason to divulge anything about Mo and Maria. If she had been found out, she would have been punished severely. I knew this and didn't push her to tell me more—but it did explain why Krys, another teen girl who lived in our room, had a matching ring like Armi's.

Sometimes Armi and I would pace the front garden for exercise, when we could exchange a few quick confidences out of the others' hearing. One afternoon I told her a dream

I'd had. "It was really weird. I tried to get this large egg and run away with it. And you jumped over the wall to escape."

She looked at me in surprise. "I have been thinking about running away and finding my parents." She stopped, and glanced over her shoulder as if we could be overheard. Confiding in each other our inner thoughts was dangerous—they'd say we were murmuring and doubting. We were trapped in that world and could do nothing. I could sense her pain and though we never discussed it again, we had a shared empathy and understanding.

Krys and Armi were put on a regular dating schedule with two adult men, John and Silas. John had been the national area shepherd before Paul took over his job, and Silas was now the shepherd of Marianne's Home's sister commune close by, with his wife Endureth.

One morning I woke up to the sound of someone throwing up in the bathroom. It was Krys. After a few days Armi and I realized she was showing signs of pregnancy. Our teen shepherd, Windy, reported it to Marianne and one of the Home shoppers was sent off to buy a home pregnancy testing kit. The results were positive.

"Who's the father?" I asked Armi.

"I think it's John. That's what Krys told me."

The leaders went into panic alert. Krys was just fourteen. There would be no question of taking her to hospital for pre-natal care. We were told not to discuss her situation with anyone or talk about who the father was. Krys was not allowed out of the house and had to wear baggy clothes to disguise her growing belly.

I was disgusted. John did not own up to his responsibilities as a father-to-be and it was obvious that Krys was being thrown to the wolves as the scapegoat. In his Letters Mo often referred to the Muslim and Indian cultures of times past, where young girls were married, as an example of how sex with children was legitimate.

He wrote:

> In India they often had child brides at seven years of age! They can get married at that age! Then they could do all the fucking they want without having to worry about any kids until they are 12 years old! We're getting young teenagers in the Family right now who are old enough to get married and have children. Why can't they have it, huh? Oh she might get pregnant! So what?

I wanted to throw these letters in the rubbish bin, but instead, we had to sit for hours reading them without question. The reality was that in our world the young girls were used to satisfy the lusts of the men without any thought for the long-term consequences of their actions. Krys would become a single mother before she had a chance to live her own childhood. I was determined not to suffer a similar fate.

It was now 1987, and Teen Training Camps were being held on every continent, following the blueprint given in *The Basic Training Handbook*. Some two hundred young members from all over South East Asia attended a camp in Manila for two weeks. Maria and Sarah Davidito orchestrated the camps for the teens and pre-teens, as it became apparent that the children were in need of indoctrination into the beliefs of the

Family. Brazenly, we were told, "Yes, we're brainwashing you—washing your brain clean of the Devil's influences and replacing it with the Word."

When I arrived at the camp, I was shown to a "girls" room" of ten other girls in my little group. We were called the "Lovelights." Each team had their own shepherd, whose job it was to monitor the teens twenty-four hours a day. I was excited to meet so many other young people, but we had little time to talk. In the morning we lined up single file and marched to the dining hall for breakfast. Our days were filled with classes, inspirations and, memorization. Loyalty to the Family and "David our King" was emphasized in skits and songs, and we all had to memorize and sign a pledge of dedication to our prophet and Maria. Every night before bed we wrote reactions and confessions in an Open Heart Report. Willingness, humility, and submission to leadership and God were the qualities we were supposed to strive for, in preparation for our calling to become future leaders of the world. It all seemed so surreal.

We had it drummed into us that we were "It"—the best place on earth to be. I had never known what the alternative was, but the adults told us horror stories of tragedy, pain, and emptiness before joining the Family and I concluded that no matter how bad I had it, it must be ten times worse in the System.

Before we left, we all filled in a lengthy questionnaire that asked intimate details about every aspect of our lives. "We want you to be completely honest because these questionnaires will be sent to Grandpa and Maria to read," our teen shepherd told us. This was our chance to say what we felt and to be heard. I dutifully and trustingly wrote down my inner thoughts, as well as the traumatic sexual experiences I had suffered, including names and when it had happened.

Shortly after we returned from camp, Marianne read everyone a memorandum from Maria and Sarah Davidito. I had not been the only girl to report bad sexual experiences, and this, together with a number of teen pregnancies, alarmed the leaders. However, they were careful not to blame Mo, the prophet.

We were told, "There is nothing wrong with the Law of Love, but sexual contact between adults and children is now discouraged"—not banned, but "discouraged." I sighed with relief. I did not care about the doctrine, I was just glad that we did not have to practise it anymore.

But I was wrong. The new laws were meaningless, as I was shortly to find out.

I had first been molested as a child of six by Peruvian Manuel in Greece, on the back double bed of Silas and Endureth's caravan. He and his wife Maria had gone with us to Sri Lanka during the big exodus. Now, they were living in our sister Home, run by Silas and Endureth. We would go over every week for Sunday fellowship, and I often went to visit Renee and Daniella and we went out busking together. Peruvian Manuel was always flirtatious and eyeing me up while I was there which made me very uncomfortable. He came over to our house one day and stayed the night. He was given the bottom bunk in my room because Armi had gone on a trip for a few days. I was extremely nervous. Childhood memories flooded back to haunt me as I clambered on to the top bunk and closed my eyes.

A few minutes later, he came into the room and started stroking my back. I kept my eyes shut and pretended to be asleep. He did not get the hint, and reached down to my vagina and pushed his finger inside.

"You're so sexy, you know that?" he whispered in my ear.

I lay there rigid and opened my eyes. "Leave me alone. You can't do this," I said, referring to the new memorandum.

He placed his mouth on mine and forced his tongue in, while still pushing his finger up me more ardently. I was scared and hated confrontation, but I refused to be bullied into this. "No! No! No!" I hissed through gritted teeth. "You know it's against the rules." I pulled away from him and closed my mouth tight. After a moment or two he backed off.

"Okay...," he said, but lingered. I stiffened my body. He let out a sigh and went down to the bottom bunk. I lay awake for the longest time, my heart beating hard as I heard him masturbating. When I was sure he was asleep, I closed my eyes but had a fitful night's sleep.

In the morning, I got up, grabbed my clothes and went to the bathroom to get dressed. Later that day, I found Marianne sitting by the pool, and asked if I could speak with her. I naively believed that if I reported it, he would be dealt with. Marianne showed no sign of shock, or even disapproval. All she said was, "I'll speak to him about it." She never mentioned the incident to me again, and I was left to wonder why or what happened. I concluded that these new rules were meaningless because the leaders were not going to enforce them.

Indeed, the one who would be corrected was me. Soon afterwards, Marianne called me to her room and sat me down on a chair in the corner of the room. She and another leader, Zadok, sat opposite me.

"You have some deep, spiritual problems," Marianne started. "We are very concerned about you and you need to be honest. You have a problem with spacing out a lot and daydreaming. Idleness is the Devil's workshop."

I never quite figured out what "spacing out" actually meant, but it was borrowed from hippie lingo when someone was on drugs and had a blanked-out look on their face. If I didn't hear what someone said, or if I was not busy doing something, or simply looking out the window, an adult would snap, "Celeste! Stop spacing out."

"What are you thinking about when you daydream?" Marianne asked.

I was at a loss as how to reply to her question. "Nothing. I don't think about anything really."

She looked puzzled, then asked me again what thoughts I had been thinking. She warned me how serious a crime daydreaming was, and reminded me of "The Last State" Letter about Mene. We had read the Letter at the Teen Training Camp. She had been a "daydreamer" and this led to her thinking evil things about her Grandfather, the letter said. The violence in the letter scared the living daylights out me. It described how Mene had come into his room and Grandpa had greeted her with a kiss and then had suddenly grabbed her and shook her violently while speaking in tongues. He'd beaten her with a rod and rebuked the devils and demons out of her. I was even more shocked when he accused her of betrayal, saying he had taken her into his bed and yet she had the gall to criticize him and refuse him.

She was his flesh and blood, and he had sex with her? Even though we were told that "all things were lawful unto us" incest was a step too far for me to accept.

In "The Last State," Grandpa also accused Mene of being insane and gave Sarah Davidito and Peter Amsterdam, his third in command, permission to beat her whenever she had bad thoughts and to tie her to her bed at night. I could not understand how the perfect girl who had been our role model could have changed so drastically into a sinful monster, possessed by the Devil who warped her mind with murderous thoughts.

After Mene, the leaders were convinced that there were other potential doubters and dissenters. Because Mene had been the good girl, all the good kids were under suspicion too. I worked hard and tried my best to keep the rules, but Marianne had it in for me in her room that day and would not give up until I had confessed to some crime.

I could not think of anything to confess to. "I don't space out," I insisted. "I'm not imagining or seeing anything."

Frustrated, she paused, and then looked angrily at me. "Well, that's even *worse!* The Devil is speaking to you and you don't even know it."

I could not believe such nonsense. I let out a laugh, and then stifled it quickly. But not quickly enough.

"You think it's funny?" Zadok chided. "This is serious and the Devil is out to destroy you. If we don't break you, God will have to do it. And believe me, that is so much worse."

Then came what I believe was the real reason for the correction. Marianne had been given the reports I had written at the camp and these showed, she claimed, that I had been harboring bitterness against God and "my brothers in the Lord." She told me I needed to forgive those I felt had wronged me. She also accused me of making an idol of Dad in my heart. She had heard reports from people in the Home that I had been talking about missing my dad. This was proof I had made an idol of him. I had to forsake him and give him to God.

"God is a jealous God," she scolded, "and he will have no other gods before Him."

I treasured Dad's rare letters and read them over and over again when I missed him. The hope that I would see him again kept me going. Now she was telling me I had made him an idol that I needed to destroy. This attack was the final straw, the hurt nerve that could not be touched. I broke down into tears. *How could I forget my own father?* All my feelings of abandonment and loss of the person I loved most in the world burst out, and I could not control it. I desperately wanted to hold back the tears but couldn't.

This display of emotion satisfied Marianne that she had finally broken my pride and rebellious spirit. She pronounced my "sentence'; I would have to spend the next month in isolation, reading and writing reactions to Mo Letters on rebellion, yieldedness, submission and demon possession. I would have an adult "buddy" who would read with me—I was not allowed to talk to anyone else.

Changing my attitude would not be enough though. I was also asked to change my name. Celeste was too spacey (because it meant "heavenly" in Spanish). My head was too much in the clouds and I needed to choose a more down-to-earth name.

"You have a few days to think and pray about it, and then you can get back to me on what the Lord shows you," she said.

For three days I could drink only soup and water. The hunger pains were my only company as I was confined in a small room apart from everyone else. At the end of the three days, Marianne asked,

"Well, have you decided on your new name?"

I nodded. "Joan, after Joan of Arc. I want to be a fighter like her."

Marianne was pleased with this. "Jesus needs fighters in his Endtime army," she said. "Good. I'll let everyone know."

During my month of isolation my mind and feelings went numb, almost as if I went into shutdown mode. I remember this time as a blur, where one day blended into another. At the end of the month, the commune gathered to say a prayer of deliverance over me. My head was anointed with oil and everyone laid hands on my head, speaking in tongues. The demons of pride, self-righteousness and rebellion were supposedly cast out of me.

I was confused. *Was there really a struggle for my soul in Heaven between God and the Devil? Why didn't I feel it then?* I still had no idea what I had done wrong or what part of the Devil Marianne had seen in me, but I was just glad and relieved that it was over.

Later I found out that I was not the only one who had gone through a breaking when I was stunned to read two Letters of Confession, published for the whole Family, in which Dad confessed his sins as part of a public demotion and retraining at the Kings house. First, he admitted his fame with *Music with Meaning* had made him too proud. During his years in college he had dabbled in the occult. The demons must have latched on to him and he asked for cleansing prayer to rid him of their influence. I was hurt when he wrote that the women in his life were better off since he had left them for the Lord.

Did he really believe that? I wondered.

In a second Confession, he said that he had made an idol of his mother, Krystyna. Mo had said that demons could "hitchhike" into your home, riding in on photographs. To break her hold and get rid of the evil spirits on her photographs, Dad had burned every picture of our grandmother. She was a Catholic and a loving mother before her death. How was anything about her demonic? I was heartbroken that he had destroyed these irreplaceable pictures that had been given to him by his father and relatives on his trip to Poland in search of his roots. The only photograph left of our grandmother is the one he gave me to keep on his return.

On the back of the Teen Training Camps, "retraining centers" were being set up in key locations around the world for the Family's teenagers and "rebel" adults to be sent to for further training. At the same time, Mo went too far in his meddling with Filipino politics and the military, and the Family wore out their welcome. The media picked up the story and Mo declared the Philippines a "reaped field." Marianne was ordered to move her entire Home to Tokyo. During this period of transition, Armi, Krys, my little sister Juliana and I were sent a nearby complex in Manila so huge it was known as the Jumbo. Krys still lived with us in the girls' teen room

even though she had just had a little baby girl. She had diffi-
culty bonding with her child and didn't take care of her properly because she wanted to share in the few fun things the
rest of us teens were allowed, instead of staying back all the
time, watching a baby she hadn't wanted.

It was here I met Paul Peloquin again. He came to film
another strip-dance video for Mo. He pulled me aside.
"Sweetie, Grandpa has made a special request. He wants you
to dance. We're not really supposed to film underage girls
dancing nude anymore, but this is just an exception."

The new rules were supposed to stop all displays of child
sexuality but the leaders wanted to make him happy.

"He thought your dance for his birthday last year was
very sexy." Paul winked at me. I didn't want to do this
dance—I felt used, put on display for some old man's entertainment. But no one said "no" to Grandpa without serious
consequences so I agreed. And just as before, Paul coached
me from behind the camera. When the song finished, I was
applauded for my humility and yieldedness to the Lord.
Everything was always about yieldedness and submission,
but I was beginning to wonder if it was really God who we
were submitting to, or the whims of our leaders.

The time had come for a team of us to move to a school
being set up in Japan. When I was told that Juliana was to
stay in the Philippines, I worried if she would be all right
without Dad or me around. I had tried to look out for her as
best I could over the years, but in reality there was little I
could do.

I was determined not to leave before seeing my father.
Even though the location of World Services was supposed

to be a secret, I knew he was still in the Philippines. The day before flying to Tokyo, I was given permission to spend two hours with him at a hotel. I was put in a van and blindfolded so I could not see where I was being taken. After driving around for an hour, the van came to a stop. When they took the blindfold off, I was greeted by my smiling dad. I was so happy to see him again, if only for a few hours.

"You've got gray hair!" I exclaimed. He had aged since I last saw him almost two years before. He kissed me on the forehead just as he did when I was a little girl. "How's my baby?"

"I'm not a baby anymore," I said, standing up tall.

"Well, no matter how old you are, I'll always be that much older than you—so you'll always be my baby," Dad teased. I smiled, half annoyed, and half enjoying his fussing. We went into the five-star hotel.

"How did you know I was in the Philippines?" He was curious to know.

"I just did. It's obvious." I didn't say that Grandpa seemed to know everything that happened in our Home, and his Letters talked about the political situation in the Philippines. I'd just put two and two together. Dad was shocked. Mo moved in an aura of such tight control and secrecy that I could see he was worried that I might inadvertently let something slip and he'd be blamed.

"Don't breathe a word," he admonished.

"Oh, Dad—I know the rules."

We went into the restaurant and ate lunch together. "How's Julie doing?" he asked.

"She's okay, I guess. I don't see her often, but she's doing well in her school work."

"She's a brain on a stick," Dad laughed. He seemed so glib about it. "You're both true Family children. And look how good you both are doing."

Well, I wasn't so sure about that. I had had a terrible year, but I didn't want to disappoint Dad or sound like I was murmuring or being negative. Our time went all too quickly, and I got teary-eyed when it was time to leave. Dad told me to be brave and that he would see me again soon, if not on this Earth then in the Millennium. He kissed me on the forehead and said goodbye. I was blindfolded again and spirited away.

CHAPTER SIX

Torn

Early in December 1987, a group of about thirty of us arrived in Tokyo airport from the Philippines. As the plane came down, I saw the breathtaking view of Mount Fuji. Capped with snow, it was instantly recognizable. We crowded on to a hired bus and traveled to a small town called Tateyama, five hours south. It was in the mountains by the sea. Japan is a series of long islands and the seasons move slowly from one end to the other—it can be winter at one end and still summer at the other. We were on the middle island, where it was just at the end of fall. Everything was miniature size—the roads, the shops, the houses and the Buddhist temples.

Our destination was the Heavenly City School. It was a large building that had been built for the Family by the Naritas, an elderly Japanese couple who supported the group financially. I learned that Mr. Narita was the wealthy owner of a nightclub called Charivari in the Ginza district, a high-class and expensive shopping and entertainment section of Tokyo. He had been targeted by some Flirty Fishers and had quickly succumbed to their charms. Perhaps even he didn't realize exactly how much he was going to spend in the years that followed.

As well as the school building, which was built in the shape of a cross, the Naritas—Mrs. Narita had quickly been converted as well—also owned a number of smaller houses within walking distance of the main school building, where the leadership stayed. Naturally, in return for his financial support, Mr. Narita enjoyed the sexual services of Family women. If the object of Flirty Fishing was to simply win souls to Christ, his soul was saved many times over. Flirty Fishing had by now been discontinued, mainly due to the AIDS scare, but there were exceptions for those whose support and protection the Family needed.

We arrived from the hot weather of Manila to a bitter cold winter. The abrupt change was a shock to my system. At night we slept on futons on the floor and took showers in true Japanese fashion in a large *ofuro* or communal bath. The school building was so large it was difficult to heat. Portable gas heaters were used sparingly to save on fuel and in the mornings we would all huddle around our one heater in the right wing of the building where we slept, to keep warm as we got dressed.

In January one morning, we woke to a dazzling view of snow. It was only the second time I had ever seen snow and I was captivated by the sparkling beauty of everything—trees, buildings and the ground were covered. We rushed outside, teenagers just bursting to break free and have fun. I had my first snowball fight since Greece. Ado, the head teen shepherd, took me aside.

"There's a letter for you," he started. "It's from England."

I almost gasped with shock and felt faint. *England! Was it from my mum?* I was too scared to ask.

Ado handed me the letter. "Let's pray together first to cleanse this letter from hitchhiking spirits."

Obediently, my heart still jumping erratically, I closed my eyes as Ado prayed. The envelope was already opened and he watched while I carefully took out the letter. He already knew the contents—nothing we received was ever private and was always heavily censored. My eyes flew to the address, and then to the signature. It wasn't from Mum.

It was from Mum's sister, an aunt I didn't know I possessed. Aunt Caryn wrote that Mum, Kristina, and David would love me to come and visit them in England. She also mentioned that David was going to school and doing well in mathematics.

I reread those words, puzzled, because Family children did not attend System schools. I was riveted by shock at the idea of actually going for a visit. All my old dreams and hopes and yearnings—the constant weight of missing my mum that I had carried around with me for a decade—flooded back. I wondered why Mum hadn't written herself, or Kristina.

"I'd love to go and visit. Can I go to England?" I asked, hopefully.

"We'll get back to you," Ado replied. I dared to hope that my dream of seeing my mother again would come true, but it wasn't to be. The weeks slid away and I heard nothing more.

Tateyama was such a beautiful place that at times the problems and the threat of doom that always hung over our heads seemed very remote. But the Endtime was always there. Grandpa had predicted the Great Tribulation, the last three and a half years before Jesus' return, would begin sometime in 1989. The call on the Naritas' purse had been great. They had built the School as a refuge, with a bunker basement deep underground, equipped to survive an atomic war. An air vent in the bunker would, in theory, filter out the radiation. They also had a large stash of whisky and liquor stored. Based on his experiences from the Great Depression of the 1930s, Grandpa believed that these items would the best commodities to trade in the event of an economic crash.

Mo had also interpreted the measurements of the Heavenly City given in the biblical Book of Revelations, chapter 21, to be the description of a pyramid structure. Mo's fervent disciples would live near the top of the apex while other Christians would be Heaven's second-class citizens.

One afternoon, we all were gathered in the main dining room. I was flabbergasted to see Peter Amsterdam walk in. Everyone went quiet as he sat down on a chair placed on a raised platform at the front of the room. He had an important message to give us.

Inspired by Mo's revelation, the Naritas had already built a pyramid structure at the top of a hill adjacent to the school building as a prayer room. Mo now decided to make it a tourist attraction, to spread the message.

"Over the next few months, artists from World Services will be working on the pyramid's interior, creating miniature models of the heavenly attractions inside," Peter Amsterdam explained. "You are not to go up to the pyramid under any circumstances, or even so much as look up at the hill during the work. Remember, the eyes of the Lord are in every place, so don't think when no one is looking you can disobey," he warned.

He looked around the hall and his eyes seemed to bore into each one of us as we sat in awe at meeting the third most important person in the Family. "You do not need to know why you are not allowed to look. And if anyone is caught disobeying, the offender will be excommunicated."

After he and the shepherds swept out and we dispersed, there was a soft, excited buzz, like a hive of bees. I was terrified of breaking the rules. I found out later that the real reason for the secrecy was that Mo and Maria were living at the Fountain House, ten minutes' walk away. It did seem odd to me at the time that at certain times during the day a message would go round that we were not allowed outside, and we were forbidden to go to the White House across the street from the school building. This was a small house also owned by the Naritas where the leadership stayed, and Grandpa often visited, cloaked in secrecy, for meetings.

Peter Amsterdam led regular evening meetings with everyone—it was a time of retraining. He also instituted a Word Date schedule. We were supposed to share God's love and read God's Word. Four makeshift rooms were built in the bunker basement as love rooms. Each one had a bed, a little table stand with tissues and lubrication, and a painting with a Mo Quote on the wall for decoration. The only person I wanted to be with was Miguel. He was my first boyfriend. We were both thirteen years old, just a month apart, and he was a Sagittarius like my dad. He was fun loving and popular and I liked his jokes and laid-back style. But of course, only being with Miguel would be considered selfish and the teen shepherds arranged the schedule for us.

Our teen shepherd, Ricky, was our daily "inspirationalist" and he got a kick out of "breaking our bottles" by getting the girls to take their tops off while playing the guitar and singing, "Come on Ma, Burn Your Bra." For his birthday, his partner Elaine got the teen girls to take their tops off and he went down the line feeling them up. That was our "birthday present" to him. I was the only one who refused to take part. Afterwards, Ricky had it in for me.

"You're just an old bottle." He would single me out in front of everyone. It made me more embarrassed and stubborn. The group pressure to conform was intense, but I refused to take my top off no matter what. Finally, I relented. For Peter Amsterdam's birthday in April, Elaine suggested the girls do a repeat performance like they had done for Ricky. I refused at first but decided last minute to do a topless dance with Armi. My true motive was to impress Miguel who was sitting with the teen boys on the side watching, but the shepherds saw my change of heart as a sign of spiritual growth.

Peter had told us there would be people from World Services around, and that if we bumped into them we were not to talk to them. They always traveled in pairs and I soon noticed a teen boy doing fix-it jobs around the school building with a Scandinavian-looking man who accompanied him. I had only seen pictures of Davidito when he was a toddler, but though he was much older now, the teen boy looked uncannily similar. His tanned skin and distinct Spanish features gave him away. I wanted to talk to him, but he kept his eyes downward most of the time, and I sensed his uneasiness at this constant supervision. Nonetheless, I continued to look at him curiously whenever I saw him.

After the pyramid project was completed, we were finally allowed to go up and see it. The inside was transformed into a showcase of Mo's idea of a Heavenly City theme park. We also started to see more of Davidito, or Pete, as he introduced himself, and Davida, the daughter of Sarah Davidito. They had been given permission to attend some of our teen activities and classes. They both were incredibly timid which surprised me. I had expected Davidito to be confident, a leader, a role model of everything we were supposed to strive for. But given his background—which we all knew about—his timidity was understandable. The children at Grandpa's Home lived in a glass bowl like *Big Brother*, where everything was reported. Over the years we had read every detail of his life, his first steps, every spanking, every reward. We knew everything about Davidito, Davida, and Techi, even though we never met them face-to-face. They had grown up knowing no other children but each other.

When I met him, Davidito was thirteen. It was the first time he had met a large number of teens and I could see that he desperately wanted to join in, but he found it very hard to talk to us after years of isolation and repression. One afternoon I got a chance to chat with him alone. He was sitting in the teen room and I sat next to him. I was a little nervous, not knowing what I could ask him and what he was allowed to say. But as we started chatting, I felt instant affection for him. He was just like any one of us, not the idol that had been built up in the Letters and *Life with Grandpa*.

"What's it like meeting so many young people for the first time?" I asked.

"It's good," he replied a little hesitantly. "I've made some friends. It's difficult, though. I'm expected to be an example all the time. I just want to be like everyone else."

We all knew that he was destined to become one of the last two Endtime Witnesses along with his mother, Maria, who had been elevated to the status of prophetess. Grandpa had prophesied that together they would fulfil this role talked about in the Book of Revelations, and that Davidito would die as a martyr at the hands of the Antichrist soldiers before Jesus' return. While I had nightmares that maybe one day I would be killed as a martyr, I could not imagine what it was like *knowing* your fate was to die on the streets of Jerusalem. I wanted to ask him how he felt about this horrible fate, but thought it might be cruel to remind him. It was a tall order having to be the perfect reflection of his parents all the time when all he wanted was to hang out with us and enjoy life.

One afternoon we were gathered together for Correction, under strict silence. I lay on a futon at the back of the room, as I had been sick for a month with swollen glands and a temperature. That summer almost the entire teen group had come down with kissing fever, or mononucleosis. But sick or not, a Correction had to include everyone. Peter Amsterdam walked in, flanked by our teen shepherds. They sat facing us.

After a prayer, Peter Amsterdam thundered sternly, "The sins of your foolishness and worldliness have come to the attention of Grandpa himself."

We looked at each other. What was this about?

He continued, "Some of you were caught listening to a compilation of System music! Sad to say, Pete was part of this. It doesn't excuse him but you all have had a part in being terrible influences, and allowing the Devil to get in."

I had no idea what Peter Amsterdam was talking about but again we were all in trouble for the actions of some. The list of our supposed sins was long. We had indulged in foolish talking and idleness instead of memorizing Bible scripture. We dressed worldly or cool. The girls flaunted long earrings and short tank tops.

At the end, the ringleaders were singled out and marched to the front. Peter Amsterdam produced a leather strap, and the guilty boys were given a belting in front of us as an example to all. We were all crying and shaking. When the punishment was over, he bawled, "Get down on your hands and knees and pray for mercy!"

It wasn't the end of it—a long list of punishments was devised for everyone for the backsliding and relaxed attitude that had led to this crime. Four of us teens who were not yet well were moved that night to the sick house, glad that we would escape at least some of the months of punishments the rest of the group would suffer. A few weeks later, I caught whooping cough. After two terrible months, and just as I was about to be released from quarantine, I was exposed to chickenpox. The shepherds told me that this meant I had to remain in quarantine for another month. It came to mid-November and I had been five months in confinement. I was going stir crazy, bored, cut off from my friends, and I was desperate to do some work, anything to keep me occupied. I hit a low of deep depression.

Then, unexpectedly, Dad arrived at the School from the Philippines. "Dad!" I hugged him. "I've missed you so much." I expected sympathy from him, but for the first time in my life, he lost his temper. I didn't feel he had the right to scold me. He hadn't lived with me for years. Raising his voice, he launched in with an attack.

"I heard you've been sick for months. You've been disobedient! You haven't taken your Get Out time faithfully like Grandpa ordered!" A Mo Letter called "Get Out" had been written about my dad, when he got deathly sick with hepatitis at Loveville in Greece. Mo wrote, "We can't have a show depending on a sick man," and ordered a regime of daily exercise to make sure that he stayed healthy. Since that day, Dad had always been faithful with his daily exercise, jogging or doing yoga exercises.

I was shocked and the tears were brimming. *He must have received a bad report from the teen shepherds*, I thought. For me to be sick for so long reflected badly on him.

Facing this angry man, in an instant the image I had of my perfect father was shattered. I thought he loved me; he had never lost his temper before, he'd always been fair. But I did not recognize the man in front of me now. *What had happened to him the years that we were apart? Was he really just like the rest of them, irrational and temperamental?*

As he continued ranting, I shut down, blocking him out. Throughout my months of illness I'd hated feeling helpless; but I hated even more everyone's judgemental attitude towards me, like it was something I had done wrong. Now even my own dad had turned against me. I couldn't believe it.

Unfortunately, I became ill again. Two days later I came down with another temperature and broke out in hives. My body swelled up with bright red bumps all over and my lips and eyes puffed up to three times their normal size. I didn't recognize my own reflection in the mirror. On the third day, Dad came to see me at the Blue House. He told me he had been praying desperately about the reason why I had been afflicted for so long.

"The Lord showed me that you have been put under a curse," he said. "Your mother is a backslider. She has left the Family."

I struggled to take it in. *Mum had left the Family!* It was devastating and shocking news. For the past year, ever since that letter, I had hung on to the hope that I would be allowed to visit her. I didn't even know if she was still in England. I had no idea where she was, or what she was doing.

"Yes, she has gone back to the System, to the pit, to wallow in the mire," he said disdainfully. "She has asked for you and wants to take you out of the Family—"

My mouth dropped open with shock as wild thoughts and emotions surged through me. She had asked for me! She wanted me! But did she even remember me? It had been so long.

"The Lord showed me that you need to pray against her and rebuke her spirit. Grandpa wrote a Mo Letter about this, called, 'God's Curses.' You should read it."

A silent tear ran down my cheek. I still felt a bond of love and loyalty to my mother that no one had replaced. *Pray against her?* It was unthinkable.

Dad was on a roll. "She's not your mother any more. You need to renounce any thoughts of her and pray against her influence in your life. This is serious spiritual warfare!"

I was torn between my love for him, my need for his approval, and my instinctive repugnance over what he was asking me to do. *Had Mum really put a curse on me?* Dad knew how much I loved her. Now he had the leverage he needed to totally destroy my memory of her for good.

I felt a wave of black despair sweep over me. I was still sick, run down, and depressed. I felt beaten. I gave in. "Okay," I said, but I had no intention of praying against her myself.

Dad laid his hands on me and prayed fervently. "May the Lord destroy your mother and take her out of the way. She's better off dead then being a tool in the hands of the Devil." The prayer went on a while, and finally he concluded with, "May the Lord to cleanse your daughter, Celeste, completely from her rebellious spirit."

It almost destroyed me to hear my Dad pray to God to kill someone, backslider or not. Grandpa had often prayed such venomous prayers against his enemies, *but now my own mother?* That day I shut her away and made a conscious effort not to think about her anymore. It was too painful to go there.

The next morning I woke up and the swelling had gone down. By the end of the day the hives had disappeared completely. My "miraculous" recovery made me wonder if what Dad had said was true. He certainly took it as a sign that I had been delivered.

I was finally released from the sick house, and like any released prisoner I was ecstatic to be back in normal life. I started a Family apprenticeship program in photography, which I loved. It was also Christmas; I joined up with the singing team again and performed at the Christmas show that was held at a fancy hotel for all our Japanese friends, over a hundred and fifty people. It boosted my self-confidence and esteem and I started to feel better after so many months of illness and isolation.

But just a month later, my tourist visa expired and I had to go to Korea for what was called a visa trip. This was common—members were often coming and going in such a way to renew their visas. It had never been a problem. I left the day before my fourteenth birthday with an adult partner, Sue, the cheerful, auburn-haired former club secretary of *Music with Meaning* back in the Loveville era. However, when we tried to re-enter Japan, immigration stopped Sue and we were both refused entry. After a night in detention we were put on a plane to Hong Kong. I was devastated and cried the entire flight.

"I can't believe this has happened," I sobbed. "I was going to out for dinner with Dad for my birthday when I got back." Sue was upset herself. She had left her lover and job in Tokyo and her future was just as uncertain. There was terrible turbulence on the flight, and this added to my anxiety. I thought for sure we were going to crash into the ocean.

At Hong Kong airport, we were greeted by Zadok and a World Services man named Isaac. Sue disappeared with the World Services leader to a Home in Hong Kong and Zadok told me I was headed to Macau.

I burst into tears again. *Not the farm!* I would have to start all over again, away from my dad and my friends. The unfairness of it made me angry. "Don't worry," Zadok tried to comfort me. "Hosea isn't there anymore. There're a lot of teens. It's different." But his words were not reassuring. For days I cried and cried. Zadok and the teen shepherds there became concerned about my emotional state and did their best to try and lift my spirits, but it was no good. I was a physical and emotional wreck.

Finally, I pulled myself together and started to make friends with the teen girls. The farm had been turned into a training center similar to ours in Japan—but part of it was like a prison camp for wayward teens. For the first time since she was twelve and had modeled for *Heaven's Girl* in the Philippines, I saw Mene. She had been sent away from the King's House to Macau in disgrace and was a Detention Teen now, kept apart from the main group. The number one crime that could land you in the Detention Teens was spreading doubts, showing a critical and analytical spirit, and questioning the words of the prophet, as Mene had done. She was the first DT placed under the charge of Crystal and her husband, Michael. They were brutally harsh.

I saw Mene with the other DTs carrying out heavy manual labor around the farm—mostly meaningless work, such as digging ditches and then filling them up again, or painting and then repainting the old barn, first brown and then green, and then back to brown again. The aim was to exhaust them to break their spirits. My childhood friend looked pale and gaunt but we were forbidden to talk to her or even make eye contact. She was under permanent silence restriction. Sometimes she would disappear for weeks at a time. I learned from the teens that were with her in the DT program that she had been put in solitary confinement in a small attic room, beaten and tied naked spread-eagled to the bed, with a bucket for a toilet, and fed only bread and water.

The thought of being sent to Detention so terrified me I did everything possible to be seen as a yielded and dedicated disciple. I just wanted to get out of the farm as soon as possible.

After three months of hearing nothing, we received an urgent message from Japan. My father had gone to the British Embassy to sign a Power of Attorney. He did not expect to be interrogated by officials, but when the consul saw the papers he demanded to know where I was. The Embassy had been alerted to look for me by the British Home Office as I had become a ward of court in London, pending a custody case. My father refused to reveal my location and the consulate had no authority to hold him. He took the next flight out to the Philippines.

This was stunning news. I had one hour to pack my things. I was taken across the border to Canton, and put on a flight to Manila to join my dad and my sister Juliana at the Jumbo Training Center. I was so happy to see my sister again. I hugged them both, delighted to be reunited with them. I had come full circle back to the Jumbo I had left two years earlier. At times, I felt I had been to hell and back. I had fought illness, loneliness, fear, and rejection. But I was far from emotionally mature or confident.

The Jumbo was closing down and we were part of the team that was left to clean up the property before returning it to the owners. For the next five months, Dad, Juliana, and I were a family once again. In the evenings we would play basketball together, or Juliana would perform for us the hula-hoop. I taught her to play badminton, and we listened to Dad telling us stories of his early days in the Family.

But I had spent so little time with Dad over the past few years that we didn't really know each other as father and daughter anymore. I was continually shocked by his behaviour and comments to me. One day I was discussing with someone in the dining hall my ambition to become a photographer, and my dad overheard our conversation. I can still remember the look of shock and disdain on his face.

"What? You're going to be a missionary!" And that was that. I did not expect his sharp response. I remained composed and kept my mouth shut, but I thought, *How dare he tell me what I'm going to do. There's no way I'm going to be a Family missionary.* It was a key moment.

Another disturbing experience was when one of my childhood abusers, Eman Artist, came from Japan for a visa trip. He asked to speak with me. Seeing him again made me break out into a sweat.

"I want to apologize," he started. "You know, for the past, if I was pushy. I didn't mean it." He smiled.

Well, this was good. He was apologizing. *Maybe he had changed and things were different now.* I was ready to forgive, after all that is what I been told to do.

"Sure," I replied.

Relieved, he began chatting to me, trying to be chummy. But as he talked, he furtively placed his hand on my thigh.

"You're beautiful," he half whispered as he bent towards me. "You've grown up…so sexy," he leered.

I saw the old lust in his eyes. *No! He has not changed at all.* I could hardly believe it after he had just apologized. I made some excuse of needing to be somewhere and walked off, deeply shaken. I did my best to stay out of sight for the next two days until he left. It came as no surprise when a few years later I heard that he had been officially excommunicated. Finally, the bastard had been dealt with. But why had it taken so long? Why had he been allowed to leave a trail of damaged girls wherever he went? His behaviour had been reported by myself and others for years. Surely the leaders bore responsibility for not doing something sooner. These questions lingered in the back of my mind.

One afternoon, Dad showed me an open letter he had written to my mother, entitled "In Defense of Our Daughter." I was appalled by the self-righteous and condescending tone he took when addressing her. He dismissed lightly any notion of sexual abuse in the Family. I knew this wasn't true, because I had experienced it myself—but of course I had been told all my life that it was "love," "God's love." Dad never even asked me if I had been sexually abused before stating so vehemently that I had received the best possible care. *How can he say that?* I thought. *He doesn't even know me.*

Dad asked me to write a letter to Mum, which I did. I stated that I was happy serving God in the Family and that this is where I wanted to be. In reality, it was the only life I knew. I had not been allowed to read my mother's or Kristina's letters. I only had my dad's version of what was happening—"The Devil is using your Mum to attack the Family and try to stop us from carrying out our mission to 'save souls for Jesus.' She'd better watch out because she's 'touching the apple of God's eye.'"

I was alarmed. Dad seemed so angry and hateful towards her. Secretly, I wanted to know more: who my mother was, what she looked like and what made her decide to leave the Family? Was she really a crazed monster possessed by the Devil, or simply a mother wanting to protect her daughter, a daughter she hadn't seen for over ten years? I had to find out.

Part Two

Juliana's Story

CHAPTER SEVEN

A Broken Family

"Julie, time to rise and shine! Up you get!"

I was unable to move, frozen with fear. If I got up, they would find I had wet the bed. But there was nothing for it. I had to get up…and climb slowly down from my bunk bed.

"What's this?" I could hear the blood thumping through my head. Someone had taken my hand and was leading me…not again…

I found myself before the Home shepherd, Uncle Dan, a large, frightening man who was my guardian at the time when I lived in Manila. I was three years old. "So, I hear you've wet your bed again, huh? That's four days in a row now. Do you remember what happens when you pee your bed?"

I nodded, trembling.

"I can't hear your brains rattle. What do you say?"

"Yes, sir," I breathed in a whisper, hoping against hope, he would let me off today. But I was hardly ever that lucky.

"Bend over and pull down your panties."

I did so; sweating heavily as I always did before a spanking, which would turn my heat rash bright red.

"Put your hands on the chair."

I obeyed even as I sobbed, "I'm sorry, Uncle Dan!"

"If you were truly sorry you wouldn't keep doing it. Now if you scream, I'll have to give you more."

I squeezed my eyes shut as the wooden board the size of a small cricket bat struck my bare bottom.

Again and again.

The swats eventually stopped. Uncle Dan put the board down as I pulled up my panties.

"Now what do you say?" No prompting was necessary. I knew the routine well by now.

"Th...thank you for correcting me!" I replied dutifully between sobs. "That's okay, sweetheart," he cooed, hugging me like a benign father. "We all make mistakes." I must have felt slippery as a slug, not to mention reeking of urine; the hugs never lasted long. I was happy to be let out of his grip though.

My story began on June 2, 1981 in the village of Rafina, Greece, where my six-year-old sister, Celeste, was living in Loveville with her father, Simon Peter. My father.

My parents had met less than a year before my birth, when my mother was asked to come and care for my dad when he was sick with hepatitis. It was love at first sight and though my parents never officially married, they started to live together as a couple.

My German mother, Serena, was a talented violin player and came from a family of musicians and artists. She was a truth-seeking hippie wandering in India when she met the Children of God. She was completely lost one day, and turned to find members of the group behind her, their beaming smiles lighting her way to salvation and a place in God's Family. She took their appearance as a sign. The free love of her hippie generation meant she embraced the group's doctrine of Flirty Fishing wholeheartedly.

The women believed their leader, Mo, when he told them God would protect them from "sperms and germs," so no contraception was used. Inevitably, they started having babies. Mo said children born through Flirty Fishing were special gifts from God and he called them Jesus Babies. My sister Mariana was conceived with one of Mum's "fish" during a stay in Turkey, so she was a Jesus Baby. Dad adopted Mariana as his own and, together with Celeste, we became a family unit.

With all the sexual sharing that was going on, sexually transmitted diseases were not uncommon. Not only did the Family members catch sperms, they also caught germs. Herpes became a widespread problem within the group. At first, Mo said just to pray for healing, but as herpes began to spread rather than heal, afflicted members eventually sought out medical help. My parents both contracted a STD early into their relationship, and were warned by a doctor to abstain from sex until they had recovered fully. However, a month into their quarantine, they succumbed to temptation.

As a teenager I wanted evidence from my father that I was even his child. There was no DNA test to prove I was; I could have been from any number of men. So Dad told me the story of how I was conceived. He looked at me and smiled fondly when he said, "We were so in love, we couldn't restrain ourselves."

"So I was born by accident through a venereal disease!" I took it to mean I had been the product of a filthy mistake and it heightened my feelings of worthlessness.

"No, honey." My dad hastened to reassure me. "You weren't a mistake. It shows how you were meant to be born, despite any obstacle."

Soon after my birth, Mum returned from a swim in the Aegean Sea, complaining of a sharp pain in her knees. Over the next few weeks the pain worsened and spread to other joints in her body. It was the first symptom of an incurable hereditary disease that makes all the joints swell with liquid so they balloon to nearly three times their normal size. All movement became extremely painful.

Poor Mum. She hobbled about and with two babies and Celeste to care for she was in constant pain. I was still a baby during the "great exodus" when we all left Greece for the Far East. After my brother, Victor, was born in the Philippines, Mum's condition deteriorated. Dad had been chosen for God's work—hand picked by the prophet himself to work for him in World Services. A sick wife and four kids did not fit into the equation. We had become a hindrance to God and His Family. After Victor's birth, the leadership split my mother and father and sent Mum away with my sister Mariana and I to another, smaller commune in Manila, where Dan and his wife, Tina, were the Home shepherds. "Uncle" Dan was a man who took pleasure in beating us.

I was three at the time. Dad and Celeste remained at the main Home and my baby brother Victor was fostered out to another couple. Dad would come to see us on Sundays and I always looked forward to his visits. Dad and Mum would lounge on the king-sized bed with yellow sheets that seemed to soak in the morning sun shining through the large windows. Mariana and I would play hide and seek in the closets while they took their time getting up, knowing later we'd all go to the zoo as a family, take boat rides on the lake and feed the ducks. It was on one of these visits that my sister, Lily, was conceived.

Mo wrote various Letters around this time on the topic of seriously ill members in the Family, in which he claimed that sickness was the result of sin. If you were sick, then you were either out of God's Will or had a spiritual malaise that manifested itself in the physical disease. Because of this some Family members did not receive proper medical treatment and died. One casualty was Peter Puppet, who produced a TV puppet show called *The Luvvets*, that aired in the Philippines. He developed a tumour on his neck, which he decided not to treat after Mo told him the tumour would clear up as soon as his spiritual sins were cleared up. The tumour did not take long to kill Peter, but his death was seen as a graduation and he joined the growing ranks of Spirit Helpers, a distinction awarded to members who passed on.

When my mother's sickness began to affect her every movement, she too was accused of spiritual rebellion and murmuring, which, according to Mo, were some of the worst sins of all. Despite that, the shepherds decided that my baby brother Victor should be returned to us. He arrived with Celeste six months after I had last seen him. He did not remember his own mother and screamed for days for his familiar foster parents.

When Victor developed TB, Mum was quarantined with him for months. Her baby's sickness was seen as just another symptom of her spiritual sins, for the "sins of the parents shall be visited on the children." While Mum was quarantined with Victor, I stayed with a German couple, Joseph and Talitha. Their daughter Vera and I were the same age and we schooled together during the day. Mariana, Vera, and I all came down with the measles and were sick in bed for weeks. I wanted Mum, but she was not allowed to see me.

No sooner had we recovered from the measles, than we came down with mumps. We never went to the doctor for treatment, nor did I ever receive a single immunization shot. The adults trusted God for our health. Instead of medicine, they spooned a daily mixture of cod liver oil, garlic, molasses, and honey down our throats. The only medicine we were allowed was worm medicine, as I remember being frequently plagued with bouts of worms. Soon after Mum was released from quarantine with Victor, she was told to return to Germany for treatment and to give birth to her new baby, as she would get free medical care. She begged to be allowed to stay where she could at least be near her husband, but she was strongly advised to leave if she did not wish to be out of God's Will, and risk His wrath.

There was a final condition. Mum was told she had to leave one of her children behind for my father. The last couple of weeks before they left were unbearable for my mother, who sat by my bedside through the long nights, staring at me and weeping. "I love you Julie," she would tell me as she stroked my hair and patted me to sleep. She suspected she would never see me again. I was their first child, her favourite, her baby.

I was not to be told anything. I was too young, they assumed, to understand what was happening. But my young brain chewed it around for some years until eventually it churned out its own conclusion: I was not wanted. I grew up with this thought deep in my psyche.

Celeste was put on distraction duty to play with me that fateful day, so I would not notice them leaving. It worked, until the minute I heard the car start up in the driveway below the window. I was crazy about any and all automobiles and this particular car was a favourite with all of us kids. We nicknamed it the "avocado car" for its pale-green color. Hearing the engine start up, I ran to the window to watch it drive out. I did not expect to see my mother getting into the car with my brother and sister.

"They're leaving without me!" I cried out. "They've forgotten me!"

"No, Julie, they're going for a trip. You're staying with me," Celeste said, trying to hold me back.

But I wriggled free and ran down to the front door and threw it open—in time to see them reversing out of the driveway. My mother did not expect to see me standing there, but her final brave act was to smile and wave goodbye even as silent tears fell on to her cheeks. I always remembered her this way.

Celeste followed me down and tried to pull me upstairs again to play. "Come on Julie! Let's go play with Lego. I'll build a castle with you!"

"No, I don't want to! I want to go with Mum in the avocado car too!" I stomped upstairs, threw myself on the bed and sulked. No amount of cajoling could cheer me up and I was angry and out of sorts for the rest of the day. Oddly though, I never cried, or perhaps that was not so odd, since I did not realize the enormity of what had just happened. It was only after some time had passed and she did not return that I understood Mum was not coming back. The realization hit me as I woke up from a nap one day drenched in sweat. Instead of getting up, I lay comatose in the drowsy heat. The door to the room was open and I could see the rest of the kids watching a Family testimony video in the living room.

They that love God shall never meet for the last time,
This life isn't the end, we will meet again.

It surprised me to realize my pillow was wet with tears, not sweat. I had only ever cried during spankings, and this was the first time I experienced a very different kind of pain. The thought that I might not see my mum and dad again in this life hurt like a knife stabbing me in the heart and I could not stop crying.

Dad never came for me as my mother had been told he would. Instead, I was assigned the first of many foster parents. I became very insecure and started wetting my bed every night. Inevitably I was led by the hand to Uncle Dan's room for a beating.

Uncle Dan would beat his sons the worst. There was a Demerit chart on the wall in our classroom, and every time we did something wrong, a demerit point would go under our name. If we earned three demerits in one day, the consequence was a beating from the board. One day his son David was very sick, and he had received a number of demerits that day. That night he was taken for his spanking—there was no mercy, fever or not.

"I'll take David's spanking for him." His brother Timmy volunteered, even though he had demerits of his own. This meant a double beating for him.

I thought this was the bravest thing I had ever seen anyone do. Even Uncle Dan was impressed. "Isn't that real brotherly love children? He's taking David's punishment, just like Jesus took our punishment for us when he died on the cross."

I was sure that because of his noble sacrifice, Uncle Dan would go easy on Timmy and not really give him the full amount. I could not have been more wrong. Timmy's beating went on and on and on. I started crying as we heard him take his punishment in the next room. Timmy never cried out. By the time it was over, his bottom was bloody. I did not understand how Uncle Dan could be so cruel to his own sons.

Other times though, Uncle Dan could be very nice. Once after my spanking he had a surprise for me. "Look what I've fixed for you!" He pulled an object out of the drawer next to him.

It was my little yellow wind-up car that I had received the last Christmas Mum had been with me. It was my favourite toy.

"Thank you Uncle Dan." I wiped away my tears, taking the car from his hand. It had been two long months since my mother left. I asked Auntie Talitha if I could write her a letter. This letter had no words, even though I usually loved writing; only a single picture, yet that picture shouted a thousand words that I could not adequately express. It was a drawing of a little girl crying, colored all in black. It was the first and last letter my mother ever received from me and she cried when she got it. None of hers ever reached me. When I was moved a few months later to yet more foster parents, she was not informed of my whereabouts. The only evidence that I ever had a mother lay in my passport. My father never gave me his name, as if not giving it would negate his responsibility for me as a parent. I had become a true child of the Family, as my father would boast in the years to come. The maternal bond had been broken.

Celeste took me under her wing as a mother hen her chick. She was a constant presence throughout my early life, identifying with my misfortunes, though usually unable to protect me from them.

Almost a year passed before Dad returned for Celeste and me. I was nearly five, and the months that followed were some of the happiest of my childhood. We traveled together, passing through Hong Kong and China, before arriving in the Portuguese colony of Macau. We might have been the remnant of a family, but we were a happy one.

We arrived at Hosea's farm in Hac Sa, Macau. At the farm, my sister settled into the teen group, while I spent my days with the younger children. In the evenings, Dad, Celeste, and I all met for dinner, and the three of us shared a room at night.

On a visit to China, Dad took us to a shopping mall and allowed me to choose between two dolls. One was a cute little Chinese doll in a traditional outfit, and long black braids; the other was part of a small set that came in a bag complete with clothes and a bottle, surrounding a sleeping doll. I chose the latter because the doll looked so peaceful. In Macau, a family visited from another Home during an Area Fellowship—their youngest daughter was around three years old. She became attached to my little dolly. I let her play with it, as we "shared all things, and had all things common," in keeping with the example set by the Apostles. But when it came time for them to leave, and she walked away with my dolly, I discovered that my sharing had its limits.

"She's taking my dolly! I want my dolly back! Please, can I have my dolly?" I hollered frantically, grabbing the doll from the little girl, who bellowed back angrily. The racket drew the attention of the adults. Dad took me sternly by the hand and led me away, one of the rare times he was angry with me. He took me to our room for a lecture.

"Now Julie, you don't even play with your dolly very much. The little girl needs it more than you do. Why don't you give it to her?"

"But I want it. I'll play with it, I promise!"

"Now honey, how do you think Jesus feels right now knowing you're not willing to share?"

"But it's my dolly." I sobbed certain Jesus would understand that.

"You're a big girl now. You don't need dollies."

Despite the fact that I was only five and in the prime of dolly-hood, that was not the issue, but I could not explain to my father that the only reason I loved the doll was because he had given it to me. That made it a treasure in my eyes. Nor could I understand why he would want me to give away his gift to me. But I gave it anyway, because Daddy and Jesus asked it of me, crying as I watched the visitors drive away, the little girl happily clutching my doll to her chest. I learned that it was not true sharing unless it hurt.

I lost many precious possessions that way, some more valuable than others, but always in the name of sharing—the silver heart locket and chain, for instance, that my Dad left with me and which had once belonged to Mo's adopted daughter, Techi. Later, there was the ring Dad sent for my tenth birthday containing a red jewelled heart surrounded by ten glittering white stones. I wore it proudly, and took it off at night, stashing it safely under my mattress. When I awoke one morning, the ring was gone, and no amount of questioning the other children made it turn up. It was a lesson well learned; people or things, nothing lasts.

A family, which I longed for most, lasted least of all.

We spent only a few months together in Macau before Dad was recalled for the Lord's service, this time to live in Mo's own home—known as the King's Household. So Dad left us behind once more. It was not that he was entirely irresponsible, or did not care. He honestly believed he would be rewarded for sacrificing us, and all the rest of his kids for God, like Abraham in the Bible offering up his only son, Isaac, on the altar. Only, unlike Isaac, we never had a sacrificial ram to save the day. I was consistently told throughout my childhood that I would be blessed for giving up my parents for God's Work. Only I hadn't given them up at all. They had been taken from me.

CHAPTER EIGHT

The Odd One Out

I was five when an adult escorted Celeste and me from Macau back to Manila to live at Marianne's Home. I was put into a group of four other children my age, under the care of a tough German woman named Auntie Stacey, who believed a healthy hiding was the best medicine for children and she dished it out regularly. Our group of five children— three to five years old—were schooled, slept, ate, showered, and "made love" together.

Everything was rigidly scheduled—from school hours to one hour of exercise time in the garden. We even had scheduled "date" times, where we each picked the partner we were to have sex with, held out our hands for a glob of pink baby lotion and proceeded to our various beds. The adults used KY jelly, but for some reason baby lotion was the lubricant of choice for us little ones. We knew what to do, as we had seen our teachers at it often enough, though we were a little lacking in the actual mechanics. Generally, the boy got on top of the girl, and a lot of sounds followed in the general rhythm of "Ooh—Aah, Ooh—Aah, Ooh—Aah."

Often I was the odd one out. Marianne's son, Pierre, regularly refused to date me, even though I always asked him first. He preferred cuddling up with Auntie Stacey, which bothered me. I would sit and stare at them, wondering why he was lying with a grown-up who wasn't his mummy and why she never invited me for a cuddle. Sometimes, I would be coupled with the youngest boy, who was only three. This was an insult even harder to bear.

Needless to say, I quickly developed a distaste for date naps, and became something of a childish prude. I did not like people touching me; even hugs I began to slink away from, subconsciously associating them with either spankings or sex. I started having terrible nightmares and was afraid to fall asleep at night. I would lie awake till two in the morning at times, fighting it. When the lights had gone out, the giant cockroaches would come crawling out of the cracks in the floor and I would lie frozen in my bed watching them crawl up the wall and over my sheets. I was afraid if I fell asleep, my mouth would fall open and one of the creatures would crawl inside, like I heard happened to one of the uncles in the home.

We were required to call all the adults "Uncle" or "Auntie" as a sign of respect. Ignoring this title was sure to invite severe punishment. We were taught good old-fashioned manners: to say "please" and "thank you," to reply to anyone addressing us with, "yes, ma'am" or "yes, sir." As I was the only child in the home without a parent, there was no one to protect me. I got daily spankings for trivial offences such as forgetting an instruction or arguing with my peers. Once again, the group operated a system of Demerits, and three marks against you in a day earned a spanking. I was so terrified of spankings that I started lying when accused of a misdemeanour. As a result, I received many unjust beatings when I was truly innocent, because, like the boy who cried "wolf," they no longer believed me.

Once, the other girl in my class, Nyna, went for a birthday outing with her parents, and was allowed to pick a present. She chose a ring and bracelet set and, to be fair, and having "all things common," they got me one too. Hers was red, mine blue. It took only one day for Nyna to break her fragile bracelet. The ring, she dropped down a snake hole in the garden to see how deep it went. It was too deep to recover.

The next day Nyna approached me. "Julie, can I borrow your ring from you? I lost mine." I hemmed and hawed, unwilling to relinquish my new treasure so soon and suspecting I might not see it again. She became angry. "*I* got it for you for *my* birthday, so you *have* to share it with me." I saw slight reason in this, so I gave it up but made her promise to give it back in the morning.

That afternoon in the garden, my ring followed Nyna's down the snake hole. Naturally, I cried over its loss. The next day, sitting on the toilet, while the other kids brushed their teeth, I decided to talk to her about it. "Nyna, I'm very sad you lost my ring." I sighed for added effect.

Nyna was a fiery redheaded Aries, with a load of freckles and a superiority complex to match, and she puffed furiously, "I'm going to tell Auntie Stacey on you!"

"For what?" But she had already stormed out of the bathroom. I could hear her high-pitched voice in the bedroom.

"Julie! Come here right now!" Auntie Stacey boomed from the next room and she did not sound happy. The other children came running into the toilet to fetch me, as excited as if someone had shouted "fight'; I was about to be disciplined and that always broke the monotony of the day.

"Auntie Stacey wants you right now!" they chorused.

"I'm coming. I just need to finish using the bathroom."

The children rushed to report an update to the teacher—and returned even quicker.

"Auntie Stacey says to come right now, or you'll be in bigger trouble." Yes, I knew that. Quick as I could, I finished my business, washed my hands and went to face whatever it was I had been accused of. But this time, I was not sweating, and my heart was not pounding. I knew I had done nothing wrong, so I would not be punished.

Auntie Stacey stood me in front of her. "Nyna here tells me that you said, 'I'm very mad at you for losing my ring, and I'm going to kill you!' Is that true?"

"I didn't say that at all Auntie Stacey. I said, 'I'm very sad you lost my ring.' That's all."

"That's not true! That's not true!" Nyna shouted. "Ask Pierre, he was there." Pierre was Nyna's boyfriend. They were the self-ordained king and queen, and very kindly granted me the role of princess, even though I was a year older than both of them. Pierre had not even been in the bathroom at the time.

"Yes, it's true," he chimed in dutifully. "She said it."

"I didn't Auntie, I didn't."

"Now Julie, I'm going to ask you again, and I want you to tell me the truth this time. Did you say you were mad and wanted to kill Nyna?"

"No, I didn't."

"Okay, we're all going to go for lunch, and you're going to stay here until you're ready to tell the truth. If you don't tell me by the time I get back, I'm going to have to give you a spanking for lying."

I was left alone, and began to cry. But this time I cried more over the injustice than the threat of the beating itself. Armi came into the room, sat next to me and asked what was wrong. I blubbered out the whole story.

Of course there was nothing she could do to help me, but she tried to comfort me all the same. Her sympathy gave me courage. By the time she left, I had stopped crying, and resolved to bear up bravely—whatever might follow.

A couple of minutes later, Auntie Stacey returned. "So Julie, are you ready to tell me the truth?"

"Yes, I'm going to tell you the truth." And I repeated my story.

"Okay, I'm going to have to give you seven swats with the board. Four for saying such a terrible thing, and three for lying. And if you are innocent, take it for all the times you deserved it and didn't get caught." That was a favourite line with many of my teachers.

I took my punishment without crying. Something inside me refused to break down. But I did not forget.

The only times I saw the outside of the commune was when we went busking. Uncle Peter—Peter Pioneer, who had been a singer in *Music with Meaning*—formed us children into a singing group. He would take us out to perform in restaurants and hotels. After our show, we would go around with the literature and posters and collect donations. Often we would be out till late in the night, tired and hungry. But we were not allowed to show it.

"Now children," Uncle Peter would chide, "I want to see big smiles on your faces, or the people will think we're forcing you to sing for them. And that would be a terrible example and make Jesus very sad!"

So we put on our big Family smiles. It was not so much the fear of offending Jesus, as the threat of having rubber bands stapled to the corners of my mouth and hooked around my ears if I did not. This was graphically demonstrated to us using paperclips and rubber bands during practice one day, and the idea of it never left my mind throughout performances.

Our days out busking were extremely tiring, but I preferred being out to the tedium of staying cloistered in the house all day. Sometimes kind people would give us treats and there were always interesting things to see. Though our singing group usually managed to bring in some money, we were only a minor part of the home's "ministry." Marianne's Home boasted some of the country's best Flirty Fishers, and the women fished some of the top generals in the Marcos government. I was five years old when Cori Aquino led the coup against Marcos. Shooting erupted not far from where we were living. I could hear the gunshots as we gathered in the living room and lay spread-eagled on the floor for hours. The adults were all speaking in tongues and praying desperately, not just for our safety, but for the Marcos regime.

It did not end the way Mo intended. Cori Aquino took over the government and the Family's infiltration into the Philippine government ended not long after due to negative media exposure and the threat of wholesale deportation of foreign Family members. Mo decided to move his operations to Japan and Marianne's Home was to relocate to Tokyo, since our ministry to the military was no longer needed.

One day Auntie Stacey gathered our little group with some news. "Guess what kids? A new Family school has opened up here in Manila. Pierre and Julie, you are both invited to go. Isn't that exciting?"

In one short week, my little bag was packed, and I was sent off to attend the first Family school, the Jumbo. They told me Celeste had gone there too, but I didn't see her again for nearly three years.

CHAPTER NINE

The Rod of Correction

It was called the Jumbo because it was a massive, maze-like structure in a giant compound with hundreds of compartments, almost like a beehive. It was the first test-tube Family boarding school. Many of the methods experimented with there were implemented in Family schools and communes around the world.

The day I arrived, I was placed in a group of thirty other five- and six-year-old children. I was six. It was the first time I had been among so many other kids my age and I was overwhelmed initially by the amount of rules we were supposed to remember. The property was huge and confusing with weird architecture. Almost every wall was a mirror, and it took time just to memorize which "mirror" was a door. The main building was in an octagonal shape, with a wooden porch that extended around the outside of the entire building. There was a separate house where the leaders lived, built in Japanese style complete with a fishpond, and an octagon-shaped pavilion that was used as a quarantine house for sick people. The garden had different levels, so that each group rotated where they would hold their exercise time; twice a week we would get to swim in the large pool. Everyone met in the giant communal dining hall for meals, and at dinner the children got to eat with their parents.

Because I didn't have a parent, I was assigned to Auntie Stacey's care once again, and spent the hour of family time with her and her daughter every evening before returning to my group for bed.

Each group was housed in giant rooms named according to the color of the carpet, with a single bathroom and shower. We slept on mattresses that folded up into low couches that we sat on during our long hours of Word time. At bedtime the couches were unfolded into a maze of mattresses that covered the entire floor, with narrow walking spaces in between.

We were not allowed to sleep with any clothes or underwear on and we had to lie on our tummies. Everywhere you looked was a naked bottom. I was very shy, so at night when we were allowed a sheet, I always covered my bum. So many naked children lying close together did nothing to discourage sexual experimentation, nor indeed, was it meant to. There was an allotted time before bed for making love.

Two brothers and a sister my age, Danny, Davie, and Anita, arrived not long after me from a World Services home where their parents worked. Danny was tall and scrawny with a mop of dirty blond curls. I thought Davie, with his brown skin and green eyes, was by far the more handsome. While in World Services, the three of them had been instructed in the mechanics of sex through watching two adults in a live class. It was the first time I had actually seen a little boy stick his penis into a little girl. I lay and watched them fascinated, till Davie sauntered over and, to my horror asked, "Would you like me to show you how to do that?"

"What? No!"

"Oh come on!" He prodded. "It's fun."

Far from seeming "fun" or natural, I was sure it involved some pain, so I refused despite his persistent prompting. Eventually he lay next to me instead and told me stories about the sexual antics different adults had taught him while we watched the other two. Both Davie and Danny took a liking to me and were always joking about how they would mount me in my sleep if I did not agree to have sex with them.

"Well, I'll sleep on my stomach then!" I replied with naïve confidence.

"That's all right." Davie laughed. "We'll just have to do it to you from behind!" The picture that conjured in my imagination was quite disturbing. I had never dreamed such a thing was possible.

Our overseers took turns sleeping in our room and always brought a date. The adults went by a sharing schedule that dictated who they were to spend the night with. Many of the people I watched on the mattresses were not exactly desirable and I wondered what the adults thought of it—like the ones who stank, or the obese ones who had sweat patches under their arms. I watched plump women, with their legs propped vertically against the desk, their fat jiggling like Jell-O, while they rocked back and forth moaning and shouting in tongues when they came, oblivious to fifty-plus eyes watching them.

One nursing Filipino auntie had a problem with excess milk, so her solution was to line us up for "breast feeding" and everyone took a turn. Her swollen nipples were huge and black. I found the whole thing repulsive, and always refused to join the line up. Fortunately for me, it was not mandatory. Occasionally a couple of our female overseers would take some of the little boys into their beds for Cuddle Time, which involved a lot of squirming, with the little boys rocking back and forth on top while the aunties held on to their buttocks. I soon noticed many of the kids around me regularly engaged in the oddest pastime, squirming about on their mattresses. I finally asked one of my friends what it was they were doing.

"Masturbating," she told me.

"What's that?"

"I don't know exactly, but it feels really nice."

So I attempted to imitate them to see what it was that felt nice, but it never seemed to work for me. I pretended to know what they were talking about, as it was very popular and, since everybody else did it, I wanted to fit in. It was a way to pass the long nap hours.

A large section of life was spent in Quiet Times. This was the term used for nap and bedtime, when there was strictly no-talking allowed. Many hours were also spent in indefinite silence restriction. We were not allowed to talk during devotions, school, and meals. If we wanted to speak, we had to raise our finger. A bathroom call required two fingers. Three fingers would be reserved for "The Revolution for Jesus!" call.

"It's a Revolution!" could be shouted out by the teacher at any hour of the day, to which we would all respond with full gusto, "For Jesus!" At which point we produced our three-finger salute in "Heil Hitler" fashion. It was the one time we were allowed to shout, so we used the opportunity to belt at the top of our lungs. Normally we could not speak louder than a whisper.

The other half of my days was spent in school, which was what we were sent to the Jumbo for. Since we children were the future of the Family, Mo came out with a letter called "The School Vision," saying it was imperative we received the training and education needed to rule the world when Jesus returned. We were to be the pure generation, unadulterated by the world, an improvement on the stock.

Every Sunday, everybody in the Jumbo would gather in the meeting hall for Sunday Fellowship. I always looked forward to it. There were many talented musicians and they would lead the rousing inspirations. Over two hundred voices joined together in song made the atmosphere electrifying and sometimes I would get goosebumps. Often people would be crying and praising in tongues as they felt the Holy Spirit come over them. Then there would be fun skits put on, which I always enjoyed most, ended by communion and prayer. Most of the skits and songs were on the topic of witnessing or the Endtime. Jesus was supposed to be coming back in 1993 according to Mo's prophecies.

I grew up believing I would be twelve years old when Christ returned. It meant I only had six years left to live. It was something of a relief to know I would not have to grow old and die. Unless, of course, I was captured by the evil Antichrist forces and they tortured me and I died as a martyr. That was my greatest fear, despite Mo's letter "Death the Ultimate Orgasm," in which he describes a dream where he is shot, and experiences dying as a wonderful rapture, even better than an orgasm. Well, I had never had an orgasm, so that did little to assuage my fears.

I would concoct scenarios in my head of how to escape if I was captured; perhaps Flirty Fishing the soldiers like in the book *Heaven's Girl*, about a young teen girl spearheading the resistance against the Antichrist soldiers in the Endtime. The story of when they threw her to the lions always disturbed me despite the fact that her guardian angel saved her and shut the mouths of the beasts. Before she was tossed to the lions, Heaven's Girl was gang raped by the guards. But she gave her body gladly and two of the guards ended up being converted and rescuing her. But then she had to Flirty Fish an ugly, old, fat government official too, so he would help her get out of the country. I did not think I could do that.

We all discussed who Heaven's Girl was going to be. I knew I would be too young, because she was about fifteen in the story and I would only live to be twelve. Nonetheless, it remained my favourite storybook to read, because we had nothing else half interesting.

During school hours, I was sent to the Teen Group for classes. My mother was a pioneer of early learning, and by the time I was three I could read fluently, write, and work out mathematical equations. The teenagers had been deprived of education, because they had been sent out busking and fundraising as children. Now they had to catch up and I was placed in the same class as fourteen- and fifteen-year-olds, which they naturally resented. I tried to be inconspicuous and sit quietly in the back of the room, but the teacher always insisted on calling on me, and would use me to create healthy competition in class. I hated that—I did not want to be noticed or show my classmates up in any way. When I returned to my own group, the other children resented me for having school with the teens.

Perhaps because of this, I had few close friends and was very lonely.

So, I kept a place inside my head where I could imagine anything I pleased, go on adventures, even be with my mummy and daddy again. Our teachers called it daydreaming and that was forbidden. "An idle mind is the Devil's workshop." I had nightmares almost every night. Giant dogs and lions would chase me and I could not run because my legs were on a treadmill, so they would pin me down and eat me. Then I wet my bed. It became my private humiliation that I hated myself for. When I awoke in the night to a wet bed, I would simply take my sheet off my mattress, flip it over and get a fresh sheet. By morning the mattress would have dried and the teachers never knew whether the stain was old or new. All the mattresses stank of urine anyway and had to be aired regularly. I would hardly get to sleep again before I was startled awake by the Family "Battle Hymn" blasting loudly through the intercom speakers:

Who will take the stand and heed
The call from Heaven above?
Who will join the band of David's men,
The army of love?
Called to live and die for the Kingdom,
As we give our all to the Lord.
Lift up your sword,
Look to Heaven's reward.
It's the Revolution for Jesus and David our King.

By the time the anthem finished, we had to be out of bed, the sheets folded, and the mattresses tucked back into couches again, or we were likely to receive a spanking from the White Stick. This was the plastic stick that the teacher carried with him everywhere, like a magic wand. A meter long and an inch wide, it looked harmless enough, but the whiplash on your bare bottom created painful welts. After a beating you would be unable to sit comfortably for a week. Once it broke on one of the boy's buttocks because the teacher wielded it with such force and they had to get a new one. I mingled with many a purple bottom in the shower. You could always tell who received the most spankings because you never saw their bare bottom sans one shade of color or another. The most recently thrashed looked fresh and bloody and you could see how badly they stung when the water ran on to them and they gave a little jump.

A milder punishment was Silence Restriction, a sentence that could be served for any length of time. I was made to walk around for days with an ignominious sign hanging about my neck that read, "Don't talk to me. I'm on silence restriction." I never spoke to some of my classmates because they seemed to be stuck on it permanently. Sometimes we had a thick piece of duct tape put over our mouths, which was only removed to let us eat.

For verbal offences like speaking out of turn, talking back, or saying something "unloving" or "un-spiritual," we would have our mouths washed out with soap. This was an old-fashioned punishment that Mo's preacher mother had practised on him. I had the bad habit of speaking my mind when I saw something unfair. My sense of justice was very strong and at times I could not help myself. I regularly gagged on soap bars. Some adults rammed the bar down my throat, others made me brush my teeth with it, but the cruellest of them made me chew it and swallow. That was usually when I gagged. Auntie Stacey especially liked using this punishment on me.

As we were everybody and nobody's kids, according to the Mo Letter "One Wife," any adult could correct you for any offence they thought you had committed. This often became confusing, as one adult could tell you to do something, and another would catch you doing it and become angry because they saw something wrong with it and punished you. If you tried to explain yourself, you would get in trouble for talking back, but if you did not obey what the first adult told you to do, you would be punished for disobedience. For the worst sins committed in front of the class, you would receive a public beating which was meant to hurt your pride as much as it hurt your rear-end. This was derived from the verse, "They who sin before all shall be rebuked before all." I received a public spanking for such offences as murmuring, arguing, talking without permission, or lying.

One day, after nap, my thin wispy hair was floating up all over the place. Pandita, who was the daughter of the school leaders, pointed it out to the other kids, laughing, "Julie looks like John the Baptist's wife with her wild hair!"

All the kids started laughing with her and I felt the blood rush to my face.

"Well you're fat and stinky!" I retorted in the heat of anger. I was feeling ill and out of sorts. Our teacher heard the commotion and pulled us out while she reported it to the head teacher, Auntie Joy. While they discussed our punishments, we sat in the closet room waiting for over an hour. I was sweating and felt dizzy. The teacher then led the entire class into the room. As it turned out my classmate who had teased me was not to receive correction with me because her parents were the shepherds of the school. The injustice infuriated me.

"But she called me John the Baptist's wife!" I cried.

"And what's wrong with that?" Auntie Joy defended her. "John the Baptist was the prophet who heralded the coming of Jesus. But for you to call someone fat and stinky is a horrible thing to say and you're going to have to take the consequences for your lack of love."

It was to be a public correction and the entire group gathered to witness it. Auntie Joy read various sections of Mo Letters and Bible verses on the subject of love, then I had to confess my sin publicly, after which the teacher ranted for what seemed like hours. The whole while I stood waiting in dread of the inevitable, wishing it could just be over. All my peers sat cross-legged on the floor staring at me and the room was crowded and hot. I could feel my hair sticking to the sweat on my neck.

Finally the moment arrived.

"Pull down your pants."

Although we all slept and showered naked together, it was not the same being the only one undressed in front of all my peers.

Slowly, ever so slowly, I pulled down my skirt, then my panties, and turned around, placing my hands on the wall as instructed.

The pain of the white stick making contact with my bare skin was nothing compared to the pain of humiliation I felt as thirty sets of eyes burned into me. But that was not the end of it. After the beating, there was still the prayer of deliverance. I was made to go down on my knees while the whole room laid their hands on me. After much speaking in tongues and a rhythmic mantra of "Thank you Jesus, thank you Lord. Thank you Jesus, thank you Lord," it was my turn to "cry out to the Lord in desperation." Then Auntie Joy said another long prayer over me, resisting the Devil and all his demons and banishing their influence in my life.

Only a couple of hours later, the teacher realized I was burning up with a fever. They discovered a huge lump behind my ear. I had a bad infection and a cold in my ears that lasted almost two weeks. When they understood my short temper that day had been a reaction to feeling ill, Auntie Joy took me aside.

"Honey, I'm sorry. I didn't know you were sick. Why don't you go and lie down?"

A private apology was all well and good but it did not offer me any vindication in the eyes of my peers. But the shepherds could never be seen to be wrong in front of the class.

For some reason, it was assumed that spiritual sins, like physical sickness, could also be contagious. A year after I went to the Jumbo we began to notice a group of older teens who were in Quarantine. They were not allowed to mingle with anyone else. They did not take their meals in the communal dining hall; the only times I saw them was when they were engaged in their daily degrading hard labor, which consisted of scrubbing toilets, drains, and massive floors with a tooth-brush. Often they would be made to do strenuous callisthenics like the Duck Walk and Starjumps, for hours at a time, until they collapsed with exhaustion. They were regularly administered the board, a piece of plywood with large holes drilled through for better leverage and a handle on the end. They always wore signs in bright red, which read "Quarantine," and often had duct tape over their mouths. They were called Detention Teens.

The youngest one—not a teen at all—was an eight-year-old African-American boy. He had expressed a desire to leave the Family, and so was imprisoned in a tiny room with an adult guarding him at all times. He was too dangerous to even mix with the other detainees. They fed him only liquids and read him Mo Letters all hours of the day and night for nearly a year. As he was so close in age to me, I often found myself thinking about him and wondering what I would do if I were in his place. A couple of times during Family Time, I caught a glimpse of him being escorted by an adult for exercise and I wished I could talk to him. Everyone avoided the Detention Teens like the plague, as if being close to them might contaminate us, and turn us into teen terrors too.

But I also had my faults, or so I was constantly told. My pride had to be kept in check. Pride was the root of all sin. Because my father was famous—thanks to his work with *Music with Meaning* and other projects—it was assumed that I must feel some kind of pride because of this. His voice was on every cassette tape, his face on nearly every video, and it was impossible to forget who he was, even if I wanted to. And

I did want to. I did not care who he was. To me, he was just my daddy who I missed.

To suppress any un-revealed pride inside me, once in awhile I found myself sitting in a bathtub full of doo-doo nappies, a present from the Nursery. Usually the Detention Teens performed this chore, but every so often I was allowed to share their load. It took hours. I never could eat on those days. The smell of shit soaked into my skin, no matter how hard I tried to scrub it off. But worse than the smell was the humiliation I felt as my happy peers passed through the bathroom to watch, and feel vindicated for not having famous parents.

I did not care who Dad was in the Family; I just wanted everything to be like it had been. I had almost forgotten Mum completely by now. The only memory of her was resurrected in my dreams. I would see her in the distance walking with Mariana and Victor and I would run towards her happily. "Mum!" I cried out. "Mum!" But somehow I could never reach her and she did not hear me calling. I would wake up crying hysterically.

Sometimes, kids were allowed to go for special sleepover nights with their parents. Sleepovers were a big deal to me because they created a semblance of family life that I missed. Once, my foster mother Auntie Stacey promised me a sleepover that I looked forward to the entire week. She had promised to pick me up after a meeting, so I lay in my bed waiting and watching the doorway for three hours, till even our teacher fell asleep. I would not allow myself to drift off, and kept awake by reciting along with the *Music with Meaning* drama tape that was playing. My eyes kept fluttering between the doorway and the clock, till they grew heavy. It was after midnight when I realized Auntie Stacey had probably forgotten about me. But I had looked forward to having that sleepover for so long that I crept out of bed and upstairs to Auntie Stacey's room. I found her sleeping with her small daughter and there was no room on the mattress for me. So I curled up on the floor at her feet and fell asleep there. It could have been a luxury bed for all I cared; I was happy, though I don't know why I should have been.

CHAPTER TEN

Adopt Me, Please

When I was seven, I was sent to Japan to live with Dad, to a very beautiful mountainous place near the sea. My new home was known as the Heavenly City School.

Although Dad lived just down the road from the school, I only saw him once or twice a week. As usual, I was put into a large group of seven- and eight-year-old children called the Shining Lights. I was surprised to see Davie and Danny there, although I shouldn't have been. Like my dad, Davie and Danny's parents also worked directly for Mo, who had left the Philippines for Japan; the World Services teams working closest with him moved wherever the King's Household moved, so there they were. As was Pierre—his parents, Paul Peloquin and Marianne, had also moved and taken up shepherding posts in Japan.

Many of the musicians from *Music with Meaning* had moved to Japan to continue recording music cassettes for the Family to sell. They had recently progressed to producing children's music videos for distribution, called "Kiddie Viddies." At night a stage would be set up in the dining hall for the inspirations and the best musicians would lead the singing. Usually, all the children would get to spend an hour with their parents after dinner and sometimes I got to have an hour with my daddy. But on these inspiration nights, we had to sit in our groups and I would miss the hour of family time. Being with my daddy was such a rare thing that I came to hate the inspirations because they took away my time with him. I would sit and cry while everyone around me joined in the singing. Because it would be a bad example to catch a child crying on the video, I was often escorted out of the hall, and had to spend the hour alone listening to muffled singing from the bedroom.

The times I did spend with my dad were cherished. We would take long walks together or climb the hill to the pyramid building. Inside the pyramid, a miniature space city had been constructed according to Mo's revelations of what the Heavenly City would look like. I could sit for hours looking at the little gem-like buildings lit up with glowing lights, and the tiny trees and people. It seemed like a magical wonderland and I would fantasize shrinking down to thumbnail size like Thumbelina and living in that beautiful little world.

After a few months, Dad and I left Japan and returned to the Philippines to meet up with Celeste, who had come directly from Hosea's farm in Macau. The Jumbo was being disbanded three years after opening, and it was our job to scrub till we dropped until the huge building was sparkling and ready to be handed back to its owners. I had my eighth birthday there, and for the first time in four years, Dad and Celeste could celebrate it with me.

I desperately wanted a music box, after a *Life with Grandpa* story came out in which Techi received a music box with a little ballerina dancing around on a glass mirror. I wanted one just like it and begged my dad for it as a birthday present. Though I did not know it at the time, this sent him into a panic. No one in The Family was supposed to know where Mo lived, and Dad assumed that if he got me a similar music box to Techi's, I would guess that the Royal Family had lived in the Philippines.

On the day of my birthday, Dad, Celeste, and I went for an outing. He promised that if we found a music box like the one I wanted, then I could have it. Secretly, he hoped we would not find it, and he encouraged Celeste to help me pick an alternative present. But I had set my heart on something, and everything else paled in comparison. We must have combed through most of the shops in the city. By the end of the afternoon, we were tired and Dad agreed to try one last shopping center. He tried to interest me in little musical stuffed toys.

"Here honey, how about this little bear that plays music when you pull the string." He held up the stuffed animal and I wrinkled my nose.

"Daddy, those are for babies!" I wandered away from him, searching further up the aisle.

And then I found it! A whole row of beautiful music boxes—some with swans, others with dancing couples, and others with ballerinas.

"Daddy, daddy, I found it! I found it! I knew I'd find it!"

I saw amazement in his eyes. Even he had begun to doubt its existence. "Well honey, I guess Jesus is rewarding you for your determination!" Dad conceded. "Which one do you like?"

I chose a black music box with a gold and red design of swans flying over a lake hedged with flowery reeds. Inside was a magnetic mirror on which two ballerinas danced to the music of *Swan Lake*. I was enchanted by it and treasured that music box for years. On the way home, we stopped for an ice cream, which was a rare treat. It was one of the happiest days of my life and I was walking on clouds.

A few weeks later, we moved to a new house with the rest of the Family members still in the Philippines. It was a time of unrestrained happiness spent with my father. I would surprise him with chocolate oatmeal balls and watch him eat them with pleasure. On the nights I slept in his room, I would wear one of his T-shirts that reached to my mid-calf like a nightgown and curl up in bed while he told me stories of his cats, his days in boarding school and how he joined the Family. Lovingly, I would study his photo album packed full of pictures of the three of us, which invoked memories of happier times. But I never found any pictures of my mother or brothers and sisters.

One picture caught my attention though. It was of a beautiful, smiling little girl around four years of age holding out a dark red apple in front of a Christmas tree. With big blue eyes, rosy cheeks, and long dark curls that glowed from the lights of the tree, she resembled a porcelain doll. "Daddy, who is this?" I asked, holding up the photo.

"Hmmm? Oh, that's your Greek sister, Davida."

"I have a Greek sister?" This was the first time I had heard of her. Dad never talked about any of his kids, and different brothers and sisters would pop up unexpectedly throughout my life.

"Yes. She's your age in fact. She was even born in the same hospital as you."

"We're twins?"

"No. I think she's a month older than you."

"Where is she?" I asked.

"I don't know. Somewhere in Greece I think."

I studied the picture for a long time and finally made up my mind. From that day on, I told people I had a twin somewhere.

A few months later, Dad announced that we were leaving the Philippines for India. This time was different from the others because Dad would be coming with us. However, when we arrived in Bombay, he promptly dropped Celeste and me at the Family boarding school there, and went to join the Witnessing Home. I saw him only a few times in the months we spent there.

We slept on bunk beds, and I had a top bunk next to the window. From where I lay, I could see out into the neighbour-hood. There was a town meeting hall across the road, where weddings were often held. They would blast loud Bollywood music from giant speakers for days at a time. I would lie at night watching the Indians dancing in their colorful wedding costumes; there were lights and flowers everywhere. It seemed like a fantasyland and I liked having a secret glimpse into that world.

One day we were having Get Out in the courtyard—which was when we were allowed out to play or exercise—when the doorbell rang. The Indian uncle assigned to answer went to the gate. A wealthy Indian family was outside. They had mistaken our school for an orphanage and had come to enquire about adopting one of us.

My heart thumped wildly. I wanted to go with them! They were a family wanting a child—I was a child without a family. I nearly jumped out and shouted, "Take me!" Dad did not even feature in the picture.

The uncle quickly put them straight. My heart sunk when they left. The rest of the day I imagined what it would be like growing up with them and I built it up so much in my mind that it became almost real to me.

Since the Jumbo, I had become a very quiet, introverted but resourceful child. I knew what made the teachers tick, and I had disciplined myself into a perfection of silence. For the first time in my life, I managed to get by without a spanking. I understood that to survive, I must become a chameleon, changing to suit every environment I found myself in. If it was silence and complacency they wanted, I gave it to them with hands folded neatly in my lap; if they wanted me to sing, I sang with gusto; I danced to all their tunes. My best disguise was transparency. I did not make many friends, however, due to my newfound popularity with the teachers.

One teacher, Auntie Peace, felt sorry for me. She was a kind teacher with curly red hair and bright blue eyes. Even when she was mad, Auntie Peace always stayed calm and never shouted at us like other adults. I had a phobia about my hair from being frequently teased about how thin and wispy it was. From the time I was a toddler I had been plagued with bad cradle cap, which turned into eczema. It covered my entire scalp and prevented my hair from growing. Bored at night, I would lie there picking at the dry skin, and my hair would come out with it. To my horror, the next morning I'd find giant bald patches where I had been picking. One of the girls in my class had long thick hair falling past her bottom, and feeling ugly, I would watch in envy as the teacher brushed it out. I never let anyone touch my hair, and always tied it back by myself into a lumpy ponytail when no one was looking.

Auntie Peace persuaded me to let her take it down one day and gently combed it out, telling me how beautiful my hair was. "There's different kinds of hair, Julie," she told me. "Just because your hair is not long and thick does not mean it is not beautiful. You are a very beautiful and special girl and you're going to grow up to do special things."

I never forgot this kindness, and always thought of her with the kind of affection I might have felt towards my own mother. In return, I would carry her baby around when she awoke screaming at night and the adults were downstairs in meetings.

"You don't have to cry," I whispered as I rocked her. "At least your mummy's coming back. My mum's never coming back for me, and I'm not crying, so you shouldn't cry either." And I'd play my music box and sing to her till she fell asleep again. It was years later that I discovered that Auntie Peace named her next baby after me.

This was the first time I became reasonably comfortable in my environment, which enabled me to form delicate strings of attachment. Just as I began to develop some semblance of routine and belonging, Dad was recalled to the Heavenly City School in Japan. He flew with Celeste and me to Thailand and dropped us at the Training Center school in Bangkok, promising to return for us in a few months.

Dad was never good at keeping promises.

Part Three

Kristina's Story

CHAPTER ELEVEN

Living a Double Life

I remember the scene as if it were only yesterday. I was five years old. The day was sunny and bright. We rose early to attend a fellowship meeting at Hyde Park, London. Everyone greeted each other by kissing and hugging and called each other "brother" and "sister." There were over eighty of us sitting on the grass singing and clapping along to "You gotta be a baby to go to heaven."

I sang with all my heart as loudly as I could. This was a happy day and I savoured the joyful atmosphere. The other children and I handed out leaflets to the growing crowd of onlookers, asking them to say a prayer with us to receive Jesus into their hearts. After "winning a soul" for Heaven, I ran back to join in the dancing. A large circle had formed with everyone holding hands and I held on tightly as we went round and round. We sang:

Come along and join our gypsy caravan
We are headed for another country, for another land…

I looked over at my beautiful mother playing the guitar, her long hair flowing down to her waist. As the Children of God we were meant to be one big happy family. She would tell me stories of the early days when they had a double-decker bus known as the prophet bus, which was painted bright yellow with the words "Revolution for Jesus" emblazoned across the sides. The bus would be filled with disciples singing and clapping as they drove to Trafalgar Square, where they would disembark and go off in pairs to witness to the youth, with a guitar, a King James Bible and some leaflets.

Happy moments like this were rare. It seems as if my entire early childhood was filled with a sense of quiet desperation with a stepfather I loathed and a mother who seemed so fey and fragile she needed protecting from the world. She was the princess chained to the rock, my stepdad was the wicked dragon and I was the one whose task it was to protect her at all cost. This was why I tried to spare her from knowing about all the abuse heaped upon me—sexual, physical, and verbal.

My real dad was my knight in shining armour. Some day, I was sure, he would rescue us. We would be reunited with him and my big sister Celeste, and all the pain would stop.

"Tell me how you met my dad," I would pester Mum when we were on our own and Joshua couldn't hear. I meant my real dad, not Joshua, the despised stepfather who abused me almost on a daily basis.

The story was always the same. Mum and Dad turned up at a Children of God commune in Kent, on the same day. They barely knew each other but she felt that the Lord was telling them to get married. Dad approached her at a large Fellowship Meeting in Central London.

"Has the Lord been showing you anything?" he asked her.

"Yes," she answered meekly. "That we should get married?"

Dad fell on his knees theatrically and clasped her around the waist. "Thank God!" he sighed in relief.

I loved that story; it always seemed so romantic which made it all the sadder that we were no longer a happy family.

I was born on June 29, 1976 in Bombay, India, where my parents were working as missionaries. Even from the earliest age, I was very aware of sex—it was impossible not to be. At around the time of my birth, our prophet Mo was publishing a series of Letters detailing a new ministry called "Flirty Fishing." In these letters Mo remembered the many years he'd spent as a lonely salesman away from his family, and felt sympathy for the needy men who had never known the real love of God. "Who better than the Family girls to give it to them?" he wrote. He boasted that he was God's fisherman, sex was the hook to catch the "fish" and the women were his "bait." Sex was the highest expression of love and if Jesus was willing to die on the Cross for us, we should be willing to sacrifice our bodies to win souls and new recruits for Him. But the letters "God's Whores" and "Hookers for Jesus" also explained how Flirty Fishing should pay the bills. Mo documented how he went with his second "wife," Maria, pimping her to pick up men in the hotel bars and nightclubs of London and Tenerife. She even had a child—Davidito—by one of the men she had Flirty Fished.

This shocking new ministry prompted many to leave the Family.

*   *   *

One day, when I was just a few months old, Mum was told that she had to go Flirty Fishing to win new souls. When she understood what it entailed, she told Dad, "This is wrong."

He laughed and tried to persuade her to accept it. "If Mo says it's right who are we to argue?"

Confused and uncertain, Mum decided to pray and ask the Lord if this could possibly be the truth. After sleeping on it, she found her feelings had changed. In theory she felt she *would* be willing to give her love and even her body to win lost souls if this would please the Lord. Then she became pregnant again with my brother David. All her pregnancies were difficult, with violent vomiting and an aversion to smell and touch, and so she was repulsed by physical intimacy with her husband while in this condition. My father told her that he wanted to find someone else to fulfil his sexual needs outside of the marriage. He made his request to the local leader, who lent him his own wife.

An article written by a visiting shepherd was published in an internal magazine, castigating the sisters for not meeting the sexual needs of the brothers in the communes.

"I was very surprised," Mum told me when I asked about it. "I hadn't realized that we were supposed to do this."

After this rebuke, sexual "sharing" was immediately implemented. In April 1978, my brother David was born. I was sixteen months old. Mum struggled to cope with three young children, while my father spent most of his time working on his radio show, *Music with Meaning*. Mum felt neglected and jealous at having to share her husband. The regional shepherdess noticed something was wrong, and Mum, touched by her concern, tried to express her feelings.

The conversation was reported to the superiors who sent her to Madras for a break and to pray about whether she should stay with my dad.

David was still a babe in arms, so Mum took him with her. While at the commune in Madras, an Australian brother, Joshua, became infatuated with her. He was asked to vacate his room for her, but he didn't leave. Feeling rested after six weeks, Mum returned to Dad to discover that in her absence he had begun an affair with an Indian sister, Ruth, who was pregnant with his child. Joshua pursued Mum back to Madras and called a meeting to suggest that he should be mated to my mother and my dad to Ruth.

Privately, Dad asked Mum, "Do you want to stay with me?"

"Yes," she replied.

The matter was ended and my parents moved away to another commune. But Joshua persisted, coming over daily to help her with the kids. After a few weeks of this, of always seeing Joshua around, Dad sat my mother down and requested a separation.

"I was completely against it," Mum told me, sadly. "But Joshua was so pushy—and your dad was so stubborn. He wouldn't change his mind."

"Couldn't you have begged him?" I asked.

Mum shook her head. "He was my husband. I felt I had no choice but to obey him and be with Joshua. Your dad insisted on keeping Celeste."

"But why didn't he want me?" I asked, feeling rejected—though going with him would have meant not being with Mum, so I would have ended up torn between my love for them.

She would try and reassure me that it wasn't because he didn't love me but that I was too young.

I would say, "But doesn't Celeste need a mother?"

I knew how much Mum missed Celeste too, so I never got anywhere with my line of questioning. I always got the same answer. "Well, I guess he thought it was fair as I got to keep two of you." This offered me little comfort.

Soon afterwards, due to negative press reports exposing Flirty Fishing, the Indian police said that all members of the Children of God had to leave the country. Joshua decided we would go to England. Before we left, we visited Dad and Celeste one last time to say goodbye. Mum was devastated and in shock at this turn of events. It was difficult for her to accept that God was requiring her to forsake her eldest daughter.

I cried as we drove through the bustle and chaos to Bombay Airport, remembering the last words Celeste said to me, "Look after baby David."

Back in a wintry England, Mum scanned the crowds at the airport and spotted her parents, Bill and Margaret, waiting for us. Tired from the long journey, and cold, we piled into the car and were driven to their comfortable house in the Midlands. We were showered with love and affection. They took us for fun outings and walks with their dogs. We spent our first real Christmas with them. There was a massive tree with presents under it, chocolates, treats, and decorations— it was wonderful because Mo didn't approve of gifts and special treats at Christmas.

I loved my new grandfather! I would crawl on to his lap and he would read me stories. I especially liked one picture book that showed how the insides of ships and planes worked. As he was a civil engineer, he could explain every detail of every machine. I loved hearing about engines, sails, and thick metal hulls.

Joshua was in his late twenties, with a shock of dark blond hair and a droopy moustache. He later told me that he had been a heroin addict in India when he met the Children of God. He flushed his drugs and cigarettes down the toilet and joined the same night. While he could be witty and charming to others, David and I suffered from his lack of patience, controlling behaviour, and violent outbursts. I was an affectionate child, but with him my instinct told me to be wary. I didn't like him and wouldn't hug him or sit on his lap. I missed my daddy at first, and resisted calling Joshua "daddy" like he insisted, which always upset him.

When he was in a good mood, he told us funny stories. "I was brought up a country boy, in the mountains. It was so isolated out there I sold Blue Mountain air to city people in jam jars." We laughed, but it was always a balancing act—how much to laugh. Too much or too little laughter got a smack. I knew that if I didn't please him, I'd be in for a spanking, or some other form of punishment. He only had to give me a look or move his hands close to his belt and I would clam up and do whatever he wanted, like a Pavlovian dog.

Our grandparents couldn't understand why Joshua would beat us as in their eyes we were little angels, but they felt it was not their place to interfere—I'm sure, though, that they discussed it at night behind the closed door of their bedroom. Granny disapproved of his harshness and would often act as a buffer between him and us. One time as I went past her,

I mumbled, "I hate that man." She didn't say anything, but I sensed quiet support from her and she was extra nice to me.

I loved being at my grandparents' and when Joshua told them that we were going to be missionaries in Poland, they were horrified. "Why don't you open up a health-food shop instead?" Granddad asked.

I thought it was a lovely idea—we'd have a home and stay in one place. But Mum just shook her head. It didn't enter her mind to tell her father that it was a sin for Family members to work in the System for money; and he probably wouldn't have understood.

My grandparents' scrutiny was too much for Joshua. I could see and hear the pressure he put on Mum. "I hate it here. They don't like me. Come on, we're getting out," he would insist, until she was worn down. All too soon, our wonderful visit came to an end. In January, we went to Blackpool to stay with a couple that had just joined the Family. In all, we lived in over forty different places over the next ten years. That meant, of course, that I had nowhere to call my home.

Secretly, behind Joshua's back, Mum wrote to Dad asking if she could return to him. I asked over and over, "Has there been a letter? Has Daddy replied?," and always she would shake her head. Time passed slowly, and still there was no letter. It was tense waiting—it felt like forever.

When Mum told Joshua that she wanted to return to my real daddy, he changed. He constantly criticized her, always looking for faults, and it escalated until he hit her. I was so small I couldn't do anything, but listen to her sobbing. Afterwards, when Joshua wasn't looking, I snuggled up close and whispered in her ear. "It will be all right, Mummy—we'll hear from Daddy soon." She nodded her head, but there was a hopeless look in her eyes. Gradually she started to switch off more and more, until she was like a ghost who lived with us but who wasn't really there.

From Blackpool we moved to London, and the council put us in a bed and breakfast in Paddington near the railway station while we waited to be housed. It was so cold and bleak. David and I developed whooping cough and Mum took us to the doctor, but she wouldn't let us have any medicine, as Mo believed that we should be healed through faith alone. The harsh whoop in whooping cough is reflexive and can't really be prevented—but because we weren't "ill" we weren't allowed to show any symptoms.

Just before our grandparents came on a visit, Joshua glared at us and admonished, wagging his finger in our faces, "Don't you even think about coughing in front of them, or you're in for a spanking."

I almost choked and turned blue trying to hold in the whoops—and as soon as I could when they left I choked and gasped for air as I coughed and coughed.

We had very little money and Mum had to go out Flirty Fishing in the evenings to make some—and to win souls, Joshua told us. I knew where she was going, and brushed her hair and made her pretty. I would often be left alone with my little brother David while Joshua went to visit other Family members, or went to the pub on the sly. Every day he insisted that I memorized a quota of verses and complete my work-books before I could go to bed, and obediently I'd settle down to my work.

One evening, after Mum had left to Flirty Fish, Joshua headed for the door. "Put David to bed, and make sure the dishes are washed," he ordered. "And make sure you pray before going to sleep," he added before leaving.

After putting David to sleep and doing my homework, I was so tired I forgot about the dishes and crawled into my bed. I woke up to the sharp sting of a belt across my body and Joshua shouting, "Get up…now!"

I clamped my little fists together and tried to scramble down from my bunk, which always hurt my feet. I hurried over to the sink, clambered on to a chair and started to clean the dishes, while he loomed behind me, shouting, his breath stinking of beer. The dishes felt slippery and I was terrified I'd drop one. It never occurred to me that he was squandering the money that Mum was earning hard.

After five depressing months crowded into the B&B, we were given a council flat in Deptford, a drab, run-down area in South London, near the Thames. The Salvation Army donated us some furniture and we moved in. A kind Scottish lady lived next door and sometimes I would be allowed to play with her daughter who was the same age as me, and some of the local children. Our flat was small, with a tiny balcony and no backyard. David and I shared a bunk bed—I slept on the top.

Many evenings after praying together, Joshua would read us a bedtime story. I was no longer allowed *Winnie the Pooh* and such tales, which had always been my favourites. I was told that these stories and fairy tales were System propaganda and a waste of our precious time. Instead, Joshua read stories about Davidito, Maria's son; these were later compiled into

The Davidito Book. This was written by his nanny, Sarah, and read like a diary that followed the daily life of the "little Prince." It became the childcare manual for The Family to follow. The chapter "My Little Fish" included pornographic pictures of Davidito and Sarah's daughter, Davida, lying naked in various sexual positions. There was even a photograph of Sarah sucking two-year-old Davidito's penis, and Maria's secretary, Sue, lying naked with him on top.

Joshua taught me that sex and nudity were natural, so that by the time he started molesting me I had no idea he was doing anything wrong. The first time was one evening in Deptford and remains with me like a snapshot. I can still see the orange curtains, covered with big white flowers, and the central light with a shade dangling down, throwing shadows. I was lying on the top bunk enjoying a bedtime story and David had fallen asleep on the bottom bunk. Mum came in, left some clean laundry, and went out of the room. When Joshua finished reading, he put the book down and stood up level with my top bunk. He put my legs around his neck and started to stroke me. He put his mouth on my mouth, and forced his tongue inside. It was wet and slobbery and I felt like gagging. I was three years old.

Then, he started licking my vagina. His beard was scratchy and I tried hard to stay still even when it hurt or became uncomfortable. It was just the beginning. He would get me to touch him and he would rub himself up against me. I was terrified of making him angry and always did what he said.

"Come!" he'd insist, getting angry when I seemed confused. "Can't you have an orgasm, damn you?" Mo believed even small children could climax, but how did I know what an orgasm was? The only emotion I felt was terror, and often pain.

It was not just what was done to me that left scars and tore at my heart, but also seeing the abuse that was inflicted on my little brother and my mother. He quoted verses and ranted for hours and hours at us and we had to sit there and dumbly take it. He ranted and raved, telling Mum her faults until it escalated into blows, or he'd throw things at her. I was embarrassed and ashamed of Joshua when he shouted or hit us in front of the Systemites or other Family members for being less than perfect. I often thought he was the one who needed a telling off. I didn't want to be or act like him. David rarely escaped his temper. As he grew older, the beatings became harsher. His childish attempts to get things right would annoy Joshua, who expected us to act like fully functioning adults.

"Stop acting like a child!" he'd shout; and I'd think, *But we are children!* To make it more confusing, the hate and anger would often be followed by phrases like "I'm doing this because I love you."

We weren't allowed to simply be children and play; we were more like his personal slaves who had constantly to be alert in case he should suddenly demand us to do something. We had to acknowledge his words with an "amen" or "yes, sir." I was always on edge attempting to pre-empt his constantly changing rules. I could never do anything right for him, no matter how hard I tried. I lived in survival mode, never quite knowing when my brother and I would be subjected to his violence.

He would explode at the smallest mistakes. "Nina! Why didn't you see that David might put that in his mouth?" Slap! "Nina! Who asked you to come in and pick David up? I'm talking to your mother."

"B-b-but he's cryi—" Slap!

These things made it very difficult for me to keep being nice to him, though I did want to be—not because I loved or even liked him; I hated him—but because I desperately wanted for us all to get along and be happy, and some instinct told me that by liking Joshua I might make Mum's life a little easier.

It was during this time that Joshua's parents came over from Australia to meet us and get to know us. They booked themselves into a hotel to be near us so they could take us out every day. They were nice, breezy Australians who seemed so kind and affectionate it seemed amazing that Joshua was their son. They told us to call them Nan and Papa and accepted us immediately as their grandchildren. I loved them because they interacted with us in a very natural way, something that Mum never did. She had the ability to go off into her own world, a kind of mental switching off. Perhaps it was the only escape she had.

Finally Mum received the long-awaited reply from Dad. When Joshua went out, I snuggled up to her in bed, and we poured over the letter. *He wanted us back!* My heart sang with joy and Mum smiled as she stroked my hair. "We'll soon be a family again," she said. "I can't wait to see Celeste—it's been so long." I nodded in silent agreement.

Using contraceptives was considered rebellion against God. Mum truly believed that God would only allow her to get pregnant if it was His Will—and when she became pregnant with her fourth child through Flirty Fishing, all our hopes of escape were dashed. As usual, she was ill and bedridden most of the time, so no further plans to join Dad were made.

A single brother living in our home witnessed Joshua's abuse of Mum and wrote to Dad about it. Dad wrote back with some concern, saying he had received this information, but that was as far as it went and we heard nothing more for some time. I would quietly ask Mum when he was coming for us and still cried at night for my daddy—but it made no difference. I was stuck in the middle of a nightmare without end.

After she recovered from the worst of her morning sickness Mum wrote again to Dad, telling him she was desperate to come back, but he replied that he was with a new sister, Crystal. "The door is now closed," he wrote in his letter. When Mum read the words to me, I wanted to cry but didn't know how.

When I had turned four, Mo issued the "Go Caravan" initiative. He decided that if Family members lived in one place too long, not only would they become tied down to the System, but they would also be easy to trace. Living out of caravans seemed the solution. Just after my birthday we had raised enough money in the streets to buy an old caravan and a car to tow it and we were off, out of London to the countryside.

We parked up at four different campsites in the south of England, always with other families who were also Family members. My favourite was next to farmland, where I would watch the farm animals. For the first time, I was given a certain amount of freedom and played outside as much as I was allowed. But at times I was called into our caravan to pose for nude pictures behind closed curtains. Joshua told me how to pose and where to put my hands.

"Smile, look happy!" he'd order; and I'd pin a huge fake grin to my face so I could go out again and join my friends.

Sometimes, when I went to use the main toilet block, a man would follow me in, and make me suck his penis while I was trying to have a wee. The first time I fell back into the toilet bowl and was stuck for what seemed like hours before I found the strength to wriggle myself out. I wasn't shocked by what he'd done, because I thought that's what men did— instead I was frantic that I would be missed and get a spanking for being late in. Joshua was always telling me off for "justifying myself" and not taking responsibility for my actions. So I said nothing and just accepted it when it happened again. I wasn't one to moan and complain; I was taught that every frown and murmur sent up a foul smell to Jesus' nostrils.

Although I was still only four, Joshua said that I was now old enough to sleep with him in their bed. He'd put on a tape of Ravel's *Bolero*. It was an old tape and hissed like a nest of snakes while he sexually abused me. It seemed to be his favourite piece of music to have sex by; he played it whenever he was "sharing" with anyone. All the hectic pace did was to set my nerves on edge and make me even more tense than I already was. It got to where I dreaded hearing the music start, knowing what was in store for me.

My brother Jonathan was born in October 1980, in Hambledon, Hampshire. He was a calm, agreeable baby, never fussy, and had the most beautiful smile and wise, dark eyes. I was glad when Mum came home from the hospital. She taught me to feed him, rock him to sleep, and change his nappies, all of which I enjoyed doing. He was my real baby doll.

Joshua was very irresponsible with money, but he never seemed to be concerned. He always said, "Don't worry, the Lord will supply!" When people were generous and invited us for meals or gave us donations, this confirmed that God did seem to take care of us. On the whole, though, there were few ways of raising money in the country. There weren't many to witness to, and we were always hard up and often hungry. Joshua never considered getting a job to support his growing family. Working for the System would be like working for the Devil, he said. Instead, he instructed Mum to apply for social security as a single mother with four children. The officer came over to our caravan to interview her. Joshua told the lady that he was just the childcare helper but she wasn't convinced and turned to me.

"So, where do you sleep?" she asked.

I knew that as a Systemite, she wasn't supposed to know about our sexual freedoms and that I slept in the big bed with Joshua. So I told the only other truth I knew and blurted out, "My Mummy sleeps with my Daddy!"

When she had gone Joshua screamed at me, "You're stupid! Stupid! What are you, Nina?"

"Stupid," I said; then uselessly pleaded not to be beaten with the belt. Mum did often plead for him to give us another chance, to be more reasonable, but this only got all of us in trouble. She did not get her benefits and to raise money we hit the streets, witnessing and busking even more.

Eventually we sold the caravan and moved back to London. I missed being able to play in the open fields, stringing daisy chains and taking my brothers on walks. Instead, I spent my days selling tracts and witnessing in Hyde Park and Kensington Gardens. I liked it when I was teamed with Mum and we would go to Oxford Street together. She would allow me to watch the giant cuckoo clock or look into the shop windows, something Joshua would never stand for.

Around this time Joshua was on edge. A grandmother had successfully won a case in which her grandchildren were made wards of court and would be taken from their parents unless they left the Family. Joshua had seen the veiled looks my Granny and Granddad had directed at him, and knew they despised him. Even though he hid most of the more serious abuse from them, he was never certain that they hadn't seen anything, so he worried that my grandparents would make us wards of court. This paranoia hastened our eventual return to India.

My father's radio program, *Music with Meaning*, had become very popular and thousands of potential recruits were writing into the show. It was decided that we were needed to go and do the follow-up. I was so proud of my Dad and listened avidly to the tapes, hearing his voice and even Celeste singing. I prayed that I would see them in Sri Lanka where they were based. Then Mum became pregnant for the fifth time. She was only twenty-five years old. The shepherds condemned her for having difficult pregnancies, but still, she was not allowed to use contraceptives. Even though I was so young, Mum discussed this with me, and I was upset by the injustice, as I struggled to change her bile bucket, make her food to eat and take care of the other children.

I was desperate to see my father and tell him everything that Joshua had done. "It's okay Mum, we'll pray extra hard for you so that you feel better soon," I'd say, as I washed her face with a damp cloth and tried to make her feel better. That fourth and last Christmas at Granny and Granddad's home in the Midlands, she was so ill she went into hospital and was given medicine that helped her keep food down.

After the holidays, we returned to London and stayed in various cheap, backstreet hotels. Mum was very weak and relapsed without the medicine, so she had to go back into hospital for a month. For the first time, she discovered what the problem was. She suffered from hyperemesis gravidarum, which meant that she couldn't keep food or water down and frequently vomited blood and bile for the first six weeks of every pregnancy.

Just before we left for India, my grandparents came to London and took us to London Zoo. I especially loved the elephants, monkeys, and giraffes. Joshua was on his best behaviour and was in a very good mood—he was glad to be finally going back to India. We believed that this was to be the last time we would see Granddad and Granny. David and I were sad about this, but confident that it wouldn't be long until the Endtime, when Jesus would return and we would all be together again in Heaven. They gave David birthday money for his fourth birthday, and he insisted on using it to buy us all fish and chips. At the end of the day, we said our goodbyes and promised to write.

CHAPTER TWELVE

A Gypsy Missionary

India was the land of my birth. I felt I was going home. But more than that, it was where I had last seen my dad and Celeste. I was so excited—perhaps I would see them again. Dad would save us from my stepdad. He would see at once how much we had suffered.

On the plane, when Joshua was sleeping, I whispered in Mum's ear, "Can we see Dad?" I kept half an eye on Joshua. He was like a mean dog, always watchful, ready to snap, but this time, tired from changing planes, he was in a deep sleep.

Knowing how I longed for my father, she placated me with a "We'll see."

After a long flight we landed in Bombay and took a taxi to a nearby hotel. I was immediately hit by the aromatic and almost suffocating muggy heat, and everywhere I looked I saw amazing sights—throngs of people crowding the streets, women with baskets on their heads, stalls selling strange foods, spices, and fruits I'd probably known once but could no longer remember—mangoes, watermelons, and mysterious dark spheres with spines on the outside.

We would spend the next six years traveling from one end of India to the other, trying to save souls before the Final Days—the Endtime. Forever driven onwards by this mission, we knew no peace, had no settled home. It was bewildering. Because of this, despite loathing Joshua, our dysfunctional family unit was the only security I knew and I clung to it with a sense of desperation.

After a few days in Bombay, we left for Poona, where many other families who had also just arrived from the West congregated at the Reception Home. I struggled to get used to the heat and developed a severe heat rash.

After a few weeks at the Reception Home, our family was dispatched to Calcutta, some 1500 miles away. The rail journey took two days. We were enthralled by the passing landscape as we looked out of the barred train windows, the wind in our faces. Hills rolled by and then the desert, and paddy field after paddy field. Everywhere, children were playing cricket; they would wave at us and we waved back.

At last we pulled into Calcutta on the north-east coast of India, a historic city that was once the capital of the British Raj before New Delhi. It's also one of the most crowded cities in the world. As we emerged from the station, the noise of traffic and Indian music filled the air and we stayed close to Mum and Joshua so we wouldn't get lost in the daily hubbub of an Indian city. Joshua rented a spacious three-bedroom ground-floor apartment for us, and some basic items of furniture. He hired a maid to wash our clothes, and when he found out how little it cost to hire a cook, he found a young man to do this work. I know Mum really appreciated this, as by now she was heavily pregnant and had to rest a lot. She was not able to get out much either, as the heat in Calcutta was very intense. On our Freeday once a week, we would often visit the nearby country club where the manager let us swim for free and brought us tea with toast and jam. The boys and I learned to swim. Unfortunately Joshua thought David should learn by throwing him in at the deep end, which traumatized him and me who was concerned for him as he almost drowned.

Even on our days out—like an outing to the zoo—Joshua made us hand out leaflets instead of enjoying a normal family day out. However we did not dare to question his reasoning, as whatever he said was the law as far as we were concerned and there was no changing it. Our lives were controlled by the whims of an impulsive, moody man—and now, we were thousands of miles away from Granddad and Granny, to whom we could have fled in an emergency.

Late one evening in August, Mum went into labor and Joshua rushed out into the street and flagged down a rickshaw. The rickshaw driver was remarkable as he only had one leg. Joshua wanted to take over driving, as we were quite a load, but the driver wouldn't hear of it. By the time we got to the hospital Mum was crumpled up with pain and breathing desperately hard. She was taken to a bare white room with just a table in the middle. Joshua ushered the boys and me into the room and we all witnessed the birth. It was terrifying to hear Mum cry out to Jesus during the painful hours of pushing. We stood in awe when at last we saw the baby's head and thanked the Lord for keeping Mum safe and giving us a new baby brother.

The name Kiron was chosen, which means "ray of light" in Bengali, though we just called him "Bubs." We made a tape to share the news with our grandparents, and our new baby brother screamed in the background. We all adored him even though he cried a great deal. There was a never-ending round of nappies and bottles to wash. It was unbearably hot and I would often sit and fan Kiron to keep him cool.

I was always required to be looking after someone, staying busy and being a shining example to my brothers and to everyone I met. I had to become a sales woman and, with so much practice, I became very good at it and would always meet my quota. But putting on a smiling face and having to suppress my feelings and emotions put me under such stress I started to wet the bed again; some of the problem was that I found it difficult to navigate myself to the toilet in the pitch black. I would think that I had found my way to the toilet only to discover it was a dream. When Joshua discovered my accidents, he would humiliate me, and threaten to put me back in nappies.

Even as small children we were told we would be persecuted for our faith, and this seemed to be confirmed when the Chief of Police pounded on our door and demanded to be let in. My brothers and I were terrified that the Antichrist's forces were coming to kill us. Mum told us to sit quietly in the bedroom. When Joshua came home, he let him in. The Chief of Police said the government had decided Dad's *Music with Meaning* show was "subversive and a front for the CIA." We had twenty-four hours to leave the district. All six Family homes in Calcutta packed up and fled. We traveled south by train to join a home in Bubanishwa.

*　　*　　*

By now Mum was under severe mental stress because of Joshua's constant cruelty towards her, and I was very worried about her and what would happen to us. She had left Joshua twice before in England, but he had persuaded her to go back to him on both occasions. She snapped once again, and one traumatic day she took Kiron and me to a cheap hotel for the night. "Mum—what about David and Jonathan?" I asked, worried that they were left with Joshua who would be so angry he'd take it out on them.

I don't think Mum even heard me. She had a frozen, exhausted look on her face and seemed to be sleepwalking.

The next day we boarded a train to Bombay—and I knew she was thinking of getting a plane home, though I had no idea how she would manage it. The train stayed stuck in the station as we sweated in steamy heat. When—when would it leave? Half of me willed it to go; the other half of me was terrified that Joshua would suddenly arrive, rampaging. And I was frantic with worry over my abandoned brothers.

"Don't be upset, Mum," I tried to comfort her, but she was lost in her own world.

We sat and waited, but the train just did not move. Suddenly, Mum stood up and said, "Grab the pushchair." She held on tightly to Kiron and we got off the train, just as the engine started up. My eyes welled up with tears as the whistle blew and the train chugged out of the station. Instead of running away, Mum took us to the area shepherd's commune to speak with the shepherds, Uriah and Katrina. When we turned up, Katrina was away and so we slept in Uriah's room; Kiron and I on the floor, and Uriah and Mum in the bed. The next morning when I woke up, Mum and Kiron were not there.

"Good morning sweetie, come up here," Uriah said, as he patted the bed beside him. Obediently, I crawled slowly on to the bed.

He pulled me towards him and I could smell his bad morning breath as he directed my hand on to his penis and started to kiss me. I was naked and he put me on top of him when I heard a knock on the door. I went rigid.

"Come in!" Uriah said casually, and to my embarrassment, a man poked his head around the door.

"Good morning, God bless you brother!" he said breezily, "Do you want some coffee?"

"Yes, sure," Uriah answered. By this time, I had slunk off to one side of him, and hid my face under his armpit. "Do you want anything, Nina?" he asked me.

"Some water, please," I answered in a whisper.

When the man left the room, Uriah placed me back on top of him, and continued kissing me passionately so it was hard to breathe. I had to masturbate him with both my hands, and holding my head, he directed it down and put his penis in my mouth. I closed up my mind and carried on the physical performance mechanically as he told me what a good lover I was. My neck hurt and I gagged when he came.

Uriah arranged for Mum, Kiron and me to go and stay in another commune for a while. Shortly afterwards we attended a local area meeting which was held in a hotel for three days. While there Mum agreed to return to Joshua, as she felt that she had no choice but to keep the family together. A few months later Uriah gave me a little card with a letter addressed, "To Nina, so sweet, loving, and sexy." When I got the card, I hid it, but Mum found it.

"Nina, why would he send you this?" she asked, surprised.

I hung my head, embarrassed, and shuffled my feet.

I became used to abuse—and sometimes it even happened during "devotions." An uncle would place me on his lap and I started to notice the telltale signs of an erection when they jiggled me up and down in time to the music.

I was aware that Mum was under great pressure to share and that Joshua was always chasing the other "Family" women. Sharing was an emotional minefield, and I knew Mum struggled with sharp feelings of jealousy, as Joshua also did at times.

While she was still breastfeeding Kiron, Mum became pregnant again with her sixth child, and as usual, it was tough. Family children were supposed to be seen but not heard and Kiron would wail loudly when she tried to take him off the breast. So to keep him quiet, she continued to nurse him, which weakened her further. She spent hours in bed. By now, Joshua made it no secret that he was in love with Auntie Crystal. She was involved in a long-term threesome with two married Family members. The leaders had noticed his violent mood swings and his Jekyll and Hyde personality, and said he was too volatile to be allowed to join Crystal and her family who were being sent to set up a "Babes" home for new disciples in Mysore. I suppose they thought his jealousy might lead to a bad scene. They told him that Mum and we children could stay—but Joshua never told us. He was so determined to be near Crystal that he took us all to live in a hotel in Mysore. We were cut off from our friends while he went to see Crystal every day.

This was hard on Mum. By now she was heavily pregnant and couldn't take us out—so we were stuck in a tiny, hot room for most of the day, bored out of our heads. But it seems that the Family leadership had noticed our situation and grew concerned. After a few weeks they sent us far away from Crystal, to Goa in the south. The journey in the train was fantastic. We hung our heads out the window most of the way. As we chugged up the mountainside, the train turned a bend and we were rewarded with the sight of a giant waterfall cascading down into the lush vegetation below. When the train idled at each station, groups of women in colorful saris would gather outside the windows selling "chai"—a sweet, spiced tea, chappatis, bananas and all manner of tasty Indian treats.

I was so excited when my sister Rosemarie was born in November 1985. With her pale complexion and strawberry blonde curls, she looked like a little porcelain doll. Everybody loved her and we affectionately called her "baby doll." After her birth, Mum and Joshua's relationship deteriorated badly. Mum was jealous because he was having an affair with a sister in the home and Joshua hated her for her jealousy.

The leaders sent Mum away on a road trip even though Rosemarie was still a baby and one dreadful day I walked into our room to find Joshua bending over baby Rosemarie on the changing table. It was obvious what he was doing and a hand of ice gripped my heart.

I heard him coo to Rosemarie, "When you're old enough, we're going to make love like your sister Nina."

Despite being indoctrinated into radical sexual beliefs, I was disgusted. I did not want my baby sister to suffer what he had done to me. I approached slowly, mumbling that I would take over putting her nappy back on. I kept her close to me until Mum returned. Two-year-old Kiron missed Mum when she wasn't around and was spanked for being clingy—all this contributed to making me anxious if I did not know where my brothers and sister were at all times throughout the day. I was a nine-year-old girl, heading for a nervous breakdown.

Now that Joshua had his own children, Kiron and Rosemarie, he became even more cruel and spiteful towards David, Jonny, and me. He constantly teased David about the gap in his teeth, calling him "Beaver," which made him self-conscious. Unfortunately, I needed glasses and would often squint. Whenever he caught me, he would slap me, saying, "You look like a rat when you do that," and often called me "rat face." I could take that. What I could not handle was when he teased Jonathan mercilessly about his dark looks, knowing full well that Jonathan was one of Mo's "Jesus Babies," born as the result of Mum's Flirty Fishing.

Whenever Joshua heard the fruitseller pass, shouting, "Mango, mango!" He would mock heartlessly, "Ho, Mango Boy—there's your dad calling for you."

Finally, to stop the bullying over my squinting at least, I told Mum I needed glasses. They took me to the eye clinic in Madras, which was a long trip. I was thankful when I got my glasses and no longer squinted. But the bullying and mocking just took a different shape.

Joshua found a spacious house in Margao, a town in the district of Goa, one mile from the beach. It was a natural paradise. Mum made sure we walked to the beach every day for a swim in the ocean. I would walk along the sands comforted

by the sound of vast waves crashing in, bringing in all manner of crabs and sea life.

Once, I was resting under the shade of the coconut trees
on the shore, gazing out at the sea, when a friendly foreign
couple came to chat with us. We were talking about their
home in Canada when I spotted our carer striding quickly
towards us, mouthing, "Selah!" This was the code word that
meant our security was in danger and we needed to split.
I had to say a quick goodbye, and the woman slipped me
their address and phone number with an invitation to
visit them if I ever found myself in Canada. We were
marched home through the back roads, to make sure we
weren't being followed. The adults were suspicious of everyone and security measures were extreme, bordering on
paranoia.

One day during devotions, an elephant walked up our
drive and stood outside our living-room window. The magnificent creature began to empty his bladder on the sandy
ground while staring in at us through the window. A real life
elephant in our garden—we were all excited! Mum halted
devotions and we all piled outside to gawk at this unusual
event. We were so small that the elephant appeared gigantic
at such close quarters. But we weren't scared—his eyes were
wise and gentle. It took him a further fifteen minutes to finish his business.

"Look we have our own pond!" I joked, pointing at the
massive puddle.

"Can we keep him, can we keep him?" Kiron, who was
two, asked, his eyes bright with excitement as he hopped
about from foot to foot.

"Don't be silly," Jonathan, a more knowledgeable four-year-old replied.

The trainer emerged from the palm trees, running towards us, frantically waving a colorful stick in the air and making clicking sounds. He chided our new animal friend sternly, imploring him not run away again or to pee in people's gardens. He apologized to us and rode his charge away.

The elephant heralded in a wonderful surprise later that day, when Mum called us into her room. We gathered around her on the bed as she glanced up, her face smiling and happy.

"I've got a package from Celeste," she said.

My heart jumped as I stared at the little parcel. It had already been opened—all our letters were censored—but I was still full of joy. This brought Dad and my big sister closer.

"What's in it—can we see? Open it quickly!" I urged. I noticed that there weren't the usual UK stamps. (Our letters usually came via the UK; I had a large collection of stamps by now—all I had of Celeste, and a faint memory of speaking with her and Dad on the phone when we were in England.)

The younger ones crawled for a position nearest Mum on the bed while she made a huge fuss of opening it. Celeste sent a pair of panties she'd made in her sewing class and a letter with a striking drawing of two mountains. On one peak Celeste stood, all alone, and on the other was Mum, David and me. In the speech bubble Celeste was crying out "Mum!" and we were calling "Celeste!" We noticed Dad was not anywhere in the picture. She had also made an A to Z with pictures cut out from posters and Mo Letters to help Kiron learn to read.

After that, when I had the time, I would write letters to Celeste and Dad. Sometimes they replied and when I got a letter of my own, it was a glorious, red-letter day and I walked around, my heart singing.

Dad wrote, "Nina, you're a shining example working for the Lord. We'll all be together again soon in the Millennium after Jesus' return. It won't be long now!"

I would fall asleep happily and dream I was running into my daddy's arms; he would scoop me up and kiss me and everything would be perfect.

But dark clouds were ahead. One day the regional shepherdess came to visit the Home. She and the Home shepherdess had a meeting with Mum in which they falsely accused her of not working hard enough in the Home. They told her that she was being demoted to Babes' status—what beginners were called. Mum hadn't been a Babe since she had first joined the Family and she was shocked and mortified.

The punishment and shame was worse than even she thought. Our whole family was to return to the UK—which along with all other Western countries was considered to be "the pit," a place fit only for backsliders and un-spiritual, half-hearted Family members.

"Nina, this is terrible. I can't believe I am being shamed like this," Mum wept.

I patted her hand. "It's all right, Mum, it's all right," I said, but inwardly I was alive with hope. *I was going home!* I would see my nice grandparents again.

We took the train to Bombay, where we lived hand-to-mouth while waiting for Granny and Granddad to send us the airfare back to England. When the money came, instead of buying regular tickets, Joshua thought he could save some cash when a Family couple who had recently arrived in India with their five children offered to sell us their return tickets for a cheap price.

On Christmas Eve, we got up at 3 a.m. to go to the airport. Soon I would see Granny and Granddad and my Mum's younger sister, Auntie Caryn, again! But I tried hard to hold back my excitement because Joshua was livid at having to leave the mission field—and somehow it was our fault. Everything was our fault—never Joshua's. When we finally got to the front of the line at the check-in desk, the lady looked at our tickets. She called in her supervisor, who called one of the immigration officers. The officer explained sternly that the names on the tickets were not the same as the names on our passports.

Joshua implored the man to change his mind, and although he was sympathetic, there was nothing he could do. If they let us fly, we would be arrested and put in jail when the plane touched down in Bahrain. We waited at the airport terrace in desperate prayer while Joshua tried to resolve the crisis. We watched luggage being loaded on to the plane through the window, growing more anxious by the minute. To our horror, the plane started taxiing down to the runway. In tears, we watched it take off, just as the sun came up.

I ran to the ladies room and bawled my eyes out. I had so looked forward to spending Christmas with my grandparents again. Now it wasn't going to happen. We were all in shock as we took a taxi to a cheap hotel. We had no money at all because Joshua had spent the profit from the cheap tickets on new clothes and shoes, so he took us children over the road to the Salvation Army hostel for a traditional Christmas lunch—and soon we moved into the hostel itself. My poor Mum had to go Flirty Fishing again to pay the bills. She hated it but had no choice.

When we had first arrived in Bombay my mother wrote a letter appealing to the leadership to let us stay in India. Several weeks after the aborted departure a reply was finally received which granted us this permission. So in March 1986, we were sent south to Madras to a large commune with many families. Later that year, in September Mum discovered she was pregnant for the seventh time. She never complained, but she must have always dreaded it. She was bedridden once again, unable to keep down food or water.

Not long after the Home shepherds informed Mum that she was to be sent back to England without any of her children. They insinuated that because she was not bright and cheery there was something spiritually wrong with her. They did not seem to understand that after six weeks of not eating Mum was still very weak and not back to her normal self. They told her that she had no rights over us children because we belonged to the Family and God. However, she begged them to let her take the two youngest, Kiron and Rosie. For fifteen years she had given her life to the Children of God, and now they judged she was a bad apple? I did not understand. She was the nicest person I knew. *Why had it not been Joshua?* My world was turned upside down. Joshua was given the choice to go with her but he chose not to. I couldn't believe this.

One afternoon, I was given a few minutes to say goodbye to my mother, who was seven months pregnant, Kiron and Rosemary, then they were gone. I had lost my dad and my elder sister. And now I lost my mum, a brother and my baby sister. I felt numb and could not even cry. But I was angry with Joshua, and blamed him for breaking up our family. I had forgiven him time and again, but this was the last straw. I closed my heart to him completely.

CHAPTER THIRTEEN

Abusive Love

I had been a confident, outgoing child, but after Mum left I became quiet and withdrawn. I did not imagine things could get worse, but they did. It felt sometimes like I was suffocating with the weight of my suppressed emotions. I missed her desperately and talked to her all the time in my mind, wondering how she was and what she was doing. Was she sad without my brothers and me? They cried into their pillows at night, but I felt like stone inside and couldn't, as that would mean my acceptance of this frightening situation.

I was now ten, and I could not help wondering the reason for it all. It seemed unlikely to me that God would approve of physical and emotional cruelty to small children as I had observed from every direction, especially from Joshua and the Home shepherds. However good and obedient we children were, it never seemed to end. Instead of behaving like a loving family—the happy, smiling face they presented to the world—behind our closed front doors, the Family created a cruel and hostile atmosphere, one driven by suspicion and paranoia. Every word sent down from Mo was an admonishment and a rant for us to do better. Joshua was no better. However hard I tried, it was never good enough.

When I began teaching a group of four- to seven-year-olds I started to realize that the way I dealt with the children differed greatly to how the adults treated them. The adults' interpretation of the rules were inconsistent and constantly changing from home to home and person to person. For example, we were always instructed to peel apples as the skins carried germs. Then a new Mo Letter said that this was unnecessary as long as the apple was soaked properly with salt water. My six-year-old brother Jonathan was eating an apple for snack, when suddenly an uncle grabbed him by the scruff of the neck.

"How dare you eat the apple without peeling it first!" he bawled. "Disobedient boy! I'm going to teach you a lesson you'll never forget!" He dragged my terrified brother into the bathroom and beat him with a flyswatter. He had not read the new letter yet and thought Jonathan had defied the rules.

Even though we knew it could lead to punishment for us, David and I were banging on the door. "Uncle—it's not what you think! He didn't disobey the rules. Please uncle!" But the sound of the whacks and Jonathan's screams continued. When my brother came out whimpering, he ran to Joshua, who was unable to do anything. Adults were not supposed to interfere with each other's correction of the children.

I glared at Joshua, panting with frustration—what kind of a man was he? What kind of a father was he? But I could say nothing.

When it was my turn to go on a "road trip," I was glad to be getting away. The commune was beginning to feel like a prison. Road trips were witnessing trips to areas that did not have any communes and could last for weeks. I went with a teen boy, Steven, and two adults—Auntie Esther, an Italian-American and Uncle Peter, an Indian national. Our bags were laden with thousands of posters to distribute and Heaven's Magic tapes to sell.

After a long and tiring day knocking on the doors of shops and offices, we returned to our hotel room. There was a double bed and a mattress on the floor. Auntie Esther officiated over the sleeping arrangements.

"The first night, I'll share with Steven," she declared, "and Nina, you can sleep on the bed with Uncle Peter. Tomorrow night, we'll swap."

I was worried. I could not stand Uncle Peter! He was always saying stupid things and scaring the younger children. He would accost me in the kitchen while I was cooking, or in the dark bend of the stairwell, lifting my top and pawing at my developing breasts. I always managed to excuse myself with some duty. Now there was nowhere to run.

Help, I thought.

I heard Auntie Esther and Steven pray before making love. They went on for hours as I gritted my teeth and tried to get to sleep. Beside me, Uncle Peter was becoming increasingly horny and inched over towards me. Suddenly, his hands were all over me, his erection rubbing into my bottom. Every muscle in my body was tense and I tried to pretend I was asleep. He turned me on to my back and his mouth assaulted me. He persistently tried to penetrate me and the more I resisted the more demanding he became.

"I'm tired," I mumbled in protest.

Uncle Peter made some strange noises then collapsed on top of me and fell asleep. He was too heavy to wiggle out from under, and I hardly slept.

After the first night, I did manage to keep him at a distance for a few days. But then, one afternoon after witnessing, we headed back to the hotel earlier than usual. I was proud of my achievements that day. I was a good salesperson and had got rid of all the posters and tapes in my bag. I felt happy and relaxed, but his words chilled me to the marrow.

Uncle Peter said, "Nina, you've done so well today, that we'll take an afternoon off!"

I recognized a look in his eye and when we got up to our room, I realized I was not going to have a nap. My fears were confirmed when I stepped out of the shower and he approached me. I dodged when he reached out to grab me and let out a slight scream. I had never screamed in my life and I could not find my voice. He grabbed me then and threw me on to the bed with his hand over my mouth, saying "Shhh."

"Why are you being so selfish?" His hot breath fanned my face. "The others have been getting all the sex while you keep denying me. I'm desperate and you're refusing to share with me!" He then implored more gently, "Come on."

I could not breathe easily and he was hurting me. I tried to wrestle myself out from under him but he clamped my two hands down over my head.

"No, no, no!" I shouted.

"You little tease!" he said aggressively, taking both my wrists in one hand and cupping the other over my mouth.

It did not take long for him to climax. Shaking, I rolled over and sobbed quietly under the sheet till I fell asleep. That evening when I awoke I went straight to the shower. It took many of them to rid me of his smell.

The next few nights were no different and I found it hard to bury my disgust. I wrestled with the concept that if I found him repulsive, it was my own fault for not having enough love. I did not mind sleeping with some of the boys my own age, but I felt sick and it was painful when I had sex with the older teens and grown men.

My best friend, Sunshine, was also unhappy and, when I got back from the road trip, we discussed running away together.

"Where will we go?" Sunshine whispered.

"England," I said confidently. "We can follow the stream down to the sea and find a boat bound for England. Then we'll find my mother—she'll look after us."

"But we have no money for our fares," Sunshine said.

"We can stowaway!" I said, grabbing her hands. "Oh, Sunshine it will be such an adventure! Let's start hiding our food now, so we'll have enough to last on the journey!"

We made a plan and squirreled away little bits of food. We were confident that we could live on the fish from the stream and peanut-butter sandwiches. The excitement of planning it all distracted us from the daily drudgery of Home life.

The night of our escape came. Still dressed, we got under the covers and waited. We were nervous but ready. When we were sure all the adults in the house had gone to bed, we got up, grabbed our "flee bags" and started to inch our way downstairs in the pitch black. I thought of unseen wild animals outside—snakes and tigers—and started to quake. We reached the front door and slid open the first lock. The noise startled us and we stood frozen for a good ten minutes, while Sunshine waited for me and I waited for her to make a move. A slight noise in the house made us panic and, holding hands, we slunk back upstairs and into our beds, our dreams of escape and freedom just ashes.

Then, for the first time in years, I had really good news. Joshua's parents, Nan and Papa, were coming to India!

We made the long journey to pick them up at Bombay airport. We recognized Papa first, then saw that Nan was in a wheelchair. She was exhausted but cried when we greeted her with hugs and kisses. They had just spent four months in England with our mother and stayed for the birth of their new grandchild, Christopher, who was born in June 1987.

When Joshua heard my new brother's name, he was livid. "Christopher! She has called him Christopher?" he seethed.

"Yes, dear," Nan smiled. "He's a lovely little baby, a real sweetheart."

But I knew without him saying that he was livid that Mum had named his child after my dad. It seemed a smack in the eye to him.

One evening Papa walked into our room as we were reading *Life with Grandpa*. We had wrapped it in a new cover so that it could not be identified as Family material, I was very aware that I needed to keep it hidden from outsiders' eyes. When Papa walked in the room, I stopped reading.

"What are you reading?" he asked, picking up the book and flicking through it. There were a few stories with graphic sexual images and strange scenarios and he stared at them shocked. He looked up and glanced at me, and I looked back guilelessly, though shaking inside. To me, these images were not "wrong"—these were the valuable words of God's prophet. However, I could see shock and disgust on Papa's face, and felt shame creep over me.

Immediately, Papa took Joshua into the next room and I could hear their raised voiced as they quarreled. Afterwards, Joshua was tense and strained and it seemed that Papa and Nan might leave. Nan stayed in her room in tears for three days and we worried that we had upset her. I'd creep in and hold her hand, and take her cold drinks, but she seemed over-wrought and could barely speak to me. But on the third day she got up, determined to give us an amazing holiday. They took us on excursions to the safari park, the zoo, and to see the other sights of the city. It was our first real holiday and we wallowed in it. I wondered why our lives couldn't always be like this—full of happiness, kindness, and fun without lectures and constant, harping criticism from adults.

But Joshua didn't change. The kinder his parents were, the more morose and hostile he became. He did not allow us to use the toilet for hours; David held it in so long that eventually, to his embarrassment, he peed himself. Nan took him up an alley to clean him up. Later, she finally exploded at Joshua. "For God's sake, just leave them alone! They're just children! You're constantly nit-picking!"

He just glowered at her and snapped, "He's old enough not to wet his pants."

For the last night of their visit, Nan and Papa said they would take us to eat at Bombay's grandest hotel, the Taj Mahal. We had a lovely meal accompanied by a string quartet. We chatted together and ignored Joshua altogether as he sat sulking through the meal. As we expected, he waved away the dessert menu.

"Well, I'm having dessert!" Papa insisted and ordered the king of banana splits.

As soon as Joshua left to go to the toilet, Papa pushed the amazing mountain of ice cream, cherries and nuts over and told us to tuck in. It was a rare moment of defiance so we quickly stuffed our faces while Nan kept watch. By the time Joshua returned the banana split was gone. When we took them to the airport, we were all in tears as we hugged good-bye. I was heartbroken to see them go. On the train back to Bangalore, I was silent. It was difficult to come down from the high of their visit.

After Christmas, we received a bulletin that Grandpa Mo was ill again and Maria had serious problems with her eyes. A worldwide prayer vigil schedule was set up so that prayers were offered for their health at every moment of the day and night. When I caught the flu and was quarantined, I was told the sickness was because of some spiritual sin of my own. But when Grandpa and Maria became sick, it was the fault of the Family members for not praying hard enough. I remembered all the hours I had spent on my knees praying for them and I knew it wasn't because of any lack of desperation and sincerity on my part. I began to wonder if there was not some sin in them.

My doubts seemed to be confirmed when I read about Mo's granddaughter, Mene, in a Mo Letter called "The Last State," which accused her of being possessed by demons for daring to question Mo. Mene had become disillusioned with her grandfather after seeing the standards he set for himself were different from those he expected of the Family.

Why she would criticize him seemed clear to me. Members had to stick to a weekly ration of an eight-ounce glass of wine, while we read that Grandpa was always getting drunk. We were punished for using bad language, but in his Letters Grandpa swore four-letter words all the time. We could never get angry and always had to show love, while we read Grandpa's angry letters in which he ranted, belittled and tore people down. When Family members were ill, God was punishing them for their sins, and yet Grandpa was always sick. How could he accuse Mene of demon possession for having a few bad thoughts, when he depicted graphically in the Mo Letters how he was plagued with demonic oppression and hellish nightmares of monsters from the Netherworld?

Like Mene, I had to pray against my mother's negative influence over me. Which meant that what I felt about her didn't count. I knew it was not natural to have to turn against your own mother because someone who didn't even know her said she was lacking faith. After my prayer of "deliverance," I had to choose a new name for my new self. Every year, a candlelit ceremony was held to usher in the New Year. Each member lit their candle and stated their resolution for the New Year. When my turn came, I stumbled through my prepared speech and announced that I had taken the new name of "Angel Dust." Though I paid them lip service, inside I was still angry that I had to denounce my mother for backsliding. Nothing made sense anymore.

I was scared what would become of me and wrote down my fears in a diary. I invented a code that was indecipherable without the key, which I kept hidden in the back of my diary. It became my way of release and a secret area that was truly mine alone. I had to share my body with men—many of them complete strangers. My diary was something I didn't have to share with anyone.

Many young girls were falling pregnant and this caused the rules to change. When a girl started her period, she could no longer have sex with a "semenating" male, and the men could only have sex with someone over sixteen, or under twelve. I was glad when I started my periods, as I became relatively safe, though I worried about what would happen when I turned sixteen. My friend, Phoebe, was about to have her sixteenth birthday and she confided to me her terror, as the men in the commune were queuing up like randy dogs in heat. I quietly sympathized with her. I was desperate to get away from these crazy communes with their irrational, sex-obsessed adults. I heard about a teen training center called the Jumbo opening up in the Philippines and worked up the courage to speak with Auntie Rose about going.

"I miss my mum and I don't get on well with Joshua." Then I told her my deepest desire. "I miss my sister Celeste, and I heard she's in the Philippines at the Jumbo. I'm wondering if there's any way I could go to the Jumbo to be with her and others my own age."

Auntie Rose replied, "Let me see what I can do."

I waited and waited. Then just when I thought I could not stand another day, Joshua broke the news to us that we were going to England. We were secretly ecstatic and he was furious at having to leave the mission field! Excitedly, my brothers and I discussed the news together in hushed whispers.

England seemed like the Promised Land. The idea of seeing my mother again was almost more than I could bear and I was tense and terrified, convinced that something would prevent it happening—as had happened before. "Jesus, let me go to England," I prayed nightly. "Please, please, make it happen."

CHAPTER FOURTEEN

Escape

On March 27, 1988, at the age of eleven, I finally arrived back in England. I was unprepared for the weather with bare legs and sandals and a red polka-dot skirt and white blouse. England was now as much of a culture shock as India had been in 1982. Gray skies, no sun, no perfumes of the East.

My brothers and I left Joshua's side and hurried our way through baggage and passport control, rushing to find Mum. She was waiting at the arrival gate holding our baby brother, Christopher. She looked so beautiful—just the same, with her long hair and lovely beaming smile. I flew into her arms and hugged her and my two little brothers and sister, laughing and crying with joy. The two years and all the pain disappeared as I looked at her. We were back together and I couldn't help but fill with tears. I still loved her—she was my Mum. But as I sensed Joshua approaching, and saw Mum look up and her smile waver, I choked back the tears. I knew he would slap me, if not there in that public place then as soon as we were alone.

We all piled into a van waiting outside and I asked Mum which commune we were going to. "No, we're going to a flat," she said. She had found a flat once she knew we were on our way back. There wasn't enough room for us all at her parents' house where she had been living. She was told that all the communes were full. No one wanted a pregnant woman and two toddlers.

As soon as we got to the one-bedroom flat in Twickenham, on the leafy outskirts of West London, we showered and rested from the long flight. The air was tense and I knew Joshua had something on his mind.

"I want us to separate," he started.

Mum nodded. "Yes, I know. Well, I don't see why not—"

His next words took the wind right out of her sails. "I want Jonathan, Rosemarie, and Kiron. I'm taking them."

"What?" Mum gasped. I almost sat bolt upright but managed to keep still while I listened.

"They're mine. And by the way Nina is to go to The Jumbo in the Philippines. You have to sign a power of attorney to keep things legal."

Mum didn't seem to take it in. She repeated, "The Philippines?"

Joshua continued, telling her that all the Family children had to be trained for the Last Days. The directives said that they were to be sent permanently to different training camps, and parents would only be allowed to visit them for two hours on Sundays. As usual he was blind to the pain of this unnatural separation. In fact he was keen to ensure that close family ties could not jeopardize the higher loyalty demanded by the group and kept waving the letter that ordained my future under Mum's nose for her to sign.

Losing Celeste had hurt Mum deeply and she had prayed every day for God to bring her children back. Now that she finally had six of us under one roof for the first time in years, here was this brutal man telling her "no, half of them are mine and I want them—and your daughter Kristina belongs to the Family." She was expected to sign the rest of her children away.

"I'm tired. I'll sign the papers later," she said. She knew that the philosophy of the group was to take children away from backslider parents and hand them over to the Family. Some children had been separated for years—and some never saw their parents again and had no idea where they were because their names had been changed.

On our third day as Joshua was sleeping, Mum came into our room and whispered to us, "Let's go out and give Dad some peace and quiet." Then, she ushered us quietly out of the front door.

She had no clear plans and it was too cold and windy to go to the park, so she took us to the local library, where we all sat down in a huddle around one of the tables there. Her next words were electric. I could hardly believe what I was hearing.

She looked at each one of us as she whispered, glancing over her shoulder as if the books had ears and would explode out of their shelves to batter us, "I've changed my mind about Grandpa. I don't believe that he really is a true prophet of God."

I sat back and gasped. Something started to grow in me like a seedling about to flourish with hope. I hardly dared to take in her words.

Mum spoke hurriedly, trying to get all her words out before her courage failed, or we were snatched away by Joshua or a Family spy. "A couple of months ago I went into the local Christian bookshop. I opened a book on religious cults, spotted an inaccurate fact, and immediately shut it. I was so brainwashed I thought it was demonic. The shop also stocked a book by Mo's daughter, Deborah Davis. It was called *The Children of God*."

I nodded, remembering the Mo Letter about it.

Mum continued. "I was scared. I almost felt that demons might be hitchhiking in it. I hesitated, opened it, then put it down. I knew that Mo had said that the book was taboo, written by his eldest daughter who had turned against him."

"What did you do then?" I asked.

Mum said, "I was overcome with curiosity, and a few days later I went back. I was so scared I was trembling. I glanced around anxiously, wondering whether a lightning bolt would strike me dead. I stood there for ages, walked around again, but that book drew me like a magnet. I had to have it. Finally, I grabbed it and walked quickly to the counter before I changed my mind. It was forbidden fruit—but I had to taste it. I found myself at the counter still trembling so hard I could scarcely count out the money. I paid and hurried out of the door."

Mum started to read the book that very night, and she read long into the morning, mesmerized, shocked, disgusted, and then convinced. "I could hardly believe what I was reading, but I knew deep in my gut it was true. It was extremely painful to realize I had been deceived for so many years. The Bible says, 'The truth will set you free,' and for me that book did just that." She looked around at us all as she quoted, "I have heard what the prophets say who prophesy lies in my name. They say, "I had a dream…" these lying prophets, who prophesy the delusions of their own minds.'"

I nodded. I knew the Bible backwards and knew that quote. "And that is Mo, a lying prophet, a false prophet," I said. The veil that had been slipping for years finally fell from my eyes.

Like Mum, I too realized we had been deceived, controlled, and manipulated. When she said she wanted to leave Joshua and the Family, a weight was taken off me and tears stung my eyes. There was no argument from me. Like her, I wanted a life in which we did not have to answer to harsh shepherds or deal with our irrational and domineering stepfather. I was exhilarated and scared at the same time—for us and for Mum, who was shaking like a leaf.

I will always admire the heroic actions of my mother that day. I know how hard it was for her to listen to her voice that had been suppressed for so long and find the courage to break free on her own. But the impetus had been the threat of losing us. She told me she had to go somewhere and left me in charge of my brothers and sister.

It was strange, sitting among all the children's books and thinking over everything she had said. Nervously, I looked at the clock. Over an hour had passed since Mum left.

I thought, "I'm all alone with five children, I hope nothing bad happens."

I kept on looking at the door. People came in, chose books, checked them out, walked out of the Exit; but there was still no sign of Mum.

Time ticked by slowly. I was growing more anxious.

After what felt like hours, Mum finally rushed in. From her face, I could tell it was good news. She explained that she had contacted a women's refuge she had read about. A white van was waiting outside to take us to their center in London. We put our books away and rushed out like spies and jumped in the van. I still couldn't believe that this was happening.

When we arrived at the refuge, to our dismay, we found there were no facilities and they did not seem interested in helping us. We were told to wait in a bare room, which had two chairs and a couple of broken toys. They had no place for us to sleep that night. I felt my courage ebbing away. *Please, please, don't make us go back to Joshua and the flat,* I prayed silently.

Mum's only option was to call her parents and she returned from the phone, looking tense but relieved. "Yes, they want us," she said simply.

The women's refuge arranged for a van to take us half way to the Midlands where our grandparents and Auntie Caryn were waiting. Granny cried at seeing us again. She hugged us all, and said, "Thank God, thank God." We had not eaten all day, so they bought us something to eat and drink. We were shattered and fell asleep as soon as we got to their house.

Once we were safely at our grandparents, Mum took the train back to London. She returned to the flat with two volunteers from the women's refuge. They climbed the stairs to the flat, quietly put the key in the lock and went in. She was relieved to find Joshua was not there and gathered as many of our belongings as she could carry. The next day she sent Joshua a letter explaining what she had done.

The only thing Mum was determined about was that somehow she would find and rescue her lost daughter—Celeste. It had been over ten years but not a day had passed when she hadn't thought about her.

Mum asked me not to talk too much about the cult at school or in front of our family. This wasn't hard to do as my whole life had been about living a double life. It was easier in some ways as my grandparents never asked about our past and we were so busy getting on with an uncertain future. Mum was worried that Joshua knew where we probably were, and at any time the Family could swoop down and snatch us children, so two weeks after we had arrived, Granny and Granddad arranged for us to go to Butlins Holiday Camp in Skegness. They rented a chalet for us and one for themselves. Joshua would never think of looking for us there. Once we had been paranoid of being around Systemites; now the tables had turned and we were paranoid of being found by Joshua. (Mo always made it clear that kidnapping the children of a blackslidden partner or spouse was necessary for the children's sake.) I would take the boys swimming in the pool every day—but otherwise, there wasn't a lot to do. Time passed slowly.

Two weeks earlier we had been in the Indian summer. Now, the wind off the North Sea bit hard and stung my face; the chill seemed to reach right into the marrow of my bones as I walked along the empty beach fighting the wind, squinting out to a sea that seemed one with the murky gray above. I had no winter clothes, so Auntie Caryn gave me some of her old jumpers and skirts. In Family style, my hair was very long with a center parting. I asked if I could have it cut. I was desperate to look different so I would not be recognized and bundled into the back of a van by the cult. Besides which, the novelty of going to a hairdresser's for the first time was exciting. I loved my new style cut into a bob with a fringe.

After two weeks we left Skegness for a women's refuge in Matlock in the Peak District. Once there, Mum gave me Deborah Davis's book—the one she had bought with fear and trembling in the bookshop. I read it through in one go. For months it was our main topic of conversation. I was shocked to hear that David Berg—the man I no longer thought of as Grandpa Mo—tried to get into bed with Deborah, his eldest daughter, after crowning her queen. I remembered the Mo Letter in which Berg goosed his youngest daughter, Faithy, under the table.

"You read that?" Mum was shocked.

"Of course." I answered. "I read everything in the Mo Letter trunk many times over."

Worried, Mum asked me if anything sexual had ever happened to me I relayed to her how I had been sexually and physically abused and she cried, feeling terrible. Devastated, she picked up the phone to call Joshua, enraged at what he had done to me.

"How could you have done that to our daughter?" she raged.

"Well, she always had orgasms!" he answered lightly.

Mum gasped at his flippant tone and I could see she was sickened to her stomach. "That vile, hateful man! How could I have not seen—I am so sorry."

"It's okay, Mum," I said, not wanting her to flail herself over what was in the past. "We're free now."

"Yes, finally, free," she said. "I was so young, so blind. So many wasted years."

We were told it could take months, even years, to get a council house. Granny and Granddad—bless them!—decided to sell their house and bought two smaller ones; one for them and one for us. I was excited because, of course, we had never really had a home of our own.

I was enrolled in school but the challenges I faced there were different from anything the cult had prepared me for. I started in the second year, and my brothers were enrolled in the local infant and junior schools. There was so much to learn and as a child who was born into a cult I had no past references. Mum helped me with the many gaps in my knowledge and I did my best to adjust.

I spoke English with an American accent and my vocabulary was completely different to that of my school mates; I knew words they did not and could quote the Bible backwards, but there were hundreds of things they said which made no sense to me. I felt stupid at times and they thought me odd. But I enjoyed learning. I spent many Saturdays reading reams of books in the local library.

One day as I was walking home with a classmate, I asked her why she was looking sad. She told me it was her birthday.

"Oh! Are you having a party?" I enquired.

"No," she said, sighing, "My parents are Jehovah's witnesses and we don't celebrate birthdays or Christmas."

That was a surprise to me. I had just come out of a cult and this was the first time I realized there were others like me. I told her I understood, because I had been brought up like that in a religious group too, and my mum had taken me out of it last year. She was never allowed to speak to me again.

Mum became something of an activist. She was put in touch with a man named Ian Howarth, who had started an organization called CIC (Cult Information Center), and in turn he put her in touch with former members as well as Graham Baldwin from Catalyst, a counseling service that deals with cult survivors. We also attended FAIR (Family Action Information and Resource) meetings and seminars. FAIR was set up in 1976 and provides up-to-date information and help for families and friends. We started researching and reading about the cult phenomenon. Though Mum had very little money, she ordered forty copies of Deborah Davis's book to send to her old friends in the group.

As soon as we left the Family we were shunned, of course. Mum was worried that if we spoke out, it would be even harder to make contact with Celeste. We wrote to Dad and Celeste many times. I told them how I had been abused and that the "Law of Love" had hurt me. Dad never replied and I had no idea if he even got my letters, as all letters from outsiders were screened and "doubts of the enemy" inked out.

Celeste was only fourteen and still at the heart of the cult and vulnerable. Mum sued for custody of her, but that did not mean much as neither the authorities nor we had any idea where she was. The judge made Celeste a ward of court. Sam Ajeiman, who had left the cult in 1978—ten years before we did—worked with Mum to produce a booklet, "Searching for Celeste," and we went on a few radio and TV programs and did a number of interviews. Our aim was to ask for help in tracking her down. Through the UK Home Office, the police and Interpol had her details and were on the look-out for her, but they failed to locate her.

I was upset Dad didn't reply to my letters; instead he issued open letters and statements to the press. He accused Mum of selling her soul to the Devil and how dare she persecute God's Family? He claimed that there was never any inappropriate sexual contact between adults and children, and that he lived in the most loving Family he knew.

How could he still believe that?

Angry and outraged, I replied in an open letter to the British press, asking how Dad, Joshua and the Family could deny our experiences, and tell such blatant lies.

In my letter I wrote:

I have read your open letter. I am sorry it has had to come out like this, especially in public . . . what you and my stepfather have said is not true. You have to remember that I was in the COG not too long ago and I know how it works. I want to tell you that I am really hurt that my own father doesn't believe I was sexually abused . . . When I was younger I used to wish that you'd come and rescue us. I was proud to tell my friends that you were my father. But your letter bought me to tears— it is hard to believe that my own father could say such things . . . You also need to understand that the reason my mother has spoken out is to warn others because she doesn't want them to fall into the same trap. Please give Celeste my love. I hope you have not turned her away from me or Mum. Please ask her to write as we have not heard anything for years. I love you, Daddy, but not what you are doing.

It was all I could do. Now we had to wait for Celeste to somehow hear the messages we were beaming to her in every way we knew, and respond.

Part Four

Journey to Freedom

CHAPTER FIFTEEN

Hide and Seek

Juliana

"You're not singing with your whole hearts!" He slammed his hand down on the guitar so suddenly my heart gave a little jump. What would he do this time? I never knew with Uncle Willing. He was unpredictable in everything; his temper would be set off by the smallest things, and usually when least expected. It was impossible to gauge his moods, and I was in no way an amateur when it came to reading our teachers. I feared Uncle Willing more than the rest of them. It was his eyes. They were wild. He always had spittle coming out of his mouth when he spoke, his nose had been broken so many times, it resembled a hawk beak, but mostly it was his beady black eyes and the crazed look in them.

Uncle Willing loved pounding out all the old Family songs on the guitar as we belted out the lyrics to his less-than-rhythmic strumming. The racket was deafening. He had the oddest habit of powdering the guitar neck and his hands throughout our "inspirations," when we had to sing wholeheartedly at the highest decibel level possible. To sing too quietly meant you were not "entering into the spirit" and that could warrant punishment. Tonight he'd decided we were going to have an inspiration before bed. So we sat cross-legged on the floor in our pajamas, singing endlessly, and we were all tired.

"The next person who I don't hear singing loud and clear is getting the paddle!" he threatened. Before the night was over, he'd singled out three boys to get the board.

Uncle Willing liked administering the paddle. His face would distort into an angry grimace, his thin lips pulled tautly back revealing crooked teeth, his nostrils flared wide. It was the same face he made when he was having sex, so I wondered whether he enjoyed beating our naked bottoms. I thought it likely.

"You can be certain of getting two things here," he would say laughing and tapping the paddle against his palm. "Room and Board!"

Only a week after my dad dropped Celeste and me at the huge Bangkok Training Center I was given my first board by Uncle Willing for rebellion. My rebellion became apparent when I refused to call my new foster parents, Joseph and Talitha, "mummy" and "daddy." Although I was glad they placed me with a family I had known as a child, I was weary of having yet one more set of "parents" whom I only spent time with once a week when I was meant to show some kind of filial devotion. My daddy was coming back for me soon; he said so. Why should I get new parents? It made little sense to me. So I called them Uncle and Auntie, like the rest of the adults.

My refusal to call my foster parents mummy and daddy was reported promptly, and I was taken in for a stern lecture and a paddling. So I called them whatever they wanted after that to save myself from further beatings. Though I had issues calling Joseph and Talitha mummy and daddy, I had no trouble accepting their daughter, Vera, as my sister. She had been my childhood playmate and I was very happy to be in the same group as her.

When Dad first brought me to my new class they made a big show of attention towards me. In front of my father, I was given the instant status of "bellwether." The bellwether in our group would be in charge of overseeing the other kids and reporting any misbehaviour.

The day after my dad left, I was stripped of my title, and it was handed over to Uncle Willing's daughter. The whole class was informed that I had "too much pride" for such an honor. Uncle Willing made it quite clear that so long as I was in that school and in *his class*, he would make sure I was given adequate correction. True to his word, he made my life a living hell.

After our customary two hours of Word time and memorization in the morning, we had school. The afternoon was for home economics, when we would be trained in one of the Home "ministries." A good Family disciple had to be a jack-of-all-trades. Ministry training was just a glorified name for being the in-house servant because all we ever did was clean, polish, wash, and scrub.

I needed some sort of release from the drudgery—and writing gave me that. I turned one of my notebooks into my storybook and filled it with tales of talking bears, mermaids, and fairies. They always carried some kind of moral. Our teen helpers and Celeste, in particular, encouraged me, and would often read them out at bedtime to the rest of the group. I kept this book under my pillow and would write when I could not sleep. Some of the other children followed my example and that started the trouble. One boy decided to write a darker tale of a witch.

When Uncle Willing found this story, he freaked out. Oddly, my classmate blamed me, saying he was encouraged to write it through hearing my stories. While I was in class one day, Uncle Willing raided my bed and found my book under my pillow. I was summoned before our three teachers—Uncle Josiah, Uncle Willing, and Auntie Hoseannah. They glared down at me with looks of fire and brimstone. My notebook lay on the table in front of them.

They opened up a Mo Letter I had never seen before. It was called "The Uneager Beaver," in which Mo blasted a woman who had drawn a little kids' coloring book telling the story of a beaver who wanders around the forest looking for his name. Mo was furious that someone had the audacity to create anything that wasn't straight from his mouth.

The letter took over an hour to read and when it was over, my teachers looked at me.

"Who do you think inspired you to write these stories?" Uncle Josiah asked, pointing with disgust to my notebook.

"The Devil helped you write these!" Uncle Josiah answered his own question.

I could not get my head around that one. "But, I don't understand. Everybody's good and loving in it, and the Devil's not good and loving. So how did he inspire me to write good stories?"

"They aren't good stories!" Uncle Willing said.

"Are they God's Word?" Uncle Josiah asked.

"Uh, no."

"Anything that is not God's Word is evil and from the Devil. The Enemy likes to come in disguised like a wolf in sheep's clothing, so you think he's harmless and innocent. But look how your stories are already leading others astray. Look how this boy's story became more evil, and he was only following your example. The Devil is always looking for a way in and you've let him in through your stories."

So far, everyone had encouraged me in my writing, and all of a sudden it was pronounced to be evil and inspired by the Devil. Because I was not God's prophet I would never be able to write anything. I could not accept that. I was proud to be the author—a credit I wasn't about to share with anyone, horns or not.

"It seems you've had far too much time on your hands to listen to Satan," Uncle Josiah said. "After praying about what to do, the Lord has showed us that you'll need a number of punishments to remind you not to let your mind become Satan's playground."

Uncle Willing rubbed his hands in glee. This was the part he enjoyed most. "You're going to receive a good paddling from the board. You'll be on silence restriction for a week, so you can turn your thoughts into prayers to the Lord. You can memorize all the verses from the section in *The Memory Book* on Daydreaming. You'll also miss all group activities and PE for a week, and spend those times reading the Word to help cleanse your mind."

"To replace the words of Grandpa, God's mouthpiece and Prophet, is a severe offence, but as you did it unknowingly, we're letting you off with a very lenient sentence." Auntie Hoseannah clarified.

As the sentence was "so lenient," I wasn't about to plead my case which would give them an excuse to add to my punishment for the offence of talking back. So I kept my mouth shut and swore I would never write again till the day I died.

The next day, Celeste had to apologize for her bad example in encouraging us to write stories that had been demonically inspired.

After that, they separated Celeste and me more than before. She was no longer allowed to help out in our group and, from then on, I only saw her infrequently.

Once a year, Celeste and I went for a photo shoot. I would be dressed up in a nice outfit, usually the same strawberry-patterned blouse and skirt I wore for witnessing. We'd pose with big smiles for pictures to send to Daddy. Then I'd write a letter telling him all the lessons I'd learned and the things I enjoyed and how happy I was. After one of my teachers had censored it, it would be sent together with a letter from Celeste and our photographs.

Dad deduced that we were happy and well cared for. Once a year he would send us a little micro tape in which he would talk to us, pray for us and tell us we would soon be reunited, if not on earth, then in Heaven. I always cried when I listened to them. I missed him and waited eagerly for the day he would come back for us. I was sure we would see him again soon.

Most people living at the Training Center did not have work permits, and had to take a visa trip every three months. They would take an overnight train across the border into

Malaysia or Burma, stay there a day or two, and return with a fresh three-month tourist visa.

I looked forward to these trips and usually went with Celeste; they were my escape from a school that I saw as a prison. On one of these trips, the overwhelming question, which had burned through my mind like a fever for seven years, finally came out.

"Why didn't Mummy want me?" I blurted out suddenly as we rode home in the back of the jeep.

Celeste was taken aback by the abruptness of the question. "What? Who told you that?"

"Nobody ever told me anything. I don't know why she left me."

"She did want you." Celeste looked at me for a minute. "She loved you very much."

"Then why would she leave me?"

"She was told to. She couldn't keep you…but she wanted to."

I wept out of relief. My mother had wanted me…had loved me.

"Told by who?"

"Well, she was sick and she couldn't take all of you with her. Also Dad wanted to keep one of you." Celeste put her arm around me.

"If he wanted to keep me, then why did he leave me too?"

Celeste was silent for a minute, contemplating an appropriate answer. There simply was none. "He was told to as well."

I began to see then that adults had as little choice as we children. We were made to give up our parents just as they were made to give up their kids. A feeling of helplessness washed over me. My every waking minute had been mapped out and scheduled; I had never been allowed to decide what to do with my time, much less what I wanted to wear, or eat, or say. Growing up wouldn't do me a bit of good after all. It wouldn't protect me from anything.

One day, about a year into our stay at the school, Celeste managed to take me out of my PE class for a walk.

"Julie, remember how Daddy said he was coming back to get us?"

"Yes, is he coming soon? I don't want to be here anymore."

"Well, that's what I want to talk to you about." Celeste paused for a moment. "Julie, I think it's time to stop waiting for him."

"What? Why?"

"Because he's not coming back." The words hit me like a ton of bricks. She might as well have told me he was dead.

"How do you know? Did he say so?"

"I asked the shepherds, and they told me he's not coming back. If you keep on waiting for him, you're only going to feel worse."

"You don't know! He's coming back; he said so! I don't want to stay here!" I burst into hysterical tears. "No, no, no!" My world was coming apart; the beatings, the humiliation, the loneliness would all be made right when Dad came back.

"Julie, honey, please don't cry. They'll see you, we'll get in trouble."

"I don't care" I lashed out in the anger of the moment. "And don't call me honey, you're not my mummy! I don't have a mummy!" *I don't have anyone.* But I did not finish my sentence, because it wasn't completely true. I did have Celeste. I just never saw her. And she could not lift a finger to protect me. I let her draw me against her chest to comfort me. But all I could think about was being stuck in Thailand forever in a frightful eternity of endless beatings, school, devotions, and marching.

The one time of year when everything seemed okay was at Christmas. It took nearly the whole month to decorate the school. We spent the week with our families or, in my case, foster family, and we'd have big feasts, activities, and dances.

It was also the loneliest time of the year. Everyone would be reunited with their families and I'd think of Dad then. Mum had long since faded out of the picture. I did not remember her face anymore, and did not even have a photograph of her since I had been made to cut out my parents from every photograph in my possession. Although my foster parents tried to make me feel welcome into their family, and Vera and I were like sisters, it was painfully obvious that I was the only child there without parents. I'd sit in front of the Christmas tree and stare at it for hours while around me everyone joined in carols. My tears turned the Christmas lights into fuzzy balls of color and I thought they looked prettier that way, so I wouldn't wipe them away.

My need for attention gave me some very odd ideas. One teacher was something of an amateur botanist and liked to describe the qualities of each exotic plant and flower that grew within our school grounds.

"This looks like an ordinary hedge, but break off a leaf," he said as he plucked one of the light-green leaves, "and the white sap inside is poisonous." Milky white sap oozed from the severed stem. "If you touched this sap, and afterwards rubbed your eyes, you could possibly go blind."

Go blind! The horror of the idea! Why, you might be attacked, and there'd be nothing you could do to defend yourself. You would not be able to get around without help; in fact, people would always have to care for you, or worry over you…

…and in an instant, going blind did not seem such a terrible fate anymore. Why, then, at least people would notice me. I plucked off a leaf and stared, mesmerized, at the thick white sap. Could go blind! Why, no one cared about me as a seeing child, perhaps they would care if I could not. Slowly I touched the sap, briefly hesitated, raised my finger and rubbed my eyes. I blinked a few times expecting a dramatic blackout.

Suddenly, as the full extent of what I had done sunk in, I realized I really did not want to go blind after all. I waited for the worst but…nothing happened. Then I started to cry in a mixture of confused emotion. Half of me cried because I might go blind, and the other half cried because my experiment did not seem to be working. I ran to catch up with the group relieved that my rash decision had not produced any disaster. Nothing was better than an unknown something.

I loved catching grasshoppers and beetles and bringing them home with me. I desperately needed something to belong to me. I'd tell my pet bug a bedtime story and drift off to sleep with a protective hand covering it. Inevitably, on waking the next morning the hapless creature was either dead or had escaped, and I'd mourn its loss until I replaced it.

Not long after I turned ten the "Techi Series" of Mo Letters came out. Maria's daughter, Techi, was now nearly twelve and beginning to experience the roller-coaster of adolescence. She had a fiery little personality, which was apparent in all the Mo Letters where she engaged in lively conversations with Grandpa.

Maria took it on herself to oversee the breaking of Techi. In the Techi Series, she was treated as the next potential Mene. Her questioning mind was seen as the voice of the Enemy trying to snare her with doubts. If she yielded to him, he could possess her. Techi's sessions of correction and prayer were recorded.

The Techi Series marked a shift in the Family's policies and methods of teen training. It was called the DTR—Discipleship Training Revolution. Things started to tighten drastically. Every evening, we had to write daily Open Heart Reports. We had to log the smallest detail of our day, down to how many times we used the bathroom and how many glasses of water we drank. Every negative thought, all the lessons we had learned, any conversation we had with our peers, and a written reaction to all the Mo Letters we read had to be recorded. We were also encouraged to report on our classmates.

Shepherds used this information to discover any doubts or potential character flaws, which they could use against you later. To write too little was very serious, but it was impossible to come up with a new lesson every day. I became a very creative writer, making up scenarios from which I "learned."

Every week an adult would be paired up as our walky-talky partner and take us for a talk where we were meant to share our hearts, or bare our souls. It was assumed we'd be more willing to talk freely with someone who was not our immediate teacher. Everything we said was, of course, reported back to our shepherds.

Two years into our stay in Thailand, Celeste and I were suddenly moved to the Service Center, a "selah" or secret home where much of the Thailand leadership was based. I had no idea why we were moving; it all happened fairly quickly. Celeste and I were packed into the jeep and driven to a mall car park, where an uncle from the Service Center home met us. Before we were transferred to another vehicle, he sat us on a ledge in the parking lot for a talk.

"How would you like to pick a new name?" he asked.

"Um, no thank you," I answered politely. "I'm all right with my own name."

"Well, in this case you don't really have a choice, honey, because you'll now be living at a selah home where everybody takes on a new name as a security precaution."

This was not entirely true, because only Celeste and I were made to change our names. She had already changed hers from Celeste to Joan and I did not see why she had to change it again.

"So, what name do you think you'd like?"

"Well, I've always liked the name Claire," Celeste offered.

"That sounds good. It suits you. So you'll be Claire from now on. What about you Julie?"

"I don't know." I wanted none of it. I had always been Julie, and it felt like a piece of my identity was being taken from me.

"Well, if you can't think of a name, we'll have to assign one to you. How about Anna?"

That was the ugliest, plainest name ever. "Well, I don't really like it much."

"Well, honey, we don't have much time. If you can't think of one, then you'll have to be Anna."

Claire and Anna, Anna and Claire. I never got used to the sound of our new names. I cried quietly in the back of the jeep. Everything was out of my control. Where I went, what I wore, who I was!

As we were driving, we were suddenly told we had to be blindfolded. Where we were going was a state secret!

The jeep finally stopped and our blindfolds were removed. "God bless you, Claire and Anna! Welcome to your new home."

My time there was miserable and lonely. Yet again, I cleaned, cooked and washed the breakfast, lunch, and dinner dishes. The other half of my day I did school work and had Word Time. As I was ten years old, and the next child under me was six, I had to spend my remaining time in the younger kid's group.

It must have been obvious that I was unhappy, because four months later, I was allowed to return to the Training Center. Celeste remained behind. She was too high a security risk to leave. I only found out later that the reason we had moved was because her mother had stepped up the search for her.

Much had changed while I was away. The school had been thrown into a state of red alert. The police had raided communes in Australia, Argentina, and France; kids had been taken away by Social Services; many adults had been arrested on charges of child abuse. A custody court case against the Children of God had begun in England. The Heavenly City School in Japan was under investigation, and everywhere the Family was being exposed in the media.

The Bangkok Training Center seemed a likely next target. The school underwent a facelift. All the rooms and classrooms were redecorated, and we received new uniforms, books, and school equipment.

We were inundated with letters and comics on the subject of religious persecution. A series for children called "Deceivers Yet True" gave examples of famous people in history and the Bible who had to lie to protect those they loved. We were told that sometimes it was necessary to lie in order to preserve the truth. Because the System was of the Devil and not of God, outsiders would never understand. Systemites looked on sex as something evil and wrong, whereas we all knew it was beautiful and good. And what the System might call abuse was not really abuse at all because it was all done in love.

The next few months we read, studied, ate, and breathed Persecution Preparation. World Services released statements on all the Family's beliefs and doctrines, which we had to learn by heart. Our teachers held mock court trials and grilled us with questions the Enemy might fire at us on sexual abuse, Family life, and our controversial doctrines. We memorized the correct answers to shoot back to the authorities.

A giant purge of all Family publications was ordered across the world. Any Mo Letters that condoned sex with minors, or of an extreme sexual nature like Flirty Fishing, were torn out and burned. Any sexual content was removed from our True Komix, books, and publications like *Life with Grandpa*. Anyone with the least talent had to draw bras, underpants, and negligees to cover naked private parts. The *Heaven's Girl* book was burned and all evidence of its existence expunged completely.

History was being re-written.

Then, suddenly, I was recalled to the Service Center. I had just turned eleven and did not fancy being stuck there again. To my pleasant surprise, three other girls my age had joined while I was away. Celeste taught us Maths and English. She encouraged me in my artistic endeavours. I discovered I could draw and became quite accomplished with oil pastels.

By this time, I had accepted that Dad was never coming back. I put him as far from my thoughts as I could. He was now just a cherished idol in my temple of memories.

One day, Celeste found a pair of his underpants tucked into one of her suitcase pockets. Dad had left them behind three years before and had forgotten them. Little bits of his cast-offs were precious souvenirs to us. One of her other treasures was a pair of Dad's holey socks.

"Hey, look what I found." She held them up for me to see.

This was as sacred an item as the Shroud of Turin and I grabbed the worn red underpants from her hand.

"Dad's underwear!" I shouted in glee. Celeste deftly snatched them back.

"They're mine! I had them in my suitcase."

"I want them! Please, I'm the youngest and you already have his socks! It's not fair!" I caught one side of the underpants and a relentless tug-o-war ensued. In the end, she got the underwear and I had to settle for the holey socks.

Not long after returning to the Service Center, the entire Home packed up and moved. They were concerned that somebody might have discovered their whereabouts, so in true Family fashion, they did the little disappearance act. The new house was much smaller, and had no garden. From this time on, Celeste and I were barred from going outside, and I found the constant indoor confinement unbearable. For exercise, we would run up and down the staircase one hundred times, or do a Jane Fonda workout video. Celeste tried to keep us girls entertained by teaching us dance routines, but we were bored brainless.

A few months later, the worldwide media frenzy seemed to subside and the leadership deemed it safe enough for me to return to the Training Center.

The night I was scheduled to leave, my departure was suddenly delayed. The Home shepherds were rushing about frantically. At 10 p.m., I was called downstairs, and my flee bag was loaded into the jeep together with some suitcases and mattresses. To my surprise, Celeste got in the back of the jeep with me.

"Are you coming back to the Training Center with me?" I asked Celeste.

Celeste looked nervously to Auntie Ami sitting in the jeep with us, as if she wasn't sure what to say.

Auntie Ami spoke up. "Anna, there's been a change of plan. Something very serious has come up. You won't be going to the Training Center yet. We're going to go somewhere else for a while first."

"Oh, where?" I asked. I had no idea what was going on.

"Well, you don't really need to know yet. Why don't you just trust the Lord, okay? Now, I know the windows are black tinted, but just as an extra precaution I'm going to have to ask that you and Claire lie down on these mattresses on the floor."

The mattresses felt and smelt damp. "What's happening?" I whispered to Celeste.

"I don't really know," she said.

My bones collided painfully with the hard metal floor as the jeep (which had no shock absorbers) hit one pothole after another. We must have driven beyond the city perimeter. It was now 2 a.m., and we had been driving in dizzying circles for the past four hours. Staring at the fleeting shadows thrown across the roof by passing lights, it seemed we had been driving forever, and would continue to drive … forever.

I could hear Celeste, Joan, Claire—my sister—breathing beside me. I often forgot what I was supposed to call her. After some time, we were finally told that bad people were trying to find us and take Celeste away. I was not being looked for, but they packed me in for the ride anyway, assuming that if I were recognized they would guess Celeste was nearby. I wondered whether I was so much a threat to her security as someone to keep her company. Finally the jeep stopped. I was relieved; the need to pee had passed beyond urgent. The jolting of the vehicle made the waiting particularly uncomfortable. But I held it another half hour as we continued to lie down, waiting for permission to sit up and tried to make out what was happening by the sounds around us.

The back door was thrown open. The bulky outline of Uncle Philip, a towering German, loomed over us and behind him I could see the night sky, lit dimly by Bangkok's polluted smog. He was joined by Uncle Paul, a stocky Filipino, Auntie Ami, and one of the head area shepherds, Auntie Christina.

"So girls, isn't this exciting?" Auntie Christina gushed. "It's almost like it will be in the Tribulation when we have to hide from Antichrist forces."

Ever since I could remember, we had been living in the Endtime, with the Great Tribulation just around the corner. Sometimes it got tiring to always be living under the shadow of the Endtime. I wished it could just be over with, one way or another, like my spankings. After a round of desperate prayer, we were informed of the plan. Quick and casually, we were to enter the motel about fifty meters away. The six of us were split into groups of two and we slunk in, a pair at a time, through the lobby. Uncle Philip and Uncle Paul were to remain with us as bodyguards. As Uncle Paul was Asian, he was the only one who was allowed to leave the room to buy our meals and pass on any messages to couriers.

There was only one double bed in the room, which we shared with Auntie Christina and Auntie Ami. The two mattresses from the car were snuck up to the room, and our bodyguards slept on the floor, one in front of the door, and one at the foot of the bed. The novelty of playing "hide and seek" faded quickly. With six of us holed up in a twelve-by-sixteen-foot room for six weeks, never seeing daylight, my eleven-year-old energy was very soon screaming for release.

I vented my raging frustrations to my sister during our daily shower time. She bore it all calmly, the level-headed person she was. I did not care anymore if they did find us; I rather

wished they would. I began to imagine running on to the
balcony, hoping someone would spot me and perhaps become
suspicious. One day, when everyone was napping, I plunged
out on to the balcony and looked down over the side, on to a
courtyard surrounded by apartments, everywhere as empty
as a ghost town. I slowly returned inside, nursing my disappointment.

We tried to find ways to amuse ourselves. Celeste would
roll up a sock into a ball, and we'd play Toss the Sock. I cut out
our milk cartons and fashioned them into a pop-up manger
scene. Six weeks passed like this, before Auntie Ami informed
us that we would be moving to a slightly bigger place. The
night we moved had its comical moments. That morning,
Auntie Ami had plaited my hair into many tight little braids,
so that when they were taken out that night, my naturally
wispy hair was transformed into a frizzy Afro. I was dressed
in a florescent orange and white-striped Mickey Mouse shirt
and fluorescent orange tennis shoes. My sister was similarly
costumed. Never mind that it was ten at night, our Systemite
disguise was rounded off with massive pairs of dark sun-
glasses that covered our entire faces. We strutted through
the hotel lobby, ignoring every turned head with the confidence only such a disguise could inspire.

After a three-hour drive, that would usually take half an
hour, we arrived at the tiny flat where we would live for the
next six weeks. We found out that the telephone number and
address of nearly every Family home in Thailand had been
compromised, which was why the Service Center was no
longer a safe hiding place. A couple of ex-members had succeeded in infiltrating a Family Home in the Philippines. They

had gained entry by imitating Mo's voice over the phone. Once inside, they persuaded the Home shepherds to leave for important leadership meetings in the US. With the shepherds gone, these two men, who had once worked in top positions in World Services, began a daring attempt to "exit counsel" the Home members by teaching them classes debunking Mo. Sixteen trunks of *Music with Meaning* archives, and un-purged group publications were stored in Manila. These two men took it all as evidence to expose the Family. It emerged just in time for the British custody case that was still going on in the UK.

The night we were spirited away, one of these men had called the Service Center in Bangkok, again imitating Mo's voice as he had done in the Philippines. Since the infiltration in the Philippines had gone so well, they thought to infiltrate Thailand next. Only this time the Home shepherd who picked up the phone became suspicious. The two impostors fled the scene, but they managed to take with them trunks of compromising material, including video footage the Family had overlooked and failed to destroy; this is the only video evidence that now remains connecting the Family to the abuses of their past.

In early December, we received the good news that an ideal house had been secured. We had the job of cleaning and setting it up before the entire Service Center moved in. Nothing prepared me for the appalling state of that property. Dirt, slime, rat and lizard droppings, spider webs, and bird feathers had combined into a hardened crust that coated every bare space of wall, roof, and floor. The smell was horrible. We got down on our hands and knees and scrubbed into the wee hours of the morning, to clear a clean space to sleep that night.

The next few weeks Celeste and I worked till our fingers were wrinkled and red. We scrubbed methodically, cleaning one room at a time. They were so filthy that it took the both of us over two days to complete one room. We wanted to have the house ready for the Service Center to move in by Christmas. We made it too, on December 23. We spent Christmas surrounded by people for the first time in four months.

New Year 1993 passed, and I was informed that I would be leaving with two of the girls to a home opened for JETTs, or Junior Endtime Teens. Within a week, we were packed off to a military-style JETT training camp. Our shepherd was a huge, ex-special forces African American named Uncle Steven. He carried a whistle around his neck and put us through military exercise drills. I came down with whooping cough and was quarantined. During this time, I received a phone call. To my surprise it was Celeste, who said she was calling to say goodbye. Now that she was eighteen, she had to go to England to confront her backslidden mother. She had asked the shepherds to be allowed to spend a day with me before she left. The request was denied because I had two days left to go before my quarantine period was over. She insisted on phoning instead.

I was too stunned to speak. It was all so sudden, so unexpected. There had been no warning of her departure, nothing to prepare me.

"Are … are you coming back?" I finally managed to ask.

"I don't know," she answered truthfully. I sat in shocked silence. "Hello? Are you there?"

"Yes." A lump was rising in my throat. I found it impossible to speak.

She tried to make small talk, but my tongue was glued to the roof of my mouth and my brain turned to mush. I could think of nothing to say. But I did not want her to hang up, knowing once she did, she'd be gone, for all I knew, forever.

"Julie? Julie? Talk to me." I wanted to tell her not to go, that I did not want to be alone, but all that came out was hot tears running down my cheeks.

"Okay, if you have nothing else to say, I have to hang up, all right? Goodbye … I love you … Bye."

When the line went dead, I held the phone to my ear, listening to the high-pitched hum. Somewhere in the distance I heard someone telling me to put it back in its cradle.

I crawled into bed, and prayed for the very first time that I would not wake up.

CHAPTER SIXTEEN

Searching for Celeste

Kristina

In December 1990, Mum was contacted by Social Services. A fourteen-year-old Swiss boy named Sammy Markos had been caught at Ramsgate, trying to stow away on a ferry to France to get back to his mother. He had no passport, but he was carrying The Emergency Survival Handbook, a Family publication. Immigration officers detained him and he was taken into protective custody. Sammy was terrified of getting the Family and his mother into trouble and refused to acknowledge anyone or answer any questions. He denied he was a member of the group.

Social Services thought Mum would have a better chance of getting him to open up. She took me with her, as I was the same age as Sammy. As soon as we introduced ourselves as former members of the Children of God, he ran into the living room and slammed the door.

Mum asked me to talk to him and I followed him into the games room, picked up the pool cue and said, "Come on! Let the adults talk. Let's have a game!" As we played, his body language relaxed and a rapport developed between us. I told him the story of my aborted escape when I was ten and showed him the article I wrote for *No Longer Children*, a magazine for former cult members. I could see in his eyes that he understood me: I spoke the cult jargon and this was a surprise to him.

But once his mother turned up, she called us "devils." She was behaving hysterically and Sammy became frightened. He withdrew again, refused to speak to me and we left. Mum left behind many of our writings and the Deborah Davis book in case he got a chance to read them. By the time the police found the training school he had been living in, everyone had already fled.

Exhausted, Mum and I dozed in the taxi home late that night. We were jolted awake by a loud bang. Wide-eyed and in shock, I realized our car had hit a bollard and spun out of control into a ditch, shattering the windscreen. The driver had fallen asleep at the wheel and apologized profusely. I was just relieved that no one had been hurt. But the scare stories I was told as a child were still fresh in my mind. The immediate question that came to me was, *Is God punishing us for persecuting the Family? Or is it the devil attacking us for exposing them?* By asking these questions, I began to understand what freedom and true choice really mean.

It was all very well for me to put my past behind me, but I believed it was also important to break the cycle of abuse. Bullies only have power through fear, and by calling them up and speaking out, they would lose their hold. The cult I had been brought up in still existed, with the same teachings and environment that had harmed thousands of families and torn mine apart. It disturbed me to know that emotional and sexual abuse was still happening every day to my friends, my sister and my family left in the group. Evil can only prevail when good people do nothing.

I sincerely believed that it could not just be left to other members of our society, like the parents and ex-members. It had to come from me, and others like me, who had first-hand knowledge as part of the second generation.

Remembering the pain of being parted from Celeste led Mum to make contact with other parents whose children had disappeared. One contact, a Mrs. Willie, invited us to visit her in Switzerland. When we arrived she explained, "My daughter—she's only nineteen—has recently joined the Family."

Mum nodded understandingly. "Her personality has changed drastically?"

Mrs. Willie seemed relieved that we understood. "Yes it has—but even more alarming, she's grown secretive and distant. I'm so worried." She hesitated and looked fraught. "I think she's pregnant. I just don't know what to do."

The only way to find out, I thought, *is to get inside.*

I said this, and Mrs. Willie looked doubtful. "How will you do that? Will it be dangerous?"

I shook my head. "They won't suspect."

Mrs. Willie had friends who lived a couple of streets away from the large commune just outside Berne and took me there. Peering through the hedge of the compound I saw telltale signs of a Family home. An inordinate amount of laundry hung from the lines and endless rows of children's tricycles were parked in the driveway. I made a plan, and walked back to where Mum and Mrs. Willie were waiting.

"I'll get into the home," I told them.

"What? How?"

"I'll make them invite me in," I replied, asking them to show me where the nearest parks to the Home were.

The first park I went to was beautiful, with a brook running through lush grass lined with avenues of trees. Something told me they would be there. To get to the playground, I had to cross the bridge. I waited, looking at my reflection in the water. When I glanced up, I saw around ten young children marching two by two, an adult in front and behind.

They were right on cue.

As they marched past me, I turned around as casually as I could. "Excuse," I said to the woman in front. "*Quelle heure s'il vous plaît?*"

"Five o'clock," she said with a German accent. She appeared to be friendly.

"Oh, English! Good," I replied. "I am actually from England."

They would have continued on their way, but I tried to keep the conversation going and commented on the number of children they had.

"Well, we're a Christian school," they replied. "So what brings you here?"

"Just traveling on my year out." I smiled, looking my "sheepy" best—the Family called potential recruits "sheep."

They invited me to join them at the playground and once we had sat down and after some small talk, they asked, "Have you heard about Jesus and that he died to save you from your sins?"

"Yeah, I've heard about religion and stuff. I don't know. It's all so confusing." I smiled feebly.

"We're Christian missionaries serving the Lord." I knew the patter, of course, by heart. "We'd give you some leaflets but we didn't bring any with us," one of the women said.

They asked me if I would like to be saved and receive Jesus into my heart. So I prayed the salvation prayer—again. *This is how we must have appeared to outsiders*, I thought.

When one of the women with dark hair called out, "Victor! Lily!" I realized that the woman was Serena, Juliana's mother, who I had seen on Family videos! I had finally met my half brother and sister whom I had only seen in baby photographs. It was a shock and I was very curious; but I had to keep my emotions in check. I had a job to do. I pretended to want to learn more about the Family's good works so they would invite me back to their home. Of course, they would not bring a stranger directly back to their "selah"— secret—commune.

After I watched them go, I sat by the lake and cried. I had been tense; but I was also very emotional having met Victor and Lily for the first time in these unusual circumstances, but not being able to say anything.

When I had recovered a little, I ran back to tell Mum I had seen Serena and she might know where Celeste was. Mum was shocked at first and then worried when I told her my new plan, but I convinced her I would be safe.

I wanted to see Victor and Lily again, and possibly find out where Celeste was, so the next day I strode up to their door and knocked. Five minutes later, a little window slid open and a pair of eyes peered out.

"Hello? Who are you?" I was asked.

"Oh, I met Serena and Ruth at the park yesterday and they said they had some pamphlets," I said, my voice full of breezy confidence.

"Oh," the voice said. The flap shut and I stood there waiting.

Eventually, I heard someone fumbling with an array of locks. Serena opened the door to welcome me. Her first question, edged with suspicion, was to ask how I had found the place.

"Oh, I asked someone," I said casually. "Everyone seemed to know where the school was."

She relaxed and smiled and stood back to let me enter. Once inside, it was like I was in a time warp. I could not believe it. I was in!

As the familiar procedure went, the children sang for me. They performed the usual routine, which of course I knew by heart. It took a considerable effort not to join in with the songs.

When the show was over, I gave a hearty clap and made a beeline for Lily and Victor. I chatted with them and ended up bouncing them on my knee. They invited me to stay for dinner and while I ate and listened, I looked casually around—and spotted a young woman who was like the photographs Mrs. Willie had shown me of her daughter. Her pregnancy was obvious. I also looked at the map on the wall because Serena had said her husband was away on "the mission field."

"Mission field?" I asked, hoping she would offer more information.

"Oh yes, Asia," she answered cagily and changed the subject.

Once the door of the commune closed behind me, I ran back to the house where Mum and Mrs. Willie were waiting expectantly. I told Mrs. Willie that I had seen her daughter who was indeed pregnant. Perhaps it wasn't the outcome she had hoped for—but at least, she knew where her daughter was.

Back in England, we got to know Ian Howarth and his wife, Marie Christine, better. Marie Christine had once been in the Children of God. She met David Berg while in the group and told me how his entire room was covered from wall to wall with photographs of naked women and children. She left in 1978 and became an open critic of the cult along with her husband. Though I was only fourteen, I, too, began speaking out against the Family and its practices. I was one of the first of their children to speak out and I gave a number of statements to the police.

Mum was scared that if she aggravated the Family they would never let her see Celeste again, so she made fewer public appearances. After fifteen years in the cult she was also trying to adjust to normal life, and with six young children to look after it was not easy. And it was not easy for me either. Mum realized that I needed some privacy as a teenage girl so I was given the box room—the first room I had ever had all to myself. I joined the school drama club and spent many hours at the local library—anything to take my mind off of the sometimes overwhelming pain I experienced. I was beginning to understand the full extent of my past and the consequences it was having on my present. We were told black was white and white was black and I had a lot of unlearning to do.

I started dating a guy called Bryan. He was three years older than me, confident and bubbly. I was immediately attracted to him. He had beautiful green eyes and I was delighted every time he asked me out. Mum thought I was too young to have a boyfriend, but I wouldn't listen. Bryan tried hard to prove his love. He was very attentive and would cycle seven miles after work to see me. When he took me out, we would have fun together. Being with him distracted me from all that I was dealing with. We fell in love.

Around this time, Dad—my real dad—wrote Mum a letter accusing her of "vilifying and degrading the good work of others, the Children of God, and causing a lot of people to get stirred up over nothing."

Mum was upset and indignant—and perhaps a little sad.

I was outraged at Dad's letter and felt compelled to speak out again and defend my mum, who was being slandered. Even though the letter hurt deeply, I now knew the techniques of mind control the cult used on its members. We had lived in the same environment that surrounded Dad and it was hard for us to blame him for his reaction.

A few weeks later we went to meet Gillian Duckworth, who lived in one of the most exclusive parts of London. Her daughter had recently joined the Family. She was pregnant, and Gillian was concerned over the unborn child's future in an abusive cult. She hoped we could show her daughter the truth and help her to change her mind about the Family. Gillian was very welcoming, but nervous. Over lunch with Gillian and her daughter, Mum started to tell her story, but the daughter would not listen. Mum thought I might be less threatening. I explained what my childhood had been like, that parents had no rights over their children, as the shepherds were in total control.

Gillian "s daughter listened, but said nothing.

We had brought some cult literature, including my copies of *Heaven's Girl* and *Heaven's Children*. I explained how both Berg's daughters and his granddaughter Mene had accused him of having sexual relations with them, and I showed her a drawing of Berg naked in bed with Maria and Techi. I outlined his perverted and incestuous behaviour, which included writing about his fantasy of having sex with his mother. After about two hours, Gillian "s daughter left agitated and angry. Her mother then told us she was going to file for custody of her unborn grandchild, and asked if we would help her by providing evidence. We agreed at once.

Gillian petitioned the court that children in the cult were beaten, denied food, humiliated, forced to stay silent and bullied by adults and peers. I became a key witness in this case, which became one of the longest custody trials in British legal history.

While the court case was in its early stages, the Branch Davidian compound in Waco, Texas, went up in flames after a bungled FBI raid, and eighty-six people died, including their leader and prophet, David Koresh. The publicity worried the Family, and they decided to file a defense with the court. But their leaders refused to give evidence in person and face cross-examination.

One morning, I threw up on the way to school. I knew at once I was pregnant, but I pushed it to the back of my mind. By now Bryan and I had split up and I used to hang around with one of my best friends, Jason. I asked him to phone Mum, as I could not face hearing the disappointment in her voice. He told her the news, and she promised she would not be angry and asked him to bring me home. The pregnancy tests were all positive. I went for my first check up and the doctor said I had about two weeks to decide if I wanted an abortion. I knew Christians considered this was murder. But what did I think? I was not used to making choices and this was one of the hardest decisions of my life.

One morning I would wake up and think, *Maybe I should have an abortion, to have a career.* An hour later, I would think, *I want this child.* One night, I dreamed of a little boy and, when I woke up, the indecision was over. I had connected with my baby and it was no longer just a fetus. I told Mum, "I'm going to have him."

I called Bryan and told him I had something important to say. We arranged to meet in the park.

"I'm pregnant," I announced.

Once the news sunk in, Bryan seemed pleased.

"I'll be the best father in the world," he promised, smiling from ear to ear. He begged me to take him back. I was impressed. *Only someone who loved me would be so happy at the news,* I thought.

Before that, I had not told him much about my past. When I did tell him what had happened to me, he cried, but he said, "I never want to talk about this again." It was too painful for him knowing this about me. I understood that, but nevertheless his reaction worried me.

Despite his promises, Bryan made no attempt to find us a house, and I was still living at home. I heard rumours he was going out with other girls, but I decided to give him another chance. I wanted my child to have a father.

Out of the blue, Debbie, one of the teens I knew from India, phoned. Her family had very recently left the cult and we chatted for hours. We had so much in common with each other and spoke the same "language." I felt less alone. I was not surprised to discover that the cult was still treating children cruelly. Debbie's younger brother, Eman, told me about his experiences in one of the teen training camps in the UK. I was filled with horror at the extreme methods being used at these new camps.

Some eighty teens had been told to write down the names of the four people they thought were the least spiritual and most worldly. One morning they were ushered into the meeting hall where the chairs had been arranged in a large circle. Four of the teens were made to sit in four chairs placed strategically in the center of the room. The Home shepherd roared, "We have read the reports from all of you, and four names kept coming up repeatedly." He paused for effect. "They have been condemned, not by us your shepherds"—he scanned the room full of terrified teens and pointed his finger at them—"they have been condemned by *you!*"

He had then read out the reports on the four. Their offences included reading an encyclopedia, wanting to be a scientist, wearing jeans, and styling their hair too much—a sign of worldliness. The boy who had committed the sin of hair styling had his head shaved. They were isolated in the shed for weeks, given hard-labor jobs, and beaten at regular intervals.

A week later Eman spotted one of the boys in the shower, bloodied, black, and blue. He had many such stories to tell. One young boy had seen his brother drown and his grief was interpreted as demon possession; they gagged him for months, only removing the tape from his mouth to let him eat. Eman's mother was not allowed to know the location of her children and was given only limited and restricted communication with them. That contributed to her decision to leave soon afterwards.

These stories only strengthened my determination to somehow right the wrongs done to the children of the Family. Debbie and Eman also joined the fight for justice and gave evidence during the court case. When I walked into the courtroom on the first day and was met by the sea of faces, I almost turned round and walked out. I had not yet gained much confidence in my day-to-day life, but once in the witness box, I had the confidence of absolute certainty. I felt like a soldier fighting for truth and justice.

After three days of intense cross-examination, the defense barrister was becoming more and more agitated because he could find no holes in my testimony. As the last day wore on, I felt his tone became more demeaning and that he belittled the trauma I had experienced. He flippantly suggested that surely I did not think they still adhered to such practices. Emotionally raw and exhausted, being seven months pregnant, I finally broke down and cried in frustration.

"This all started with David Berg! He's the one who decided it all!" I said in indignation. "It's all his prophecy, so how can he suddenly change it all? Is he saying it's all wrong, saying that he made a mistake? Where's all the counseling for the victims he's made? Has he done anything to help stop the suffering that has happened and will keep on happening?"

The judge got some tissues and handed them to the official for me. I looked over at Gillian Duckworth and she gave me a look of encouragement, in contrast to her daughter, who sat staring stony-faced at the floor. I wiped my eyes and continued.

"How can it have changed?" I asked. "It's changed on the outside so that we don't persecute them. It hasn't changed his heart. It hasn't changed his mind. It's just made things more covered up, more secretive, that's all. He hasn't said sorry for any of the things he started in the first place. People are still suffering for what he's done to us. It'll be with me for the rest of my life, I know that. If you do wrong to someone or thousands of people, you should help if you really believe in your heart that you've done wrong and I don't believe he does."

I was the longest witness in that box, being cross-examined for four long days. The judge was kind and assuring, giving me breaks when I became emotional or started to cry. He described me in his judgment as "a very important witness." Later, he ruled:

> Time and time again, I was impressed with the wealth of detail which came pouring out in a way which did not suggest either invention or the recounting of the experiences of others. There were too many occasions when she was given the opportunity to embellish facts to the disadvantage of The Family and refrained from doing so. She gave credit where credit was due. (Lord Justice Ward, 1995)

Two months later we were having a family meal at our grandparents' house one weekend when I started having slight contractions. They began to come every fifteen minutes and I could not get hold of Bryan, so Auntie Caryn drove me to hospital. I was wheeled into the maternity suite. I wanted Mum with me, but she had to stay with the kids. At one in the morning, Bryan turned up. They broke my waters and gave me an epidural, both of which were extremely painful. Exhausted, I fell asleep. I was woken at seven in the morning.

"Miss Jones," the nurse said, "your contractions are very close now. The baby's almost ready."

I just wanted to roll over and go back to sleep. The nurse laughed and said it was it was very unusual for a woman to be sound asleep during labor. I turned and gazed into Bryan's eyes, which were full of joy, and felt like this was the happiest, yet most daunting moment of my life.

At 8.25 a.m., I gave birth to a little boy with curly dark hair. His father and I were both moved to tears as they put him on my stomach. Jordan was born on September 13, 1992. I loved him instantly. He was absolutely adorable—and still is.

I was happy, happier than I thought possible after so many years in a dark and manipulative cult; but always at the back of my mind was the thought—*We have to find Celeste. She has to know the freedom I now enjoy—freedom I will never take for granted.*

CHAPTER SEVENTEEN

On Opposite Sides

Celeste

After Dad's close call with the British Embassy in Japan, we were aware that every British consulate had instructions to look out for me. For Dad, there was no question of going back to England to fight it out in court. He hated England and leaving the mission field was worse than death for him.

"Now that your passport is renewed we don't have to worry, we can lay low until you are of legal age," he said with some relief.

Dad had always talked about going back to India if he was ever given the choice, and now that he was free from World Services, he announced to Julie and me at the dinner table, "I've decided to go back to the mission field of India. You know I've always had a love for India."

"Well, I'm not going to India," I replied. "I don't know anyone there."

"Sweetie, you have to go. You're my daughter."

This sudden assertion of his authority as my parent after so many years of being apart aggravated and annoyed me. "All my friends have gone to Brazil. I'm not going to India!"

Despite my protests, Dad was right; I had no choice but to relent, and we flew Air India to Bombay a few weeks later. But in the back of my mind I wondered how long it would last. I was sure that Dad would be snapped up again for another World Services project and we would be dumped yet again. It seemed too good to be true that after all these years he was being "let go" to just go back to being a normal Family member.

My suspicions proved right, when four months later, Dad broke the news. "Honey, I've been asked to go back to Japan. They need me to help script a new video series for children called *Treasure Attic.*"

"What about Julie and me?" I asked. I knew we couldn't go back to Japan because of what had happened with the British Embassy there. It would be too risky as the authorities were aware of the Heavenly City School as a Family location.

"There's a training center in Bangkok. Joseph and Talitha are there—you remember them from Dan and Tina's Home in the Philippines? They'd be good foster parents for Julie, and Silas and Endureth are the CROs." The term CRO stood for Central Reporting Officers. Silas and Endureth oversaw the South East Asia area, reporting directly to Peter Amsterdam and Maria.

"And don't worry, it will only be for six months."

The assurance that it was not a permanent separation stopped me from kicking up too much of a fuss. I wanted to believe Dad's assurance that he would be back for us as soon as the project was completed. But six months turned into five long years!

For the first year-and-a-half Julie and I renewed our tourist visa every three months by taking a train journey with our legal guardians over the border to Malaysia and then back again two days later. But when the police raided communes in Sydney, Australia in May 1992, and Mrs. Turle filed for custody of her grandchild in England, they considered it too risky for me to cross the border anymore.

Persecution paranoia was at an all-time high. When it was discovered that my mother and sister Kristina were involved in giving evidence for the British custody case, their names appeared on the Worldwide Prayer List to pray against. It deeply disturbed me because Jesus said to love your enemies and to pray for them, not against them, and I could never bring myself to do it.

For so long I had bottled up all my emotions and feelings or simply ignored them. But on the morning of my seventeenth birthday, everything came flooding out and I spent most of the day crying. All of a sudden it hit me; I only had one more year before I was officially of legal age—an adult—and I didn't have a clue what I wanted to do with myself. I felt completely lost. All my life I had been sent from place to place, whenever and wherever the leaders decided. I had always wanted to grow up fast, to be an adult so no one could boss me about or treat me like dirt, but now that it was almost here, the thought that I would have to find my own way scared me. There was no one I could talk to. That thought brought on another burst of tears. I was in a terrible mood the whole day. I just wanted to curl up into a little ball and disappear.

One evening, Ami had announced, "We've received instructions that we need to purge our personal belongings of anything that could identify someone else other than yourself and your immediate family. If the police were to raid the home, we wouldn't want them to find information they could use to hurt the Lord's work."

That evening I sat with a pair of scissors in one hand and my photos in another, cutting up my pictures. Personal letters were put in a large black bin in the middle of the room to be burned later. It was heart wrenching to have to destroy everything that connected me to my past. Everything that was dear to me, and every reminder of who I was, was being stripped away.

We were supposed to be in a state of readiness and alert twenty-four hours a day should the police knock on the door. Everyone took this very seriously. During one of our evening prayer meetings we heard the doorbell ring. Everyone went silent. Who could it be so late? The bell rang again. Christina told everyone to wait while she went to the gate. "Who is it?" Christina asked over the intercom.

A gruff voice spoke in Thai. "It's the police. Open the door."

"Who?" She asked again.

"The police," came the reply.

Frantically, Christina ran back into the room and told us it was the police. Everyone sprung into action. The Mo Letter library was locked and hidden away. Everyone scanned the public areas for anything that would betray us as the Family. We all ran to our rooms, held our breaths and waited.

After an anxious ten minutes, Ami gathered us all back to the living room and told us, "It wasn't really the police at the door. It was John and I." John was a Thai national. "I wanted to see how prepared you all were and how you would react."

No one knew whether to laugh or cry. Ami had not expected her test run to provoke such panic and tried to calm us. One brother went pale and clutched his stomach. "What's the matter?" Ami asked him.

"I went to my room and saw that I had forgotten to burn my selah trash in the basket. I didn't know what to do, so I ate the paper," he explained. Selah trash was any kind of paper with writing that could possibly give away information to outsiders.

"How?" someone asked incredulously.

"I swallowed it down with water …"

We all burst out in laughter. His dedication, I thought, went a step further than most of us would have gone.

I was not allowed out into the garden for the next six months during the day in case detectives were staking out the place. Then, three months before my eighteenth birthday, Juliana and I were bundled into a van in the middle of the night and taken to an apartment in the city. While there, the shepherds took me aside and told me that my mother had sent a letter demanding my immediate return.

"Do you want to go back to your mother? It's your choice. But if you decide you want to stay then we'll protect you," Ami said.

I was confused. *Hadn't I been in hiding all these years "for my protection'? And why hadn't I been given this choice sooner? Why now?*

For the last four years I was not allowed to have pictures taken of me apart from the rare photo for Dad, and I was told to burn all photographs of my friends and family. I had had to change my name to Claire and was not allowed to correspond with anyone. None of these security measures seemed necessary to me. Now, just before my eighteenth birthday, and after all I had suffered in an effort to avoid my mother finding me, I was being given a choice!

I felt like a piece of property that was being fought over. I was my own person and could make my own decisions. No, I would not be sent back to my mother now. She was a stranger to me.

"It's not long before my birthday," I replied. "I'll stay."

My only image of the outside world was the one the Family gave me. I had read the *Traumatic Testimonies* series, with their horror stories of rape, wife beating, violence, and drug use in the System. If we left God's wonderful Family of Love we could expect much worse. The first young person who had tried to leave had been beaten and thrown into solitary confinement; he had to escape in the middle of the night with nothing but the shirt on his back. But now, due to the court cases, such harsh tactics were discontinued. The "choice" we young people were given went something like this:

"Sure, you can leave any time you want. We're not forcing you stay. You can walk out the door anytime. But...if you leave, you're a backslider, God will spit you out of his mouth."

I wanted to please the Lord and serve Him. I did not want to be the next one on the Prayer List with everyone praying for me to be killed because I was an enemy of the Family.

After my eighteenth birthday I received a visit from the CROs, Silas and Endureth. For them to come and see me personally meant it was something important.

Silas said, "Your mother and sister, Kristina, have been appearing on television and in newspaper articles and there's a big media storm in England. We might need you to go there to meet your mother and defuse the situation."

I wasn't sure what "defuse" meant exactly. However, first I needed to go through media training. "Oh," I responded nonchalantly. But inwardly my heart began beating faster. Meeting my mother was one thing, but I wasn't so sure I was prepared to face the media. What will I say when I see them? Will I be convincing enough? But everything had been set in motion and I was caught up in it—a small pawn in a very large game.

Whether I met my mother or not depended on how well I did in the media training. Three other young people were chosen to go through this training with me. We had to spend hours in classes and read all the controversial Mo Letters—most of which by this time had been burned. The few copies left were under lock and key. We were told that these letters had to be purged, not because we did not believe in their message any more, but because we had to appear to conform in order to survive. Our wording was carefully scripted. We were not to denounce the message, just the Letters themselves, a strategy devised by Maria.

We were also shown videos of how to speak with the media, and drilled in question and answer sessions. Despite my fear of being kidnapped, I wanted to see my mother, and hoped I would be allowed to go to England. I must have passed the loyalty test. After a month of training, Silas and Endureth prepared a send-off lunch for me and everyone gathered for prayer and prophecies. They received visions of me being a warrior in spirit, like Joan of Arc, fighting for the faith. These prophecies were given to me as a parting gift.

But in my heart the inner conviction that I was doing the right thing was lacking. I felt like an impostor, playing a role that wasn't really mine. I hoped that somehow, miraculously, when I got to England the conviction would come and I would feel "the anointing of the Spirit" like the prophecies said I had.

I have no idea how much they had to pay as I had over-stayed my visa for over a year, but Silas and Endureth and my legal guardians dealt with it. I was driven to the airport and rushed on to the aeroplane at the last minute. I arrived in London accompanied by Galileo and Dawn, the CROs for Europe. The first thing that struck me about England was that there were no walls around the houses. In Thailand and the Philippines, most of the well-to-do houses were enclosed by high walls and gates.

We took a taxi to a three-storey mid-terrace house on Finchley Road, a well-to-do part of North London. A tall, well-built American named Matthew opened the door. He had a neatly trimmed beard and moustache and a strong presence; it was his job to coordinate the Family's defense in the custody case of Mrs. Duckworth's grandchild. Matthew told me a meeting with my mother had been arranged on "neutral" territory—the house of Professor Eileen Barker. She was Professor Emeritus of Sociology at the London School of Economics, with a special interest in the study of religion and author of many books about cults, including one on the Moonies. She was acting as mediator between us and my mother due to her position as head of INFORM—a non-governmental organization set up in 1988, which supplies information about alternative religions—or cults. Her credentials were impressive and I was curious about her when, a few days before the all-important meeting with Mum, I went to her house accompanied by Matthew.

Professor Barker greeted me at the door and invited me in. Her house was full of bookshelves and books lying everywhere. She seemed friendly, though I was extremely nervous. She invited us into the living room. I don't remember doing much talking, as Matthew mainly carried the conversation. Professor Barker played the video of myself dancing when I was six years old in Greece.

"How do you feel about this?" Professor Barker asked me.

I was really uncomfortable seeing my dance, though it was by far the tamest one I had been asked to perform. But I kept to the scripted line. "I don't really remember it. It wasn't such a big deal."

Professor Barker nodded, but didn't confront me on any issues. Perhaps she was afraid that she would scare me away or anger Matthew. Throughout, I was surprised that no one ever asked—not Professor Barker, nor any journalist I spoke with—whether I had performed more explicit dances. I had, of course, and these were much more damaging.

Matthew told me the meeting with my mother was scheduled for the following Sunday for two hours. The hype that surrounded this "reunion" was incredible. The night before, Matthew drove me to a phone box. My father wanted to talk to me. He was still in Japan, at the Heavenly City School, and I had not spoken to him since the day he had left three years ago.

My joy at finally being able to talk to Dad quickly turned into agitation. The call lasted over an hour, as he went on and on about my mother, telling me every horrible thing he could about her. I had been given to read much of the same already in a dossier written to discredit her—a tactic learned from Scientology to damage the reputation of outspoken critics. The dossier dredged up every negative little snippet of supposed information from people who had lived with her in India. They pulled no punches. Apparently, she was dirty, slovenly, lazy, and actually enjoyed Flirty Fishing. She had even pulled out a knife one night in a violent argument with Joshua. (I found out later he had been the one to wield the knife.)

I could not accept my father's below-the-belt tactics, even if she was an "enemy." I was relieved when the call was over. The conflict of divided loyalties made me ill. I could not sleep well and a knot in my throat stopped me swallowing properly. I had always been thin, but now I weighed only 48 kilos.

The next day we drove back to Professor Barker's house. Matthew immediately freaked out when he saw it was not just my mother who had turned up, but Kristina, David, my grandparents, Auntie Caryn—and a pastor friend. "Your mother has brought a deprogramer with her!" Matthew fumed as he stormed out of the house. "The meeting cannot go ahead unless he leaves," he demanded. This made me even more apprehensive. After the pastor left graciously, Matthew made everyone wait in the garden while my mother was invited in for lunch.

When Mum entered the room the first thing I noticed were her clothes. She wore an ankle-length bright, flowery patterned skirt and a bright-green suit jacket with a button-up blouse underneath. I disliked anything hippieish, and the colorful skirt screamed "flower child" all over. She had gained weight from the description I had been given by Dad and that one photograph I had seen years ago. Having seven difficult pregnancies had taken its toll. The childhood image of my mother that I carried in my head starkly contrasted with the woman that stood in front of me.

I had no idea what to say to her, except for, "Hi, Mum." That word was so strange to say to someone I didn't know.

Mum looked nervous herself, but she greeted me with a kiss on the cheek. "You've grown," she smiled. Professor Barker invited us into the living room. Mum asked me, "What shoe size are you?"

I stuttered, "I'm not sure, really." I had no idea.

Then she commented, "You look so thin." She looked me over, a little concerned.

I wasn't sure how to reply to that either. The small talk seemed forced, with awkward gaps of silence. Professor Barker invited us to sit down at the table in the kitchen that had a spread of tuna and cucumber sandwiches, coleslaw, and cold meats. I felt like I was in a daze the entire time and had no idea how to react to a mother overcome with emotion at finally seeing the young daughter she had been apart from for almost fifteen years.

"I want you to know that I never wanted to leave you," Mum said, and then burst into tears. I was unsure how to respond. I should have gone to hug her, but instead I sat awkwardly.

Professor Barker asked, "Are you okay, Rebecca? It seems to me you're struggling. Perhaps you might want to go for counseling."

I looked at Mum as she dried her eyes with a napkin from the table and tried to regain her composure. The focus seemed to be on Mum, that somehow she was in the wrong. I did think that was a bit harsh. Even though I remained poised on the outside—as I had learned so well to do—it was me who needed the help; help to form a connection with my mother who was a stranger to me.

After lunch, Mum said, "Kristina and David are here, and your grandparents, outside in the garden. They would love to see you."

Professor Barker interjected, "You don't have to, Celeste. It's up to you."

"It's okay," I replied, "I'm fine to meet them." I was curious especially to see Kristina and David. Mum and I walked out together to the back garden. Everyone greeted me with hugs and kisses and questions.

"Celeste!" Kristina smiled and hugged me. I noticed she had a little boy on her hip. "This is my son, Jordan. You're an aunt."

"He's so cute with his curls," I replied.

"Where were you? We missed you!" Auntie Caryn hugged me.

"Did you get the presents we sent you?" Granny asked as she clasped my hand.

Their attention was overwhelming and I wasn't so sure Granny had ever sent me presents, because she never had the address of where I was. I was suspicious of their motives after all the brainwashing I had received over the years against them. Did they really love me, just for me, and without any hidden motives?

Matthew had warned me that they might try to kidnap me, but despite what I had been told, my true, flesh and blood family that stood before me did not seem the type of people who would have thugs around the corner ready to jump on me. I wanted to get to know them better and I agreed to meet them again.

CHAPTER EIGHTEEN

Bittersweet Reunion

Kristina

As we parked outside Eileen Barker's home, another car pulled up across the road and Celeste stepped out with her chaperone, Matthew. We watched her walk into the house, looking drawn and very thin.

A few minutes after she disappeared inside, we piled out of the car. Mum, David, and I were excited and nervous to finally see her after all these years. I knocked on the door. It opened sharply.

Professor Barker was surprised to see that Mum was not alone and that she had brought a pastor for moral support. Matthew, the Family spokesman, who had been waiting indoors with Professor Barker, freaked out—ranting and raving and accusing the pastor of intending to kidnap Celeste. To calm the situation our friend left. My baby had started to cry and for a moment things were tense and confusing. Professor Barker told us that only Mum could stay in the house. We were welcome to wait in the garden. Having no choice, we walked outside and waited impatiently, wondering how Celeste and our mother were getting on together after all this time. Mum had been so nervous that morning she could barely speak. Perhaps I had built it all up in my mind after so long, but it wasn't as I'd imagined it would be like. I thought we would get together as a family— and talk and cry and catch up. Experience should have warned me that cult members were so conditioned to be suspicious of outsiders that it was hard to break through their defenses.

We waited for over an hour while they had their lunch. When Professor Barker finally came outside and said we could meet Celeste, she told us, "Don't talk to her about the Family. Keep it light."

"I haven't seen my sister for fourteen years and I will talk to her about anything I like," I said, nettled.

Celeste came out with Mum and she smiled weakly, as one by one we gave her a hug and a kiss. She started to relax a bit. I had a few moments alone with her at one end of the garden. As much as we both wished to stay off the subject, it was inevitable.

"I'm not lying," I assured her. "Everything I've spoken out about is true."

She nodded. "Joshua has been excommunicated, you know."

"It wasn't just him—" I started to say, realizing that she had been given the impression that it was only Joshua who was responsible for everything that had happened to our mother and me—and not the policy of the cult. "You must remember what Berg did to Mene."

Celeste became uncomfortable. "Mene? She's crazy!"

"But she was your friend!" I was saddened by the fact she could dismiss her friend's agony so flippantly. "Why do you think she's turned out that way?" I said.

We both stared at the ground. There was so much to say and not enough time in which to say it. I sighed; it seemed insurmountable. We had Celeste at last—but she was like a ghost. Instead, I looked down at baby Jordan resting on my hip and smiled. He was real.

Taking my lead, Celeste relaxed. "I haven't congratulated you, Nina," she said, using my old, familiar name. "He's lovely—really cute."

When Matthew and Professor Barker said our time was up, I quickly told my sister I loved her and had always missed her. There was so much more to say but I wanted her to know that much at least. As we all said goodbye, we were desperate to know when we could meet her again.

Soon after this first meeting, Mum phoned Celeste to arrange another meeting, asking if Jonathan could come as well. We took the train down to London and knocked on the door of the Media Home on Finchley Road. A "sweet auntie" opened it with her best "Hi, God Bless You" smile. Eventually Celeste came down, but they refused to leave her alone with us. This time, she seemed much more relaxed and happy to see us. She talked with David and Jonathan and played with baby Jordan. Mum and I just watched, glad to be there with her.

While we waited for lunch, Celeste put on lots of Family PR videos for us, and we gave her the gifts we had brought. My present to her was a bound diary with the names, phone numbers, addresses and birthdays of all her family. Mum had a plan and before leaving home, she had enlisted me as her accomplice. I was to distract Matthew so Mum could have a few moments with Celeste. She wanted to read her a significant Bible verse to give Celeste a new perspective.

Berg always said that you should judge someone by their "fruits" and interpreted fruits to mean the number of souls they'd saved. But Mum wanted to explain that the correct interpretation of "By their fruits you shall know them" was very different. Jesus meant the fruits of the spirit: love, joy, peace, longsuffering, and temperance. On the other hand, the works of the flesh were adultery, drunkenness, wrath, and hatred (Galatians 5:19–23).

She wanted to say more; but hard as it was to leave her there, the Home made it clear our time was up.

"I'll write or telephone— " Celeste said hurriedly as we left. As we half expected, she didn't do either.

I desperately wanted to see my sister again and the next time I was visiting my friends in London, Eman and I plotted over a game of chess to visit Finchley Road together. The next day, we turned up uninvited to the Media Home. Eman knocked on the door as I stood nervously behind him. The curtains twitched and eventually the door was unlocked. Begrudgingly, we were let in. As we sat down in the front room, we noticed that a baby monitor on the coffee table was turned on. It was not the half that parents use to listen—it was the half that listened in on the baby. We were not surprised they would try and eavesdrop on our conversation with Celeste.

After a long wait, in what felt like the Lion's Den, a rattled-looking Celeste came downstairs. I gave her a hug and kiss and introduced her to Eman. People were hovering around us and I was surprised to see Solomon, my old boyfriend from India. We asked Celeste if she and Solomon would like to walk with us to the local garage three doors down to buy some treats.

They did everything to avoid leaving us alone with Celeste. Finally, Solomon was allowed to go with Eman, while I stayed with Celeste. We ended up having dinner there, but it was stiff and difficult. Before we left, Matthew, the Family spokesperson, made an extraordinary request. He asked me to write an affidavit, basically saying everything was "hunky dory" in our meetings with Celeste—that we hadn't been refused or restricted access.

I stared at him and my mouth must have fallen open with surprise. Quickly, I said, "I'll contact Gillian Duckworth's solicitor."

In the end I agreed, and gave my honest opinion in the affidavit. I said that our communication was monitored and Celeste was not allowed to go out unsupervised, even for one minute to the local shops. The group might be smiling but not everything was fine. After this, we heard nothing more from Celeste and soon discovered she was no longer at Finchley Road.

I started to appear on talk shows and in newspaper and magazine interviews. I was also interviewed for BBC news. I learned that Celeste had been moved to a mansion in Dunton Bassett and I turned up at the Home's doorstep with the BBC reporter, cameraman and soundman. Matthew stormed out, ranting, "You traitor! We trusted you, welcomed you into our home! Under no circumstances are you coming inside! You'll only tell more lies in an affidavit."

"You asked me to write one," I calmly replied. "And I'm not going to lie!"

This sent him into a hopping frenzy and he could barely string a coherent sentence together. He was right in my face, so the reporter stepped in.

"Woa! Steady there. She just wants to talk to her sister."

Angry as he was, Matthew realized he could not afford to look like a maniac on TV and eventually agreed to fetch Celeste. Tears in my eyes, I sat on the wall shaking and trying to recover myself. We waited, and waited, and waited. When Celeste came out over an hour later, she looked tired and on edge. She gave me a wan smile and we strolled around the grounds with arms linked. The BBC crew put themselves between us and Matthew, who was hopping about like a cricket.

I bared my soul to my sister and explained why I had to speak out. I told her I did not believe she had not been sexually abused. I ended by saying how great it would be if every now and again we could meet up for a movie or a meal. All our numbers were in the diary I had given her.

She nodded. "I'll be in touch," she said. I knew she wouldn't; she wasn't ready. On the way home I felt that the visit had been worth it, that the cult knew we were "watching" them—I hoped it made a difference—but it also haunted me as I turned to leave.

CHAPTER NINETEEN

A "Deceiver Yet True"

Celeste

Matthew arranged for a lawyer to help me draft an affidavit, stating that I wasn't abused. However, I was not on the list to take the stand as a witness in the custody case of Gillian Duckworth's grandchild. The leaders were well aware of what went on at *Music with Meaning*, and it would be too risky to put me on the stand. I was not prepared to lie outright about my past. It was one thing to sign a document drafted for me, but I neither would nor could say on oath in court that I had never been sexually abused.

Matthew took me out to lunch to introduce me to the lawyer. During the meal, the lawyer looked directly at me and asked, "Have you ever been abused sexually?"

I shifted uneasily in my seat and looked down at my plate. "No, I haven't," I replied.

"You know," he said, half-jokingly, "they say that if you look away when you answer a question that it's a sign that you're lying."

I looked at Matthew and then at him, and we all broke

out into a laugh. Mathew said something about me being nervous and shy and we continued our conversation. The lawyer never again questioned me on the matter. I only wish that I had been pushed a little further, because I was nearly ready to break.

What was important about my affidavit is not what I said—that I had a fun, happy childhood, and that I had never been abused—but what I did not say. I never stated specifically that no adult men ever touched me in a sexual way. This hair splitting on the definition of "abuse" was a successful tactic that Family leaders used to convince us that denying abuse was not "lying." I had been brainwashed for so long to accept that even our worst sexual experiences were "loving" compared to the real abuse that System children suffered.

One day I sneaked a peak at Kristina's affidavit when I went into Matthew's room. He had left it on his desk along with an affidavit from Mene, Mo's granddaughter. I felt sick at the things Joshua had done to my sister, and I knew she wasn't lying. I had gone through similar things. But Matthew had told me Joshua had been excommunicated. I wanted to believe the Family had changed. This was the only world I knew, and I was terrified that if I spoke up my friends and Dad would have to turn on me and I would be cut off like my mother and sister had been. Dad had told me on the phone, "I'm so proud of you, honey, for standing up for the faith." Isn't that what I had always wanted? His love and approval? I had it now, but my conscience nagged at me.

I also read parts of Mene's affidavit—it was horrifying what she had endured—but Maria had said in a Letter to the Family that Mene had gone crazy and talked to demons, and that her word should not be believed. After I saw Mene in Macau, she had a complete mental breakdown and was finally sent back to her grandmother, Jane Berg, in the States for treatment. Maria did not tell the Family the full story, however—how her breakdown was due to years of solitary confinement and physical and mental torture. Part of me was angry at how her life had been destroyed, and secretly I hoped her testimony in court would do some good. By denying publicly that any abuse had occurred, I felt like I was betraying my sister and childhood friends who had suffered terribly, and the mental struggle was relentless.

Over the next year and a half, I appeared on a number of television programs, including Sky News and on the BBC, to deny the stories my mother and Kristina were openly talking about. Police raids on communes in Argentina and France had put the Family in the news, and a Home was set up especially for the purpose of interacting with the media and dealing with public enquiries. I was asked to stay and help Gideon and Rachel who were the Media Spokespersons for Europe, and I did their secretarial work. Every time I was requested to appear on television I found it nerve wracking. I dreaded having to give some lame explanation of how I felt about dancing nude when I was six.

My memorized line was, "It was like a hippie commune in Greece by the beach and everyone walked around naked. It was no big deal." Of course, it was rubbish and I hardly gave a convincing performance.

Then Lord Justice Ward, the High Court judge, made a key request. He could not allow Gillian Duckworth's grandson to remain with his mother unless the Family denounced the teachings of Mo that promoted child sex and incest. Everything was done to avoid it, but when it was clear that the boy's fate depended on this, Peter Amsterdam and Maria wrote a very carefully worded letter to the judge.

As spokespersons, we were briefed on this letter and held a press conference where it was read to journalists. However, Matthew stressed to us, "We're not really denying the teaching of the Law of Love, but this is just another case of Deceivers Yet True." The Family could not afford to lose the custody case, but they also could not afford to allow their members to think that the prophet might be wrong. I am sure there would have been no repudiation if it had not been for this pressure from the judge. For the first time I saw that our leaders were not just accountable to God alone.

Then one day, I snapped. My body and mind had been destroyed. I couldn't lie anymore. I felt so low that I even contemplated suicide. I had struggled with severe depression for the past five years, sometimes not speaking for days at a time, but now I reached breaking point. But it was too much to face the truth, and instead I decided to run away from it all.

I went to Matthew's partner, Joan, who was second generation and only a few years older than me. I could talk to her and I knew she would understand. I burst out, "I've got to get away from this place, or I'll explode. I've got to go *now*—today!"

She heard how desperate I was and arranged for me to go to a commune in Liverpool uninvolved with the media and court case.

Then in late November, the shocking news came that Moses David, our prophet and leader, was dead.

Maria told us in a series of letters that he had passed over to Heaven. But we were not to feel abandoned because he would be leading us from the Spirit World through the voice of prophecy. I did not feel sad; rather, I hoped that the Family, finally free from his fantasies and whims, would change for the better. I was sure that the now Queen Maria—as she had been crowned by Jesus in prophecy—would be different and more reasonable.

The drama of the court case had overshadowed the fact that 1993 had come and gone and Jesus had not yet returned. All the prophecies we had been indoctrinated with had been left unfulfilled. Queen Maria said that God had given the Family more time to win the world for Jesus, before the End-time. Many speculated that Jesus would return in the clouds to rescue us in the year 2000.

In the middle of all my confusion and agonizing over what I really believed and what I wanted to do with my life, I received word from Dad. He was coming to England for two months to sort out his passport situation. I desperately wanted to see him after five long years.

In London I arrived at a young people's home headed by Ricky and Elaine, my former teen shepherds from Japan. Dad and my sister Juliana had arrived from the Heavenly City School the day before. I was so happy to see them again. "Dad, it's been so long, I was wondering if I was going to see you again," I said as I gave him a hug.

"I'm sorry, honey," he apologized and gave me a kiss on the forehead. "I had to overstay my visa, so I was hiding out at the school. It was a risk for me to leave and I was needed to work on projects." Dad was now blacklisted, and had to change his name and passport to have any chance of returning to Japan.

"Look at you," I said, as I touched his hair. "You've gone gray since I last saw you."

"I know," he chuckled. "It's part of getting old—but I still feel young at heart."

"And Julie, look how tall you are! You're taller than me now." Julie was at least 5 ft 9 in and her hair had grown longer since I had last seen her.

I was excited to hear about the projects that Dad was working on. He had been scripting for the children's video shows *Family Fun* and *Treasure Attic*. My eyes lit up. "That is just the sort of thing that I'd love to do," I told him. "I'd love to go back with you to Japan."

Dad liked the idea, but did not have the authority to grant me permission. I had to write to the leaders directly and I would have to raise the money for the plane ticket. He told me he would put in a good word for me when he got back. That gave me hope.

Before leaving, Dad decided he wanted to meet Mum and Kristina before he left.

"Are you sure?" I said. "I hope you're not going to argue with her. Her version of events on your separation is very different. I think all she wants really is understanding and an apology."

But he refused to apologize. "I have no reason to. She decided to go with Joshua and I waited two years. I did nothing wrong," he insisted.

I cringed at having to accompany him knowing it would not be pretty. My fears were not unfounded. As we sat in a

McDonald's in London, Dad was confrontational and condescending. "How could you persecute the Family?"

Mum defended herself.

"Celeste has been abused; I was concerned for her safety," Mum said.

"Abused? Ridiculous," Dad retorted. "She's a virgin."

I wondered why neither of them asked me that question directly as they battled it out.

"No she's not. She's been made to have sex with men; it was the belief of David Berg. He molested his own granddaughter, Mene."

"That's ridiculous."

The discussion made me uncomfortable and I excused myself to go to the bathroom, and came back twenty minutes later to find them still arguing. I saw that Mum was clearly unhappy but had to leave and get back home. She handed Dad a letter detailing her thoughts and feelings.

Mum gave me a hug and handed me a bag with a couple of books about cults and the Children of God. "I've highlighted some parts that I thought were good. Please read them if you get the chance." I nodded. Of course, I didn't read them—I was too afraid that I would be poisoned by the Devil's doubts.

As Mum walked away, I pulled Dad aside. "I can't believe you actually think I'm a virgin," I said.

"Well, aren't you?" he asked.

"Well, no actually, I'm not. You should have asked me before saying it. Things did happen."

"Really?" Dad stuttered. "I…I didn't know."

Dad did not pursue the subject further and I did not offer any more information. In fact, I realized that the only time we had talked about sex was once in India on my fifteenth birthday. He told me he thought fifteen was a bit young to have children. There were quite a few fifteen- and sixteen-year-olds in the Family who were falling pregnant, and Dad didn't want that to happen to me. I agreed.

Later that evening Dad called his parents, Glen and Penny. It had been fifteen years since they had seen him, when they visited us in Loveville, Greece. Glen invited us to stay over the Christmas holiday week, and Juliana and I met our extended family and relatives for the first time. My sister Kristina lived not too far away, and Dad and I went over to spend an evening with her and my brother David at her small, but cosy house. Her son Jordan was now three years old. "His curls are gone," I said, remembering his adorable ringlets from before. Kristina cooked us lasagne, and that night was the first time I truly enjoyed talking with my sister, reading her poems, looking at family pictures, and getting to know her. When we left, I told her I would stay in touch.

A week later, I had to say goodbye to Dad and Juliana when they left for Japan. As I waited for clearance to join them there, I decided to start raising money for my fare. I was tired of busking or going shop-to-shop being a Family salesperson, so I did something daring. I persuaded Ricky and Elaine to let me join a temping agency, Office Angels. Before, under Mo's rule, this would have been unheard of. But now the group was more flexible. They agreed I could give it a try. The next day I was called to fill a PA position at JVC headquarters.

Up to this point, I had not really known what it was like to interact normally with people outside the group. Instead of mean, backstabbing, evil people like the *Traumatic Testimonies* had said all Systemites were, I discovered that I enjoyed my conversations with my co-workers, who were considerate, decent, and hardworking.

This was my first taste of freedom, of earning my own money and *truly* being appreciated for my work. I realized that I had skills that could support me, and my confidence grew.

Something else happened too. For the previous six years, I had remained celibate. I was lucky that I had been able to avoid any unwanted dates for so long. But a few days before my flight to Tokyo, I ended up talking late into the night with Elaine's son, Richard. We had first met in Japan when I was thirteen. We got on well, and I found him cute and engaging. He also happened to be sleeping on his own in the living room that night. One thing led to another and we ended up having passionate sex until five in the morning. As the dawn broke, we were starving and snuck out to the kitchen for a snack.

This was the sex I wanted—mutual attraction and true desire, spontaneous and enjoyable, not a physical chore that had to be scheduled. And when I arrived in Japan in April 1995, I had a new outlook and perspective on life. I tried my hardest to remain true to myself and my feelings and not just follow the dictates of others, but standing up for myself took every ounce of strength in me and I didn't always succeed. Sometimes the pressure would get to me and I would give in.

*　　*　　*

It was the most surreal feeling going back to the Heavenly City School I had left eight years earlier. Everything was the same as I remembered it.

Over the next two years, I threw myself into my work, scripting *Family Fun* shows and planning the filming schedule. However, there were many things that unsettled me. I met again men who triggered painful memories from my childhood: Michael, Patience's husband, Jeremy Spencer, Peruvian Manuel and Paul Peloquin. I was disturbed that they still so brazenly flirted with me. I avoided them as much as I could but there was a part of me that was desperate to confront them about what they had done. I suffered from bouts of depression and often fantasized about killing myself.

I desperately needed someone to talk to and I found an unlikely friend in Francis. He was fifty years old and a single father to his ten-year-old son. He was like a big teddy bear and I felt safe with him. This friendship was important because up until this point I had had a deep-seated mistrust of men, and thought all "older" men were dirty and sleazy with ulterior motives. But with Francis I could be myself completely without the fear of being taken advantage of. During my most difficult times, he was a shoulder to cry on.

This is what I had missed and wanted in a father. For so many years I had missed my dad terribly and longed to be with him, but it was too late to regain what had been lost. Even though we lived together at the School, we barely saw each other. He was busy with his new family, and I had my own life and work.

The only times I would speak with him were at the dinner table. One evening he told me that he had received a letter from Davida, our half-sister in Athens. The letter she wrote was angry and hurting. She felt abandoned by her father. I asked him what had happened.

"Well, honey, she wrote to me a few months ago. She wanted to know why I never sent her birthday cards or letters," Dad explained. "I wrote back saying that I had a new family now."

"You said that?" I was shocked at his insensitivity. "You should have let me help you write the letter to her, Dad," I said. "No wonder she was hurt! You should have apologized to her and understood why she felt that way."

"Well…" He did not have an answer to that.

"You need to write to her again," I said. "She needs to know that you care." Dad assured me he would.

Two years later, I found out that Dad had not kept his word to stay in contact with Davida, and she had become severely depressed and had turned to drugs. I could barely look my father in the eyes. I was angry that he had neglected his children and refused to acknowledge that the children he fathered were his responsibility. All he had were excuses.

"If this is what resulted from the Law of Love, then it was wrong," I told him, but he never took me seriously. Dad could not consider the possibility that anything our prophet said might be wrong.

In reality, I found that I had little in common with him anymore. I was no longer daddy's little girl.

CHAPTER TWENTY

A Tale of Two Fathers

Kristina

My campaign continued. Together with Ian Howarth, who had started Cult Information Center, I was a guest on the *Richard and Judy Show*. As the camera turned on me, my heart pounded so much I feared the mike would pick it up; but once we started talking I felt more relaxed, knowing Ian was beside me.

During the show Richard asked me why it was that the perpetrators of the abuse had not been jailed.

"It's very hard to bring them to court," I answered, "because in the cult, they change their names many times. The cult hides them from the outside world and moves them around within the communes."

"Was it difficult to adjust to life outside the cult?" Judy asked.

"I did not know what was right from wrong. Your whole foundation of life is suddenly taken from you and you don't know what to believe." Once I started talking, my nervousness faded.

Richard ended the show by asking me, "Would you cate-
gorize yourself now as basically adjusted and normal?"

"I'm a survivor," I answered smiling.

After the show Ian commented that I had spoken with
conviction and clarity. This gave me more confidence to confront the Family's spokespeople, Gideon and Rachel Scott,
alone on *GMTV*.

To my surprise, a few days before the show, Dad called
me. He was in England! I was pleased to hear from him and
updated him on my latest news. Then the conversation
turned to the inevitable—why was I persecuting the Family,
his family?

"Didn't you read my letters?" I asked.

He skirted around the subject, so I asked about Celeste
and his other children. I was delighted to hear that Celeste
was also with him. I informed him that I would be in London
to appear on a TV program and suggested we meet at my
hotel for dinner.

I put the phone down, very excited.

The big day that I had been waiting for my whole life
finally arrived. Before I left for London, I dressed carefully
and stared into the mirror. I felt I was a daughter he could be
proud of—and I wanted that so much. I checked into the
hotel and waited anxiously for Dad in the restaurant, but I
got a message to say he was running late, so I ate on my own.
I hoped he wouldn't flunk this—I had waited so long.

Wandering around the lobby I spotted him by the lift. I
recognized him immediately. He apologized for being late
and we hugged somewhat awkwardly. We sat down and I had
so much to say, I cut to the chase. I explained—just as I had

done in my letters to him—about my traumatic childhood. He looked genuinely upset when I described what Joshua and a lot of the men had done to me.

"That's horrible, I am so sorry." He was shaking and said, "I could hit them." This reaction was the one I had hoped for.

"But David Berg started the whole thing, Dad! He wrote it down in black and white in the Mo Letters!"

Dad looked cornered and started to shake his head in denial. What I had learned about cult members was confirmed when I saw how he had suddenly "switched" as soon as I accused David Berg and criticized the Law of Love. His loyalty to the leader was total and illogical. He would not accept his spiritual father was a pervert, insisting that he was motivated by love.

"Love?" I almost spat. "That wasn't love. It was a perversion. You really have no idea, do you, Dad, because you're in total denial, what that type of 'love' did to me—how badly it damaged me." I broke down in tears and went to the Ladies to recover myself.

When I got back, he had bought us both a drink. I stood just out of sight, watching him. His shoulders drooped and his head was forward—he looked so sad and alone. I saw then that he would find it almost impossible to deny what he had spent a lifetime defending.

I sat down and picked up my drink and sipped a little. At some points, his own personality shone through, a funny, engaging man who was good company. But when I mentioned anything negative about the cult he would just shut down and trot out the party line, which was so ingrained in him.

I told him with heartfelt sincerity how much I had missed him, how as a child I had treasured his letters and was proud when I listened to *Music with Meaning*. I still had a copy of the *Child of Love* drama he narrated, which I played to my son at Christmas.

He smiled and looked happy. "It's wonderful being a grandfather! I'd love to meet my grandson," he enthused.

I sensed that he was vulnerable. He had devoted his whole life to the group. Part of me felt sorry for him. The other part was angry and needed answers. It hurt knowing that as an "enemy," he would always be two-faced towards me and I wished that he could be as honest with me as I was trying to be with him.

I noticed that he did not ask too many questions. What I thought or felt did not seem to matter and he made it clear that I would never change his mind.

At one point he said, "Can't we just agree to disagree?"

I nodded. "Okay, if that's what you want."

We showed each other pictures of our families. I asked if he had any pictures of David and me as children. Eagerly, he fished into his pocket—and it made me smile that he kept them on him.

As I looked at pictures of Celeste, I said, "You know, Dad, it was really sad being separated from her for so long. We just weren't allowed to be sisters—and it's hard to undo the past. All those missing years will never be recovered."

"I'm sorry," he said simply.

"And you can have no idea how it hurt me to know that you didn't protest when I was put on a list to be prayed against. Did you actually want me to die or be harmed in some way?"

He could not answer, and just gazed steadfastly at his feet. I wondered what he was thinking, what strange thoughts must be going through his mind—or perhaps he was thinking of nothing. Or he might even have been praying against my words.

We lost track of the time. The hotel bar was closing.

"Oh no, I've missed my tube," he realized.

"You're welcome to stay in my room," I offered. I could not believe it when he agreed. On the way up in the lift, I said, "I'll sleep on the floor, and you can have the bed."

"No, I don't mind sleeping on the floor," he replied. "I was a hippie. I'm used to roughing it."

We laughed. He had twisted my arm. I was so happy to be spending time with Dad my head was spinning. Then he remembered, "I better phone Celeste or she'll be worried."

He was on the phone with her for nearly an hour. He allowed me to speak with her and when he put the phone down he chuckled. "She's a bit worried and maybe a bit jealous that I'm here with you."

He gave me the impression that they were as tight as net curtains and said that she and Juliana wrapped him round their little fingers.

We laughed again and while we brushed our teeth he said, "You're a nice person."

"So you don't think I'm a witch or a demon?" I raised my eyebrows.

"I…never thought you were a witch…I didn't…believe," he mumbled.

"Don't believe if they ever say it again, Dad." I shook my finger at him.

He said he wouldn't, hugged me—and said goodnight.

Dad was up at 5 a.m. the next morning. Room service brought my breakfast of coffee and croissants. He asked if I would pray with him and I said yes. With his eyes shut tight, he started reciting whole portions of the Bible and Mo Letters for the next half an hour. I quietly nibbled a croissant and occasionally chimed in an "Amen." When he had finished, I complimented him on his impressive memory.

"One day in the Endtime all that will be left of the Bible is what is hidden in our hearts," he said.

The car was coming at 7 a.m. to take me to the studio, so we decided to grab a coffee in Covent Garden. I was tired and jittery. As we crossed the Strand, instinctively he took my hand. I smiled. At the age of eighteen I was finally holding my Daddy's hand.

We said our goodbyes as I jumped into the car waiting to take me to the studios. I pondered how cults demand unconditional love for the group and leader, which takes the place of their own family, and it made me incredibly sad. But this meeting gave me hope. Before I went into make-up, an "excited little Nina" told Ian Howarth about the last fourteen hours with Dad.

He knew how much this meant to me. "Does that mean you've changed your mind?" he half teased.

"Don't think so," I said. I was happy to have met my father but I had not changed my mind about the Family. *Bring it on* I thought.

That year I was awarded £5,000 by the Criminal Injuries Compensation Board for the abuse I had suffered in the cult whilst a child in the UK. The money did not matter to me as much as the precedent it set. This award was to be part of the discussion on the show.

The hosts of *GMTV*, Eamonn Holmes and Anthea Turner, opened the show with a picture of me on the front page of the *Daily Mail* and the *Guardian*.

"The front page of the *Daily Mail* yesterday focused on the story of eighteen-year-old Kristina Jones. Kristina is here with us in the studio this morning," Eamonn Holmes introduced. "The leaders of the group, Gideon and Rachel Scott, are on the show with us too."

He turned to me asking, "Will the money in any way go towards easing your pain?"

"I don't think any amount of money will make up for the twelve years that I lost," I answered. I was nervous with Gideon and Rachel sitting so close to me.

When Gideon was asked what he thought about it, he answered, "It's difficult for us to comment on Kristina's allegations, because even though she has been awarded this £5,000, these allegations have never been tested in a court of law."

Eamonn Holmes thought this statement was bizarre, considering it was a court that awarded my compensation. "Surely there must have been some validity for the judge to make the award," he commented.

"I presume someone believes her story," Gideon replied self-righteously. "And I doubt…cannot comment on the story as I don't know the details. But I do know that I have been in our group for twenty-three years, and have never once seen any sexual abuse of any child and this is born out by the evidence around the world of over five hundred of our children who have been intimately and thoroughly examined by court appointed officials. Not one single case of child abuse has ever been found," he answered. "In fact, the evidence is entirely to the contrary—that our children are happy, well adjusted, well brought up and educated."

I shook my head in disgust as I listened to Gideon. I felt anger welling up inside me and my face felt as if it was on fire.

"Kristina—," Eamonn cut him off and turned to me. "They say members are free to leave the group. Does this comfort you?"

"No it does not!" I exclaimed. "When all their lives David Berg has instilled in them fear of leaving, fear of the System, fear of what will happen to you outside their elite group."

"And will you continue your campaign?"

I looked directly at Rachel and Gideon as I answered, "Yes, I will."

I was determined to continue speaking out, but had just broken up with Bryan and I needed to relax and get my head together from the difficult and drawn out break-up. I also needed some peace and quiet, without the emotional stress of everything that was going on around me, and I arranged to go to Australia with my son to visit Nan and Papa for a few months.

At Sydney airport I spotted Nan and Papa straight away. We were all in tears as we hugged. They still called me Nina and I did not mind a bit; it reminded me of the good times in my childhood. Jordan took to Nan immediately. Being with Nan and Papa again made me feel safe and loved.

I was saddened when I saw all the pictures of us hanging on their wall. It struck me how much it must have hurt them that their only son had abandoned them and how lonely it must be with their grandchildren half way across the world. I spent many hours telling them about my brothers and sister in England.

The four of us went on many outings to the zoo and parks and the incredible Blue Mountains—and I remembered the air in a jam jar, one of the few amusing stories that Joshua used to tell us. They took us to meet their welcoming friends and relatives. It was good to know they had a wonderful set of friends and family to keep them company. They took an active part in their church community and Nan sang in the choir. While I was there, they asked me if it was okay for their son and his Greek wife to come over. They had been in Sydney for a few months; he was driving a cab to raise funds so that he could go back to the "mission field." I assumed he had been forgiven his "excommunication"—and I wondered if it had ever happened at all.

Joshua greeted me as if nothing had ever happened. He ruffled my hair. "You've grown," he said.

I flinched. Suddenly I felt like I was a little girl again. We all had tea and made polite awkward conversation. Over lunch Joshua complimented me on my toddler and at one point admitted to everyone that he had been very strict with us as children. It was hard for me to hear and say nothing and I felt uncomfortable when he was around my son.

After lunch, while Nan and Joshua's wife were in the kitchen doing the dishes, Joshua came out and sat with me on the porch. We got into a heated debate about Mum. He criticized her for backsliding and running off with his children. I explained that she did what she had to do, and that I thought she was very brave.

"You were wrong and a hypocrite because you were the one who had wanted to split us up," I said.

"I guess I shouldn't have pushed your mum into leaving your dad. I am sorry for that," was all he owned up to.

Our conversation led into a discussion about the "Law of Love" and "One Wife." I told him that those teachings had led to untold abuse and I relayed my childhood memories to him.

"You remember that?" he asked, surprised.

"Of course I do."

He started the usual patter of prepared responses about how the Family was free from the bondage of the System, who wrongly viewed it as abuse. "See, it's not really abuse—," he started to defend himself.

Suddenly there was a roar from inside the house. Papa burst out the back door on to the porch, trying to steady himself with a cane. He had overheard us from his room, where he was in bed resting from a recent hernia operation.

"How could you?" Papa said. "I heard every word!"

He lifted his cane and struck his son on the shoulder with the little strength he had. Nan came running out and Papa told her what he had heard. She looked shocked and I was reminded of that time when she stayed in her bed in India for three days. It must have been very painful for this kindly woman to have suspected what was going on, but not been able to say or do anything.

I jumped up in surprise and concern for Papa. I had never seen him so angry before, much less heard him raise his voice.

He was livid. "Don't you dare criticize her mother! I am warning you! Get out! This is my house and I won't hear a word against her!"

A general uproar followed and Nan and Papa ordered Joshua and his wife to leave the house.

That night I gave them my side of the story in detail for the first time. It was painful for us all and we never brought the subject up again.

That week Joshua sent me money to buy a new pushchair for Jordan. But I had no desire to ever see that man again. He wrote a letter to me wanting to repair the relationship and continue being my dad. He said how it had torn his heart to have lost us that day in London when Mum fled with us. I didn't remind him that he had threatened to take her children from her and send them to the cult to bring up. There was a place in my heart that pitied him, but though I had forgiven him, it was too late. The past could not be undone.

CHAPTER TWENTY-ONE

Rehabilitation

Juliana

Winds of change were blowing through the Family in the early 1990s, beginning with the announcement of Mo's death. The entire Bangkok school gathered in the large meeting hall and the letter detailing our leader's "graduation" to Heaven was read. He had died in his sleep after years of prolonged illness with Family members around him, just like he wanted it. There was hardly a dry eye in the room; everyone around me was weeping in tongues and prayer. I knew I probably should have been joining in more, but I did not feel the least bit sorrowful. Mo was just a name without a face, a phantom whose writings dictated my life in every way, and yet as a man, prophet, or saint, he meant nothing to me. The meeting dragged on for hours with songs, anecdotes about our late prophet, prayers, and pledges of love and dedication. I was bored out of my mind.

The atmosphere was sombre for an entire week. No one was sure what the fate of the Family would be, or whether Maria, Mo's chosen heir, would rise to claim "the mantel of anointing." We heard that a new guiding law book was being written for the Family. There was a feeling of hope, that things would begin to change for the better and that Maria would modernize and improve the Family rules and way of life.

I was nearly thirteen when, during this time of uncertainty, I was given unexpected news. They were sending me to Japan to live with my dad! I had long ago given up hope of seeing Dad again and I could not believe it when I was told. At the same time, I was given a letter from my mum with a photograph of Mariana, Victor, and Lily. The letter was short, and I briefly glanced over it; it was the photo that interested me most. I stared at them—my brother and sisters— for hours. Mariana stood a head taller behind Victor and Lily. They were in a beautiful wood in Switzerland and I was sure their smiles were for me. I must have showed that picture to the entire school. My heart was so full of joy at this sudden turn of events; it was like Christmas!

The Heavenly City School housed all the stars of the modern Family of the 1990s. They were commissioned by Mo and Maria to produce new modern music and videos that the Family around the world could use for witnessing, both to sell and to air on television. In order to appeal to Systemites, and especially the youth, the Family young people dressed up and wore make-up, like they did in the outside world. It was seen as a necessary evil, to win the lost for Christ. *Kiddie Viddie*, *Treasure Attic* and other Family production videos had created a new set of young Family celebrities. It had also brought some outside or worldly influence previously absent. The Heavenly City School was the cool place to go, where the cool people gathered to out-cool each other. It took months for me to begin to fit in.

It was only after arriving at the School that I learned that Dad was not actually living there. He was in a small World Services Home in Tokyo, where he lived with his new Japanese wife, Sunshine, and baby son, Kingdom.

In 1995 Maria crowned herself Queen Maria in a series of letters explaining how Mo's mantel had been passed on to her. This was followed by the crowning of her new consort, King Peter or Peter Amsterdam, Mo and Maria's former business administrator. Mo loyalists found it difficult to accept the reign of a woman with a very different style from their former leader. But many of us young people in the group remained hopeful that with the change of leadership, things would get better for the second generation. It did seem, at the time, that things were loosening dramatically, and there was much more freedom of expression. It was this hope of a different future that kept many of us hanging on. I was happy to be given a certain amount of choice in my day-to-day life under the new regime. I could wear what I liked within reason; I was not watched twenty-four hours a day and marched around in a group. I was given more responsibility and more free time to myself.

Hope can be a powerful instrument in the hands of the one who can both give and withdraw it. The one with that control was Queen Maria.

After about a year, Dad left the World Services Home in Tokyo and moved with Sunshine and Kingdom to the Heavenly City School. Dad told me Sunshine was pregnant again and he was kept busy with his new family and scriptwriting for the video productions. I only saw him occasionally at the dinner table. Although I seemed outwardly cheerful, inside I felt lost and worthless. I no longer knew where I fit in the grand scheme of things. I hated Dad. For leaving my Mum; for abandoning me; but mostly for pretending it was all okay.

The illusion worked for him. But it had never been okay for me.

I had grown up alone, and now that I finally had a parent, I was still alone, friendless, at war with the world and at war with myself. I decided it was time to end the crushing rejection that had dogged my life. So convinced was I that I had been a mistake, I wrote a note giving away my belongings to one of my few friends. Then I climbed on to Dad's second-storey windowsill and talked myself into jumping. The pavement below stared up at me, and suddenly it seemed a very short way down. The disjointed thought struck me that I might not die after all, and might survive as a paraplegic, or a vegetable. The thought froze me long enough for Dad to walk into the room.

He hardly glanced up as I quickly jumped back inside, wondering what he might think. But he never thought. He never even reacted.

Until I told him, "I want to leave the Family." It was only then that he panicked. I really said it to get his attention, and I did. But not in the way I imagined. When he asked me why I wanted to leave, I told him I was unhappy. His solution was to send me to India—being on the "mission field" would cure me. For Dad, out of sight was out of mind. Perhaps seeing the mess of a teenager that I was disturbed him too greatly and showed up his glaring failures as a parent. I had lost all respect for him as a father.

To the rest of the Family, anyone coming from Japan was worldly and out of the spirit. By this time, I had learned to dress to fit in. I wore cut-off jeans just over my knees, and a vest. The shepherds in India wrote a scathing letter to my dad saying I came off the plane looking like a whore. They brought me some long flowery skirts and said I could only wear feminine clothes in the spirit of a true Bible woman.

No matter where I went, I could never get it right. I had tried so hard to fit in at the Heavenly City School, and had succeeded. Now, I was being condemned for it.

I had only been in India a few days when I came down with serious diarrhea and a dangerously high fever. I slipped in and out of delirium for a week. The only relief my stomach felt was when I hugged a scalding water thermos to it. As a result my stomach was covered in welts. I could not even keep water down. By the time I began to pull out of my sickness, I was a skeleton. The minute I was well enough to sit up and eat, I was given the usual talk. Why was God punishing me? What lessons was I learning? I had to start reading a list of Mo Letters and write reactions to whatever spiritual weaknesses had triggered such a violent physical manifestation.

My months there were a nightmare. I worked scrubbing, cooking and taking care of kids from morning to night, or pounding the streets to sell the tapes and videos. We only had a day off every other week. There were other young people there, but the shepherds did not like me talking to them, as they were afraid I would contaminate their pure spirits.

Often, the shepherds would take me into a private room for correction—for the usual sins: rebellion, worldliness, and lack of hunger for the Word of God. It seemed to me that they just had it in for me. The Home shepherd, an Indian man named Matthew, scared me. He would shout at me until he got me to cry, and then he would smile. "Now tell me you love me. Do you love me?"

"No." I looked at him hatefully.

His eyes grew fiery and he grabbed my head with his two hands and held my face an inch from his own. "Tell me you love me, or you can't leave this room."

He played this little power struggle game until he had wrested the words out of me. Then he would kiss me all over my face and hug me for what seemed like hours before finally allowing me to leave. He tasted and smelt like curry. I would lock myself in the bathroom afterwards, hold my head back and scream silently. That gave me some small relief.

After three months of this, I was desperate to leave. Japan seemed like heaven in comparison. Every day I begged to be allowed to go back to my dad. They had failed to retrain me, so they eventually wrote to my father telling him to come take me off their hands; they could do nothing more for his little terror.

Dad came running to get me with fire under his ass. I tried to explain the truth, but he was having none of it. He was still a giant celebrity in India and I had disgraced his good name. He told me in no uncertain terms that he was both ashamed and disappointed in me. On this note we flew home to Japan in time for Christmas. I was looking forward to going home.

At immigration, the officers pored over our papers. They believed Dad had been working illegally in Japan and refused us entry. All the flights out of Tokyo were fully booked for days. So Dad and I were driven to prison in a caged bus.

We passed Christmas behind bars. During the day, the jail was fairly empty, and we sat in the dining hall playing snap with the guards. It was a lark watching them all stiff and serious as they stared at the pile of cards and jumped to attention with a brisk "Snapu!" when two cards matched. Dad and I became very popular with the guards. They were sympathetic, knowing Dad had a Japanese wife and two kids, and that we were missing Christmas with them.

After four days, we were put on a plane to Thailand. My heart sunk when I heard our destination. I was going from the frying pan back into the fire. We went back to the Bangkok Training Center. Once again, Dad left me in the Junior Teen group. He seemed relieved to have me off his hands and hardly ever bothered to check how I was doing. I caught up with my foster sister Vera, and we became close friends once again.

But the shepherds in India had blacklisted me as a potential "rotten apple" and the Central Reporting Officers gave the Training Center an immediate update on my serious state. They decided to continue my retraining where India had left off. I was put on silence restriction and worked like a slave. It was my job to sweep, mop, and buff the entire school, nearly a quarter of a mile long from end to end. This was a monumental job, by the end of which I could hardly stand up straight from bending over for so many hours.

After this, I had to wipe every window and there were hundreds. I had to keep the entire serving area, kitchen and dining room and visitor areas clean at all times. I had to work seven days a week, with no day off and no school or play. This was the only form of discipline they could inflict and they went the whole nine yards. Anything I enjoyed was forbidden. The few times I saw Dad, I would ask when we were leaving. We were only supposed to stay a couple of weeks, but the weeks were dragging into months, and a terrible fear seized me that I might be stuck there forever.

In February, the Family-wide yearly three-day fast was held. Usually it was at this time that the newest "revelations" from Heaven were passed on. This year, we were in for a real treat. The "Loving Jesus Revelation" was revealed. There were hundreds of pages to read and it took the entire three-day fast to get through. It was revealed to us, God's chosen End-time Brides, that Jesus was lonely and craving our love. The Bible made it clear through books like the Song of Solomon, that we, God's last church, were the Bride of Christ. He wanted more of us than just to love him as a father, or even a big brother. He wanted us as His lovers.

The Revelation explained in extremely graphic detail that, in "the spirit," we were all women, regardless of our physical gender. Even men could make love to Jesus in the Spirit.

In the Spirit, in the Spirit,
You can sing our brand-new song
In the Spirit, in the Spirit
You don't need to have a dong!

For in the Spirit, in the Spirit,
You can be anything you want!
In the Spirit, in the Spirit,
You can even have a cunt!

The letters gave many examples of how to Love Jesus. But the ultimate expression was Loving Jesus when having sex with a partner. You were each to pretend your partner was Jesus and to shout out how hot and horny you were for God's Dick and Jesus would indeed be there, possessing the other person in the flesh.

I thought it was the strangest doctrine to date. I wanted to laugh at its absurdity, but of course, I did not dare. This new "revelation" was not mandatory, but something people could slowly become used to in their own time. I was relieved. As minors, we were only to Love Jesus up to masturbation. However, we were told that Loving Jesus together as a Home would increase our unity as One Wife.

When many of the adults shouted out in prayer sessions how sexy Jesus was and how badly they wanted his seeds, I just kept quiet. It went beyond unorthodox in my eyes; it rather seemed sacrilegious. We had just come out of serious court cases, and I had thought we were finally going to be more normal, doing good works and telling people about Jesus.

But with a strange belief like this, who would ever take you seriously as a religious organization?

To sort out our visa woes, Dad and I flew to the UK. Dad was changing his passport so he could enter Japan again, with a new name and a clean record. Because I was not allowed to change my name, as I was minor, Dad informed me that I would not be able to return to Japan with him. I walked outside the British Embassy while Dad was filling in forms, and sat down on the pavement feeling like a lost orphan. I just stared at the feet walking by me, and thought that I was just one of billions of feet walking this planet. One pair less wouldn't matter. I must have looked desperately sad because three different people stopped to offer a word of cheer. I just wanted to be left alone.

Dad decided to send me to my mum who was living in the south of France. She would help me change my passport so I could try to re-enter Japan. Mum, Victor, Lily and Mariana, my family I did not know, met me off the plane. When I walked out of the terminal, I knew who Mum was immediately, even though I had not seen her in ten years. She was smiling from ear to ear and she gave me a huge hug. Time had been good to her, and unlike Dad she still looked young, without a single gray hair. "Look at you! You're so beautiful!" She exclaimed proudly. I was nervous, but my brother and sisters put me right at ease. They were living in a gite in the beautiful French countryside. Mum had remarried a French man named Luke and they had a daughter Corina together. But my biggest shock came when I discovered there was a third partner in their marriage. Her name was Crystal. She was madly in love with Luke and Luke was madly in love with Mum and the three of them were living in a tangled triangle.

Crystal had known my parents back in Loveville in Greece. She had run the Detention Teen program in Macau where Mene was tortured. One of the other detained teens there was Ben Farnom, who committed suicide shortly after.

Crystal was now no longer in a leadership position. This made her insecure and she took it upon herself to shepherd our little family, gathering us daily for Word Time and lectures. We begrudged this intrusion into our lives and our family. She was constantly belittling Mum and saying that our dad had been hers first, rubbing it in that if she hadn't been sent away from him in Greece, none of us would be alive today.

I stayed outdoors as much as I could with Lily, Victor and my stepbrothers and sisters. It was the first time that I had been allowed to run relatively free and we would take long hikes up the river that ran behind the house, explore old empty houses, or build pine lodges in the woods. For the first time, I got to know my little brother and sister.

Which was more than I could say for Mum. She had longed for the day when I would come back to her, but it was not playing out as she had imagined. Mum had not realized that by leaving me so young, she had severed the bond that would otherwise have grown between us. It was not that I did not love her; I did, very much. I simply did not display any attachment to her, and the disappointment cut her deeply.

Eventually because of this, she withdrew from me, hardly daring even to hug me, for fear I would pull away. She felt the guilt of leaving me, and imagined I hated her for it. In reality, I was not sure how to react to my mother, who I did not know and could not talk to. I felt the invisible barrier between us, but did not know how to remove it. I was no longer a cuddly child who could nuzzle into her neck. I was an angry and confused teenager who never seemed to belong anywhere—not even in my own family. I did not share any memories with my brothers and sisters, which left me on the outside of many conversations. I was the eternal outsider.

One day, a solution occurred to me. I could simply remove myself completely. I had already balanced on the edge of Dad's windowsill, but this time, I felt ready to jump. One day when everyone was taking a siesta, I took the kitchen knife and locked myself into the bathroom.

I sat on the floor and began sawing with the blade across my wrist. To my irritation the knife was blunt. I sawed frantically at my wrist, but the knife would hardly pierce my skin. Eventually I managed to cut a ribbon of flesh, but I could not get it deep enough to cut the vein. I felt squeamish and scared of the pain.

I gave up, lay down on the bathroom floor and cried till I fell asleep. I was ashamed that I was too cowardly to live and ashamed that I was too cowardly to die. I woke up in a pool of sweat. The heat in the tiny room was suffocating. I snuck upstairs, and bandaged up my wrist. I always wore long sleeves, so no one ever noticed.

Once my passport was changed, I returned to the Heavenly City School in Japan. After a few months, news came from Mum that my stepbrother, Philippe, had died from a brain tumour. He was only fourteen and his passing hit me hard. I was overwhelmed with guilt. I had not got to know him as well as I might have, and now I would never have that chance. He might not have been my blood brother, but he was still part of my family and I should have cared more. But more than anything, I felt angry with myself that I could not cry. Not long after Philippe's death, Windy, a girl I had known in

Japan, committed suicide. These two deaths affected me deeply. I had always grown up thinking the world would end before I got too old. Now I decided if all our lives would end anyway, whether through unexpected death, or when the world ended, then what was the point of anything?

I kept up a correspondence with my foster sister Vera after leaving Thailand and I spilt my guts to her in a letter, telling her just to "live and let live," because all we had to look forward to was death. Much of the pain I was feeling went into that letter. If I had known my correspondence was being censored, I would never have written what I did. A couple weeks later, I received a letter from my former foster parents, Joseph and Talitha. They said they did not want me writing to them or Vera any more. I was a negative influence on Vera, and they made it clear that they no longer considered me a daughter. This letter wounded me deeply. Once I had given up all hope of seeing Dad again, I clung to them as my family. This sudden cold rejection was like a slap in the face.

After this something in my heart shut down. I no longer wanted to let anyone near me to avoid the pain people I cared about inevitably brought me. I became profoundly angry and sometimes erupted in violent outbursts. If people did not seem to like me, I no longer saw any point in making myself likeable. My personal hygiene went out the window. I wore my hair in an unbecoming bob, so I would not have to brush it. I was always looking for fights and one day even hurled my teacher across the dining-room table, which broke in two.

I lost all my friends. No one gave me the time of day unless they were cheering me on in a fight. I was too tall, too rowdy and had a mouth like a machine gun without a safety switch. My sarcastic wit became a defense to hide my lack of self-esteem. It is little wonder I was on the school list of "the last ten people in the world to be caught hanging out with."

I rarely saw Celeste. Even Dad stopped caring whether I came down to dinner or not, which was the only time he might see me. I needed to get away. One day, a notice on the school bulletin board caught my attention. A Family couple in Tokyo needed help with their children. I applied and was accepted for the three-month post.

I was met at Shinjiku station by a young man named Marcus, who lived at my new Home. I was pleased I was not going to be the only young person there. Marcus quickly developed more than a mild interest in me. I was completely uninterested, however. No one had ever liked me in that way, and I did not read the signs of attraction because I had no experience in reading them.

The couple's oldest son, Miguel, came to visit. He had left the Family shortly before and worked at a bar in Tokyo. He was handsome and I was flattered by the way he openly stared at me. It was a new feeling for me, and although I did not understand it, I knew I liked the attention and perhaps unconsciously even encouraged him. Nevertheless, it was a surprise to wake up in the middle of the night and discover him in my bed. He was tugging at my panties, his hot breath reeking of cigarettes.

"No," I whispered quickly.

"No?" He was rubbing himself frantically against me.

"No."

"C'mon, you want me. I know you're hot for me."

I was still half asleep and a part of me was telling myself, *this is all a funny dream.*

"Don't. The kids," I mumbled in protest. His brothers and sisters slept in the same room as me and I hoped this would stop him.

"Then you'd better be quiet."

I was too terrified to do anything but lie there silently, and the dream continued like a nightmare for the next two hours. When he finally pulled away I was raw and in pain.

Early the next morning I slunk out of the house, took my bike and stayed out all day until I was certain he'd left. Sex with an outsider was an excommunicable offence at most and a partial excommunication at least. The thought of being excommunicated, especially for something that had been forced on me, was terrifying. I was only fifteen after all.

I decided to keep the nightmare in my chest of secrets that I locked inside my head. Only, secrets have a way of revealing themselves.

In my case it was sooner rather than later. The next day, in fact. Marcus came home from work and barred my way at the head of the stairs with a beefy arm.

"What's up, Marcus?" I tried to sound casual, but my voice betrayed my concern.

"You little slut!" He spat. "You don't even know him and you jump into bed with him the first night."

"I don't know what you're talking about. We didn't do anything."

"Really? He said you were panting like a little bitch in heat. He said you wore him out, you could not get enough like an insatiable whore." This lie hurt even worse than the actual rape.

"What! He's just telling you that to make you jealous."

There was a terrible heat behind my eyes and the room was spinning around me.

"I'm going to report you, and you know what'll happen then. You're in big shit now."

"Marcus, it wasn't like that. He forced me," I tried to explain.

"Bullshit. I don't believe you." Nor did he want to, because he had his own agenda.

"Look, believe me or not, it's true. Please, I'll do anything; just don't report me. It wasn't my fault."

"Of course it was your fault and you're right about one thing; you will do anything, or I will report you."

He came to my bed that night, and every night after. Sometimes I tried to pretend I was asleep, or on my monthly, or feeling sick. Eventually he stopped buying my excuses. My life there became a misery, so I jumped on a train back to the Heavenly City School.

When I arrived back, one of the teen shepherds approached me.

"What are you doing back here?"

I was shocked by the question. I had always thought the school was my home.

"You didn't ask permission to come back. We don't even have a bed for you."

"I can sleep on the floor."

They quickly found work for me, however, I could hardly manage to take care of myself much less eleven rowdy kids from nine in the morning to seven at night. After a few months I was bordering on a nervous breakdown and asked for a break.

I was sent to work in the Nursery instead. Here, I was frequently on my own with four young babies, which was not easy. Then the two shepherds in charge of the teachers summoned me.

"We've been having trouble with some of the children using bad language," they said.

"Oh?" I could not see where this was going.

"We feel that you are probably the one responsible, so we're going to have to ask that you step down from your ministry in childcare."

I was shocked by their logic. "I work in the Nursery all day. How in the world could I be responsible for children who I don't even see using bad language?" I said.

"We prayed about it, and the Lord showed us that you're to blame."

I thought that was ridiculous. Why did they always use the Lord when they needed an excuse to do something?

"It just seems that there's a lot of lessons you need to be learning and you could best learn them elsewhere where you can't be a negative influence on the kids."

I just kept quiet. If I was honest with myself, I did not mind being taken off childcare. I was tired. What hurt was the way I was being sacked after working very hard with very little help.

"Instead of Childcare, you can report to staff. Maybe a bit of physical labor will do you good."

"A bit of physical labor" meant joining the men renovating the park, hauling blocks of cement from the construction area.

I ran outside into the fields where no one could hear me and wept bitterly. "Why, God," I screamed to the sky, "do you hate me? Why does everyone hate me? What have I done?" I was having it out with the great Creator this time. "Why is life so hard to live? Do you enjoy seeing my pain? Do you enjoy seeing me suffer? Speak to me! Are you even there? Why don't you ever answer! God, I'm your child, speak to me!"

But no answer ever came. Maybe God had turned his back on me too.

All the biggest singers and musicians from around the world were gathering in Japan for an artists' summit at the Heavenly City School. There was a big push to start recording *Loving Jesus Music*—love songs to Jesus. King Peter was visiting the biggest communes around the world to make his and Queen Maria's presence felt, and he was going to attend.

I was working on some art project for the school when King Peter walked by with his entourage. The first thing that struck me was his towering height. He wore his long hair in a ponytail and was trying to dress hip in jeans. I knew they were trying to give the Family a new image of modern, cool and endearing leaders. King Peter showed photographs of Queen Maria. This was the first time most of us had seen what she looked like and I was shocked when I looked at the pictures of Queen Maria posing naked or in a skimpy negligee. Supposedly, this was to show her revolutionary spirit.

All the leadership followed Peter's new look. They made a big push on uniting the generations and the first generation was encouraged to marry into our second generation. All the top pony-tailed leaders took young brides—now that they were of legal age. Following King Peter around like a faithful little puppy was his second-generation secretary, Rebecca. She was Celeste's age; it was no secret that she took care of Peter in every way.

During this visit, Celeste was recruited to work in World Services. I knew she was having difficulties of her own and I could see she was not happy. I knew she had pursued a love affair with a young man who was only using her for sex. I watched him make the rounds with all the women in the school and I knew he was bad news. This young man had already impregnated three separate women, and coldly messed about with my sister's emotions. I could see how deeply Celeste was hurt by him. No doubt, she wanted to escape as much as I did.

Dad was elated at the news. Only the best ended up in World Services and his daughter had made it, his little darling in whom he was well pleased. But I was upset with her for it. She was going down the rabbit hole, and who could say when she might reappear. Some people ended up staying the rest of their lives in World Services. I'd never know where she was, or what she was doing.

"If that's what you want, then go! We're not a family anyway, so it won't make a difference." I did not want to sound mean, but that's how it came out. Once again, I was left behind. This time though, I did not cry. All the tears in me seemed to have dried up.

After Celeste left, Dad had the sudden inspiration that, as his daughter, I should audition for a voice recording and before I knew what was happening, I found a script in my hand and headphones on my head. But at the crucial moment, I lost my voice.

I felt the immense pressure of Dad's expectations and I froze up. The studio informed him that I did not do well. After dinner, he found me outside.

"Honey, what happened?" It was more an accusation than a question.

"What do you mean?"

"I set up this great opportunity for you and you just blew it!"

"I'm sorry, Dad." I whispered. "I just froze up."

"Sweetheart, I'm very disappointed in you. I put my neck on the line and I expected a little more from you. You're not going to have a second chance with this one."

Those words cut me to the heart and I responded angrily. "That's fine, Dad! Be disappointed then. I never can do anything right for you anyway!" I ran away from him. He could never just love me for being his daughter.

CHAPTER TWENTY-TWO

House of the Open Pussy

Celeste

As I pushed my luggage cart out into the airport lobby, I glanced nervously around, looking for a smiling face, any sign of someone waiting for me. Eighteen hours earlier in Tokyo International airport I had been given an envelope with a plane ticket and $300 and told, "Your plane leaves in forty-five minutes so you'd better get going."

The moment I was through passport control I looked down eagerly at the ticket in my hand. My eyes fell on the word "Porto." *Where on earth is that?* I thought as I rushed to the boarding gate. It was only after take off when I heard the pilot mention Portugal that I knew where I was going. I had never been to Portugal and had no idea what to expect, let alone where I would be sleeping that night. My stomach was in a knot the entire flight, a stir of anticipation, excitement, and dread. It was like something out of a spy novel. I was twenty-two years old, and more curious than scared. It was exciting yet terrifying at the same time.

It was early evening when I walked into the small Porto airport lobby. I spotted them at once, a man and woman standing together, both in their late forties.

"Welcome, honey." The woman greeted me and proceeded to give me a large hug. I had no idea who she was but there was a certain look that gave her away as a member of the Family—especially a member my parents' age: the overly beaming smile, straight fringe and long hair and little make-up.

"Did you have a good flight?" she asked.

"Yes."

"My name is Vicky, and this is Terry," she said smiling.

"So, do you know where we are?" Terry asked me. He had silver hair and in his youth would have been a handsome man.

"Well, I wasn't sure where Porto was, but this is Portugal, right?" I asked, just to make doubly sure.

"Yes…we're in Portugal…But do you know what Home this is that you've come to?"

"Well, I'm pretty sure it's Mama Maria's home," I said.

"How did you know?" Terry asked, a little surprised.

"Well, I had a hunch," I replied.

"Isn't it exciting?" Vicky chimed in. "You've come to the Queen's household. You probably won't meet Mama for a few weeks, but Terry and I are the shepherds of the home here and take care of everything."

Queen Maria was affectionately called "Mama." Her location was always kept secret. All my life I had read about Mama, and every part of my life had been ruled by her dictates, and now…finally…I would get to meet her in person. It was considered the highest honor to be chosen to live in her household, the next closest thing to being with

God, as she was His voice and representative on earth since Mo's death. But even in her own house, Maria rarely met those working for her. Terry and Vicky were her eyes and ears; they carried out her instructions and ran day-to-day business. It was their job to make sure everyone complied with the rules and had their personal lives "in order" spiritually.

"We live about a half-hour away in a small village by the beach. When we get in, we'll take you on a tour of the house," Vicky said. Vicky was a bubbly person, a little on the heavy side, rather plain, I thought, but dressed well and she had done a lot of sun tanning by the look of her weathered skin. We drove from the airport to the house in the dark so I could see very little of where the house was located.

I could not wait to see who lived in Queen Maria's house. I felt like I was about to walk through the dividing curtain, and discover who and what was on the other side. *What was it really like at the apex—the heart of the Family?* I was about to find out.

"You'll need to choose a new name for security. Have you thought of any names you would like to be called?" Vicky asked. "If you decide before we get home, then we can introduce you by your new name."

Not again, I thought. I had been Celeste, Rebecca, then Joan, then Joanna, then Claire, than back to Joanna. I was so confused it did not matter to me anymore.

"Well…I sort of like the name Michelle," I replied.

In World Services, even more than in the regular Family, you weren't supposed to know anyone's legal name or last name. Security was paramount.

"Michelle…yes, that's a good name," Vicky replied. "Okay, Michelle…"

"We're here!" Terry announced, as we drove up to a set of large gates. Once inside, Terry grabbed my one suitcase and Vicky led me through the kitchen entrance. The house was a large villa with an extension on the side. I was taken aback by the size of the living room, which looked more like a hotel lobby. At the far end was a set of mismatched couches and a video set up in the corner. To the left was a large wooden dining table that could sit about twenty-five people.

"We move so often," Vicky explained, "we don't usually invest in furniture that we have to leave behind. We got these at a secondhand store."

A magnificent stairway led upstairs. On the second floor a corridor to the left was blocked by a curtain. This led to the inner sanctum—Queen Maria's quarters, which, of course, were off limits. Another spiral staircase led to the third floor, but first I was taken to the extension to the right of the house, which had four additional rooms. At the very end was the visitors" or "date" room. A bowl of fruit was on a table in the corner with a sign saying "welcome" and a double bed with a small table and lamp beside. Terry explained the usual induction procedure for newcomers. I would have three days off to read and get acquainted with the rules of the Queen's Home before starting work. I was tired and it was late, so I fell asleep quickly.

The next morning, I woke up to the strong smell of the sea and the sound of waves lapping on to the shore. Out of the window I saw the property was right on the beach. The sight was breathtaking. And yet a sadness fell over me. I felt a sense of isolation. It finally sunk in that I was far away from my family and friends; they did not even have a clue where I was or how to contact me. And I could no longer contact them.

I spent most of that first day reading the large stack of material that had been left for me. Then, around mid-afternoon there was a knock on the door. A woman in her forties introduced herself as Misty and invited me for a walk. I recognized her immediately as I had briefly met her a few years before in Japan—she looked the same except that her waist-long hair had turned almost completely gray. She was my first boyfriend's mother. She had disappeared one day in Japan, just like I had, and no one had known what had happened to her. As we walked in the garden, Misty explained to me some of their projects. She worked with Maria to produce the publications and letters that were sent out bi-monthly to the Family.

"The Lord is leading the Family in exciting new directions," Misty enthused. "Our dear Lover even recently gave us a special name for the Queen's household in prophecy. He called us the 'House of the Open Pussy!'"

I stopped walking and gulped. I could not believe what I had just heard, but I managed to hide my disgust. Misty went on to explain that Jesus, our Lover, was pouring down his "golden seeds" in such abundance to His insatiable brides who had spread their legs wide to receive it.

My heart sank. I had hoped that things had changed, and that the focus of our group had moved away from its obsession with sex. I had been invited to come and edit a magazine for children called *Heaven's Library* and I was eager to do the job and use my creative talents. However, I was not prepared to participate in sexual escapades or vulgar talk and imagery.

But my worst fears were soon proved right. The "open pussy" analogy was not just a spiritual metaphor, as everyone, married, betrothed, or single was bed-hopping with everyone else. It led, of course, to jealousy among the women especially. I remained determined not to allow anyone to pressure me to have sex with them. Maria had said that Jesus had wanted us to have a "marriage of the generations," but the thought of having sex with many of the same men who had violated me when I was just a little girl was repulsive. As I listened to Misty, I had flashbacks of having to perform oral sex on men as a child. I would not be bullied or guilt-tripped into that again, no matter what. I made that a solemn promise to myself. In fact, I had thrown away every mini-skirt and short top I owned and packed only baggy, conservative clothes.

I was even more nervous when Misty showed me a gold ring on her finger and said that in a few days I would have a "marriage" ceremony and be given a ring to symbolize my union with King Peter and Queen Maria. *Dear God, it better not involve any sex*, I thought, as I remembered Armi and her ceremony with Mo and Maria that was a physical union and not just a metaphor.

"What's going to happen at the ceremony?" I asked gingerly.

"It will be during a fellowship. You'll kneel and say a pledge to the King and Queen. Don't worry, we all did it." Relieved that there would be no sex required, I went through with the ceremony in front of the whole Home on the following Sunday.

The next evening Vicky informed me that the owner of the house and his family were coming for dinner so I should stay in my room and that my meal would be brought to me.

We had to stay out of sight while he visited. He owned a large casino in town and was well known in the area.

There were only three young men in Mama's house; one of them, Vince, had a small room right across the hall from me. We started chatting, and he offered to keep me company. He brought up our dinner and two glasses of wine and we ended up talking for a couple of hours.

Over the next few days, as I got acquainted with my new job, Vince and I spent more time talking. He was an excellent carpenter and carver and showed me a beautiful bedside lamp he had made out of a large seashell he had found on the beach. One evening, after staying up late talking, he finally said goodnight and left my room. A few minutes later, I knocked on his door. Dressed only in a short T-shirt, I said "goodnight" to him and gave him a kiss on the cheek.

A few minutes later, I heard a knock on my door. It was Vince—eager to finish what I had started. I had in my purse a condom I had brought with me from Japan, but it broke. We went ahead anyway without protection. I figured I was due in a few days so I would be safe.

Things escalated from that point on, and Vince kept coming to my room every night. After about two weeks, I started to worry that he was getting too attached, as he was already talking about marriage. I was looking for friendship and solace, not something serious.

Vince must have "confessed" to Terry and Vicky that we were having sex because I was called in for a "chat."

"We've heard that you've been having dates with Vince. He seems to be quite taken with you, and we're wondering how you feel about it?" Vicky asked me.

"Well, yeah…I like him," I replied. I was embarrassed about discussing my personal life with people I barely knew.

"Vince told us you've been having unprotected sex. You realize the consequences, don't you?" Vicky raised her eyebrows for effect.

"Yeah…," I stammered.

"It's not really recommended that you get involved with someone so soon on coming here. You need time to get to know everyone and bond with the team. Vince has been sharing with Jackie, you know. She's been a dedicated member of Mama's team for over twenty years," she explained.

I learned quickly that there was most definitely a pecking order. In fact, Maria made it a policy that after a scheduled date, the younger woman had to write a "thank you" note to the older woman who was the partner of the man. Jackie was a woman in her early fifties and had been a lover of my father some fifteen years earlier when he was in World Services. Dad had talked about Jackie to me over the years and had even shown me a thong that she had given him as a keepsake. Jackie had talked to me only a few days before and told me stories about my father when he lived with them, and she still remembered him fondly.

I cringed when I heard that Vince was having sex with my father's ex-lover at the same time as with me. It was beyond what I could accept.

Vicky interrupted my thoughts. "We don't want her to get jealous, or for this new friendship you two have to interfere with Vince and Jackie. Besides, you should tell Vince that you need to share with the other men, too."

I did not respond, other than give an unintelligible grunt. I had no intention of having sex with anyone else, but I would keep that to myself. I left as quickly as possible. But it started me thinking. I thought I fancied Vince, but now I was not so sure. *Was I prepared to get pregnant, marry him and spend the rest of my life with him in World Services?* The thought scared me more than anything. I had jumped in way too fast and now I wanted out. I knew telling him would break his heart.

The next night Vince came into my room, and though I wanted to say no, that I needed some time and space, I could not do it. *I'll wait and tell him next week*, I thought.

But it was too late. I was already pregnant.

I was throwing up everything and feeling sick as a dog. I could not hide it any longer and had to tell someone. It was one of the hardest things that I've ever had to do. Vince started to wonder what was going on, as I was being very stand-offish, so I had to tell him.

"I'm pregnant, Vince," I said finally, "but I can't do this. I can't continue our relationship. I don't mind being friends, but I can't give you more. It wouldn't be fair to you to lie. I don't see a future for us."

Those words hurt him deeply. I could see it from his expression, from his body language. He had told me how he had been praying for a wife and he wanted to be a father so desperately; he thought my arrival was the answer to his prayers, his Godsend, and now I was telling him that it wasn't going to happen. I felt worse than I had ever felt in my life. I did not want to hurt him. If there was any way I could have made myself love him, return his love, to want his child,

I would. But I could not. I could not even fake it. I knew then and there that I had to leave, to get out from that place. Vince's loyalties lay with World Services and I was not going to raise a child in isolation, apart from my family.

By seven weeks, I could barely crawl to the bathroom. I kept nothing down, not even water, and I was getting severely dehydrated. My weight dropped dangerously to 47 kilos. I could do nothing but toss and turn on my bed. The nights were long, lonely, and agonizing. All I could do was think, reflect and pray that I would have the strength to make it through another torturous day.

I wept, begging Terry and Vicky to let me go back to Japan. I missed my family terribly and I wanted to tell them what was happening to me, but I was told that I could not.

"We just brought you here so it's too soon to go back. When you came here, you knew it would be a commitment. Just hang on, okay?" Vicky told me.

I was not allowed to write to anyone to say that I was pregnant, as they said it would reflect badly on them. I felt totally isolated. There were times I wanted to die; nights when I cried for endless hours wishing this were all a bad dream. At nine weeks I was near death, and had to be taken to hospital and put on a drip for three days. I recovered enough for Terry and Vicky to take me home, but relapsed again and stayed bedridden for six months. I had low blood pressure, severe heartburn and anaemia. The doctor warned there was a high risk of severe blood loss during childbirth.

Finally, on August 9, 1998, Cherie was born. After eighteen hours of labor, I was exhausted but happy it was over. When I held her in my arms, she hummed sweetly. Cherie was my "little miracle." Despite everything, she was a healthy 4.1 kilos with the chubbiest cheeks I'd ever seen. The hospital staff nicknamed her "Gordo," which means "fat" in Portuguese.

I loved everything about being a parent, but my difficult pregnancy had left me traumatized. I didn't know at the time that I had the rare condition hyperemesis gravidarum, and that my mother and Auntie Caryn had suffered the same condition during their pregnancies. I could not bare the thought of ever going through another pregnancy again or being physically intimate with anyone. Vince shared the responsibility of caring for our child, but we were not a couple. At first I didn't want Vince to be part of her life as I feared he would expect too much of me, but I changed my mind when I thought about my childhood and how much I wanted a relationship with both my Mum and Dad. I resolved that no matter what differences we had between us, Cherie deserved to know her father.

I had come to World Services to work, so soon after Cherie's birth I went back to editing *Heaven's Library* stories, while a Brazilian woman named Tina baby-sat her, or Techi, Maria's daughter, who had a three-year-old son. But my resolve to leave World Services had not changed. There were people in World Services who triggered painful memories. Dan, whom I had lived with in the Philippines with his now ex-wife, Tina, worked for *Activated*, the Family's monthly magazine sold to the public. I was a firsthand witness to his cruelty in violently beating my little sister Juliana and his wife and children. Did he realize and was he sorry for the scars that he had left and the damage he had done?

Then there was John, the man who had impregnated Krys when she was only fourteen. His consistent pedophile behaviour over the years was well known and yet he was in a top position of leadership. He made decisions on who should be excommunicated for breaking the Love Charter rules—including sexual offences. What a complete farce!

Another man in the Home was three months into his partial excommunication for having sex with an underage girl. Partial excommunication meant no movies, no sex and no alcohol for six months, and spending long hours reading Mo Letters—missives from the pedophile prophet himself. The irony of it smacked me in the face. Partial excommunication was a meaningless slap on the hand.

More upsetting still, if a parent wanted to report sexual abuse of their child to the police or take the offender to court, the Love Charter stated they would have to "give up" their Family membership. I had seen more than once how "devoted disciples" chose to call their own child a liar, rather than give up their life in the Family.

Eman Artist, though "officially excommunicated," received a "salary" from World Services as he continued to do artwork for children's storybooks published by Aurora Productions, the Family's publishing front.

I told Terry and Vicky I wanted to leave World Services but they kept telling me to "stick it out." The rare times I heard from Queen Maria were when she would send me a prophecy that said I was making progress in the spirit, and great things were in store for me if I just "held on to my crown" and continued to fight the Devil.

We hardly ever saw Queen Maria in person. She communicated with her staff via an intercom system. She stayed in her room and had her meals made according to her specific requirements—no fat, just organic and whole grain foods, as well as an assortment of vitamins and supplements like Royal Jelly and calcium. Except for the occasional meeting, only a few saw her daily, like Misty and Rebecca and her personal assistant, Becky. Rebecca told me how she washed Mama's hair for her and clipped her toenails. Those she handpicked to serve her seemed eager to please and were willing to pay the price for their position of leadership.

We had very little time off and the only recreation we had was the occasional dance night. One particular dance night the living room was set up like a nightclub, with a booth in the middle of the room with peeping holes. The women did strip dances, and people made out in the booth. I quickly excused myself to my room where my three-month-old daughter was sleeping. "I don't want to leave her alone," I said, but the truth was there were too many flashback memories to deal with. I had to constantly struggle and fight against the pressure to conform and I was tired of it.

I was the oddball—the one that didn't fit in—as was Davidito and his girlfriend, Elixcia. Davidito was still called Pete in his mother's Home, and straight away I noticed the sadness in his eyes. He was depressed and restless, living under his mother's shadow. After his short time at the Heavenly City School when he was thirteen, we all discovered a few months later what had happened to him when he "disappeared." In a letter we read Mo's stern "correction" for hanging around the "bad crowd" and getting into worldliness. Mo threatened him with physical violence and he was punished severely. I felt terrible for Davidito, because he was a normal teenager who just wanted to have fun. The next time we heard of him was when he was twenty years old and, accompanied by an adult minder from World Services, he was allowed to visit normal communes once again in Eastern Europe, where he met Elixcia.

He finally had been let out of his cage, but even away from the watchful eye of his mother, he was constantly monitored and the shepherds were instructed to write her reports on his actions. Inevitably, he began talking about his life in Mo's household, and of his resentment of a childhood shut away like a prisoner. His mother had to do some major damage control. He was publicly corrected and made to write a Letter of Confession and Apology for "spreading doubts" and murmuring.

Reluctantly, he returned to his mother's Home at her request, bringing with him Elixcia. One evening Terry and Vicky announced that for an activity, we would have dinner in pairs to "get to know each other better." The girls picked a name out of a hat, and I got Davidito. He set up a small table in his room and lit a candle, and we brought up our plates. We spent the next hour and a half chatting. I had remembered him from Japan as a thin and slightly built teenager with acne, but he was now well toned and had obviously worked hard on building up his physique. He was still timid and quiet, and like me he hated confrontation.

We got on to the subject of leadership, and Davidito told me he had made a deliberate decision not to be a "leader." He despised the way Grandpa and his mother operated, controlling their flock and demanding money, loyalty, and unquestioning obedience.

"If I wanted that, I could have it," he said, "but there is no way I could live with myself."

I agreed that I, too, had been given many opportunities to rise within the ranks, but was not willing to pay the price of my conscience.

"And the whole 'Loving Jesus' thing, it's wrong. I don't agree with all these weird new 'revelations.' The Bible should be enough," he said.

I never accepted "Loving Jesus" either, and found a kindred spirit in him.

It was not long after that Davidito and Elixcia were finally given Queen Maria's permission to leave Portugal, the same month I did in January 2000. Terry and Vicky realized I was not going to change my mind about leaving. As the Home was leaving to a new location, I would no longer be a "security risk" to them.

A few days before my departure, I was invited to have dinner with Queen Maria herself, in her new Motor Home she traveled in with Peter Amsterdam that was parked on our property. Six months earlier we had moved from Porto to the sunny Algarve, in the south of Portugal. Besides the main villa, our extensive property had three other bungalows, a swimming pool, sauna house, basketball court, and further down a two-storey house next to a football field where the Motor Home was. In the two and a half years I had worked for her, I had never been invited to her personal quarters. The only time she had come to see me was a few days after my baby was born—for ten minutes. Now that

I was leaving, I was to receive the special honor of her attention.

I was escorted by Becky, her personal assistant, who knocked on the door to the Motor Home.

"Come in." I heard a voice say.

Maria greeted me and invited me to sit at the table. I nervously sat down on the sofa couch.

"I thought I could share my dinner with you," Maria said. The specially prepared organic food had already been brought in by Becky and Maria heated it up in the microwave in the small kitchen area.

The portions were small. "I hope you don't mind," Maria said, "I can't eat very much at a time, so I just have little meals every few hours."

"No, that's fine," I replied. I wasn't that hungry anyway.

As we sat at the table, I could tell she was making an effort to be personable. But to me it felt awkward and contrived.

"My son Pete and Elixcia are leaving too," she told me. "We got some prophecies for them. I'll ask my secretary to give you some of them, as they were really important messages from the Lord and Grandpa to prepare you for all the new things you'll be faced with after you leave."

I didn't really know what to say. I had so much on my heart, overflowing with questions, but I was riveted by fear and uncertainty. What do you say to the woman who has affected your life so profoundly? I wish I could have asked her why. *Why were we experimented with as children? Why did she allow Mo to abuse his own granddaughter, Mene? And why did she cover up for him? Why the Detention Camps, and why was our father taken from us when we were just children? Did she care? Did she even remember?* Some part of me already knew what she would say if I did confront her on these painful issues and it would only hurt to hear it again: "All things work together for good to them that love God"—that was the verse used to excuse everything. Don't question your leaders, just put up with abuse, violence and intimidation because, well, God has a plan and it's for your good in the end.

"You have a pioneer spirit like your Dad," Maria told me, interrupting my thoughts. "He wasn't good at being behind the scenes. Just be yielded and willing to the Lord's will and everything will fall into place."

That really irked me and I couldn't let it slip by. I summoned up the courage to ask her something that had played on my mind for a long time.

"But how do you know what God's will is? I've always been told to be yielded to the Lord's will, but what does that mean? I've never heard God's voice booming out of the sky telling me, 'This is my will!'"

I figured if anyone should know it would be the prophetess of the Endtime. Maria looked a little baffled at this question, though.

"Well, sweetie." She smiled and paused for a moment. "The Lord usually leads us through his shepherds. Just be yielded to the Lord's will and you'll be fine." She smiled even more.

She didn't answer my question at all, but like a light bulb it became clear as day for me—it was not yieldedness to God she wanted, nor was I "following God" as I had been told all my life; I was following the whims of a leader who played with her devoted followers like pawns on a chessboard. I saw how she had completely detached herself from reality and lived in a protective bubble that shielded her from the consequences of her decisions.

I didn't feel any real concern for myself and my daughter. I felt the leaders were trying to appease me, to keep me on their good side. But it was superficial. As I was driven away in the car to the airport, there was a part of me that grieved as I waved goodbye to Cherie's father Vince, and the few friends I had made, knowing I might never see them again. The other part of me was happy—happy that I was finally being released at last. It was the first step of many to my final freedom.

The Central Reporting Office for Europe was located in the little village of Fluelen in Switzerland. Galileo was there to greet me—he held the same position of leadership as when he had met me at the age of eighteen and accompanied me to the Media Home in Finchley Road with Dawn. The next day he was off on assignment to England. The Office Home was small, just fifteen people, and the jealousy and rivalry in that house with double the ratio of women to men was compounded by the fact that you could hear every noise in that three-storey creaky wooden house. I had many sleepless nights, tossing and turning.

I felt alone—completely alone. The beauty of the rugged mountain peaks that surrounded us, and the tranquil lake of Lucerne, was lost to me. I was cut off from the friends I had just left behind in World Services, and I could not be in contact with my family and friends in normal Family Homes.

I might as well have been stranded on an island in the middle of the ocean, completely cut off from the outside world. This was not how I was going to raise my child. Cherie had such a bright, inquisitive mind and raising her in the Family would crush the unique, independent personality I so loved in her. I had only agreed to go to Switzerland temporarily—though it wasn't really a choice—but after six months I finally caught on that Queen Maria seemed keen to keep me locked away and within her reach.

I was through with being polite and "yielded," and finally, I snapped. Galileo had returned from a trip and I approached him. "I need to leave now," I told him. "I'm not staying here another week."

"Where do you want to go?" he asked me, concerned at the sound of urgency in my voice. I felt comfortable talking with Galileo even though he was a CRO. He was different from many of the men I knew, a gentle spirit and respectful. If he hadn't have been caught up in the cult, or in a position of leadership to enforce cult doctrine, he would have been a decent man.

"I'm not sure what I want to do," I said, "but I'd like to visit my dad, and from there I'll decide. All I know is that I can't stay here another minute without going crazy."

Galileo agreed to let me travel to England and then on to Uganda to visit Dad and my sister Juliana, who I hadn't seen for nearly two years. I was given enough money to buy a three-month round-trip ticket from London to Kampala and headed off to the continent of Africa.

CHAPTER TWENTY-THREE

Anorexia

Juliana

Deep sadness like a shadowy blanket of spiders crept over me. I needed my fix; craved it with the obsession of a hungry addict. Locking the door so my roommate couldn't surprise me, I stripped in a hurry, longing for a glimpse...the mirror was so close; my body tingled with anticipation. I reached for the handle to the bathroom door, swung it open and slowly raised my eyes to the reflection in the glass.

My bones jutted out in every direction, my stomach was so concave, the hip bones so prominent. I stroked them lovingly, allowing my hands to travel slowly upwards to stroke my tiny shrunken breasts and frowned slightly. If only they had not disappeared with my weight. But it hardly mattered; the rest of me was beautiful—a nearly perfect skeleton.

The desire for food had faded long ago, and all that remained was the obsession. I could stand it no longer. I stepped gingerly on to the scales, feeling the bumpy texture under my bare feet. *Mirror, mirror on the wall, who's the thinnest of them all?*

The scales did not disappoint; down another little red line, another little unit of weight, down to 43 kilos. The shadow receded; I could breathe again. I even allowed myself a little smile of pleasure, while my body shivered in its bony frame.

I turned back to the bedroom and tugged on my baggy clothes. The clothes did not matter, only what was underneath. The clothes had never mattered.

I had never mattered.

Nothing mattered anymore.

I was sixteen years old when Dad sent me away again. Only this time he dismissed me to protect himself. That alone hurt more than anything else. Our visas in Japan had to be renewed, and Dad feared if immigration officials investigated they would discover he had changed his name to re-enter the country, after which we would be blacklisted and deported. It could re-open a can of worms. So I was the sacrificial lamb. Dad's quick disposal of me had wounded much deeper than I liked to admit. I felt like a worthless, ugly person; the obvious reason no one had ever wanted me, or loved me.

Dad wanted to send me back to my mum who was now in India. I begged him to send me anywhere in the world but India! I did not ever want to end up there again and my relationship with Mum was not close. I applied to a commune in Ireland, and was accepted.

I arrived at the large house in the suburbs of Limerick. It had a sprawling lawn, tennis and basketball court, and was surrounded on three sides by Irish bog. There were five other young people there, plus three families. The Home shepherds had nine kids. We were under no illusions who the boss was—Uncle Elkannah, who ran the place like a "mom and pop sweat shop."

It quickly became obvious how he could afford the rent for such a large property. We young people raised it through ballooning and face painting in malls across the country. I got to see a lot of Ireland; well, a lot of Irish malls anyway. We traveled to wherever we had bookings and spent twelve-hour days twisting balloons into shapes, animals, cartoon characters—you name it, we made it.

And we raked in the money!—all for a psychopathic Home shepherd. One minute he'd be hugging and kissing me, the next shouting and cussing. He had long stringy hair and a large bulbous nose with purple veins running through it. His face turned two shades redder whenever he erupted into one of his unpredictable furies. His constant fits were turning me into a nervous wreck and my weight started dropping drastically.

Over twenty people lived in that house and the noise was constant. One day, I awoke early on my day off, after a long weekend of ballooning. The racket made sleep impossible, so I got up and made my way to the kitchen for a coffee. Elkannah was in one of his chirpy moods and greeted me with a cheery hug.

"Hello, Julie! And how has your night been?" He gushed in a singsong voice that betrayed far too much enthusiasm. I should have guessed then.

"All right. I'm a bit tired though," I answered. "Couldn't sleep, there was too much noise." What followed was completely unanticipated.

His face changed color as quickly as a chameleon. "You ungrateful little bitch!" He suddenly shouted.

"What?" I was completely bewildered. Was he kidding with me? This had to be another joke. You could never tell with him.

"I feed you, house you, take care of you, and you dare complain that you can't get a little sleep! You murmuring, rotten little terror!" He grabbed me suddenly and started shaking me. I was sure he was going to hit me, so I pulled away.

"Please, you're hurting me." I mumbled.

"I'm hurting you? You don't know what pain is!" I could feel his spittle hitting my face. I had enough. I had done nothing to warrant such treatment.

"According to the charter," I said to him, "you can't touch me!" I spun on my heels and ran from the kitchen to my room and locked the door. Elkannah followed close behind and pounded at the door. "Open the door this minute!" he yelled. "Open up, or I'll kick it down."

My roommate looked at me wide-eyed. "What's happening?" she asked.

"I think he's gone insane," I whispered.

"I have to open it." She looked at me. "If I don't, he'll kick it down. I know him. It'll only be worse for you."

"Okay. Open it then," I said, and slipped into the bathroom, locking the door behind me.

"Where is she?" he shouted.

"She's using the toilet," my friend explained.

"You come out of there this minute!" He hammered on the bathroom door. "Or Charter or not, I'll slap some respect into you! I mean it! Open it now!"

I could hear his wife Tamar beside him. She was gentle, motherly and the only person in the house that he listened to. The racket had alerted her, and she came down to discover the cause.

"Honey, calm yourself down first, and then you can talk to her," I could hear her whispering.

There was absolute silence for a minute. I could feel the beads of sweat running down my neck, but I did nothing to wipe them away. I did not move at all. Then his voice spoke with calm menace.

"I want to see you in my room within the next five minutes, and that's not a request."

The entire house was holding its breath. I slumped down on the toilet and sat there, willing courage into myself while my stomach churned with terror. It was the same fear I had felt as a child when the teacher called me for a spanking.

I squared my shoulders, clenched my fists, and walked straight upstairs to his room. To my relief, I saw that Tamar had insisted on remaining in the room to prevent Elkannah doing anything he would regret. The minute I walked in, he resumed his tirade. He started throwing insults at me. His hair stood on end as if he'd been electrocuted; his face was a livid purple and when he called me demon possessed, I thought that if anyone was possessed it was most definitely him.

After listening to Elkannah bluster for nearly half an hour, Tamar finally managed to discern the cause of his fury. I had mentioned that there was too much noise in his house. Obviously she thought there was some truth in this because, between Elkannah's incoherent ranting, she told me this was ridiculous and I was free to leave.

Not only did I leave their room, I left the house. I could not breathe. I yearned for air and light and freedom. I climbed through the window in my room, and started running through the bog, allowing my legs to carry me wherever they pleased. I lost track of time. When at last I felt well enough to return, I strolled slowly back to the house, climbed in through the window and lay down on my bed.

My roommate found me there soon after and gave a little yelp of delight.

"You know, you've thrown the entire house into a panic. Tamar has been driving around every back road for the past two hours looking for you."

"What? Why?" Up until that point, no one had paid me much attention at all unless I was late for work.

"Well, after Elkannah freaked out, Tamar felt really bad and she came down to see if you were okay. You weren't here, or anywhere else in the house, so we panicked and thought you'd run away."

"Just tell Tamar I'm here, please, so she won't worry."

"She's still out looking for you."

I felt bad then. Tamar was a good person. If I had wanted to run away, just knowing what I would put her through would have prevented me. She returned five minutes later, and hurried straight to my room.

"Julie, you're okay? You had me so worried!"

"I'm sorry. I just went out for a walk in the bog."

"You gave us a scare. Listen, whatever Elkannah said to you, he didn't mean it. He just had a bad day. He really does love you."

"Sure." I found that particularly hard to swallow. She left the room and I lay down on my bed, exhausted.

Suddenly, the door burst open and Elkannah's overpowering figure filled the frame. I sat up quickly, bracing myself for another outburst.

He fell dramatically to his knees, grabbing my feet and kissing them while he blubbered. "Julie, I'm so so sorry. Please forgive me. I love you Julie. I would never want to hurt you. Never! You're a Gemini like me. You understand we have moods. You know I love you, right?"

His hands were fawning all over my legs, and if I hadn't thought so before, I was now certain that the man was insane.

"Yes, yes, Elkannah. It's all right, I forgive you." Cringing, I tried to extricate myself from his paws. I just wanted him to leave. Tamar returned to the room and, seeing her husband's ridiculous display and the pained look on my face, interrupted.

"Okay, honey, that's enough. She's forgiven you."

After a few further reassurances on my part, he got up and left the room to my relief. I now desperately wanted to leave Ireland. But I had no money and was completely reliant on Elkannah, who was loath to let me go. I was trapped in a world that I did not want to live in, with no purpose for an existence I found unbearable. Like a caged bird staring longingly at the freedom of the skies, every time I tried to break free, my wings were clipped a little more. They had wanted to break my spirit and finally they succeeded. There was no fight left in me. I was tired of picking myself up every time I was beaten down, tired of fearing where the next blow would come from, tired of wishing for dreams I could not realize, tired of bouncing back from countless disappointments.

I was tired of living—and I was only seventeen.

There was nothing left but to wait while I faded away a little more with each passing day. Eating less, talking less, laughing less, until I became a mere remnant, a flesh and bone shell of myself. And when that too was gone, then the mistake that was my life would finally be over.

I could only write how badly I felt:

It's madness to think I'd stick around now;
Your insanity's the cause, you know.
Inside's a festering wound
And you ask me why I'm looking pale.
You're so dense, don't you see?
You call this liberty!
I want to get out!
Why don't you let me go?
Keeping me will kill me. I'm too young to die.
They say I'm losing weight; what's hunger to pain?
Why don't you just leave me be?
I'd don't understand, can't understand
The twisted workings of your mind.
Freedom and happiness are an illusion;
A midnight rendezvous, or a fairy-tale
For people who have never lived.
One day I'll escape—
But your nightmares will bring me back.
They won't let you forget, you know.
Won't ever let you forget.

Luckily for me, Mum returned to Europe with her family. They had had enough of India and the small-minded Family members they encountered there. They were back to raise money to go to Africa.

I wrote to Mum saying I was not well, and asked if I might visit her. I knew I had to get out of Ireland before things got worse. I flew to France and she met me at the airport with Luke and Crystal. The transformation in me was shocking. I was in such a bad state that Mum sat in the front of the van for the ride home so I wouldn't see her crying.

My family united to help me get better. My half sister Mariana had just flown in, and for the first time our broken family lived together. For the first time too, I was shown unconditional love and acceptance. We lived in a big old stone farmhouse in Vigy, southern France. I spent most of the days on long walks through the fields and forests with my brother and sisters. It was a time of uninterrupted peace for me.

Mariana literally force-fed me at mealtimes. She put the food on my plate herself, despite my angry protests, and watched me until I had eaten every last bite. Sometimes I would dissolve in a pool of tears and wanted to gag, but she wouldn't back down. I thought she was being cruel, but she followed through relentlessly for my good. If it had been anyone else, I would have dug in my heels.

Then unexpectedly, after two years of being hidden away, World Services allowed Celeste to visit briefly. She came from England with Dad and brought her baby, Cherie, whom we had never seen. It was the first time since the Philippines, fifteen years before, that we spent a day all together.

This visit should have held more importance for me, but I was oblivious to everything. I walked around zombie-like, unable to express any kind of emotion. I could not feel. I did not experience joy at their arrival, or sorrow at their departure. Because of this, that visit remains a blur in my mind. I do remember taking a short stroll with Celeste and relaying to her my experiences in Ireland.

I celebrated my eighteenth birthday in France with my family around me. The few months spent with them had rallied my spirits, but I still was not strong enough to venture back out on my own. I lacked any self-confidence. I was wafer thin and continued to battle depression.

By now my family had raised enough money to move to Senegal. I was invited to join them and I jumped at the offer. There was a quote that stuck in my mind from one of Mo's stories, of his mother when she was contemplating suicide: "If you're going to throw your life away, why not give it to some cause." I decided that that was what I was going to do. Before I knew it, I was on a plane heading for West Africa.

The care my family gave me started me down the road to recovery, but Africa cured me. It took seeing people much worse off to put my troubles back into perspective.

Senegal was hot, dusty, and wonderful! It carried an exotic blend of Arabic, African, and French culture. The Senegalese people are tall and striking. It was a land rich with color, music, and life. We started working with a home for street children, which was a big problem in Dakar. We would put on clown shows to entertain them, and raised regular sponsorship for food and clothing for the kids.

New Year 2000—Y2K—was to be dramatic. A prophecy announced that this could be the beginning of the End of the World—again. All over the globe, we were to pray and rededicate our lives to the Family in "The Footwashing Ceremony." Someone acted out the role of Jesus and washed each of our feet and then we read out our pledge of dedication.

When midnight struck on New Year's Day 2000, and no lights went out in the city, we were mildly surprised. Queen Maria explained it away through prophecy that Jesus was delaying the inevitable Endtime so we would have more time to "spread the gospel." The turn of the millennium was seen as a milestone, for we were now "ordained warriors" wielding the greatest power in the Universe.

One day, quite unexpectedly, I received a phone call from Dad. He was moving to Uganda to start up a radio ministry and wondered if I'd like to join him. He thought I could put my talent for writing to use scripting the shows. Before I might have jumped at such an offer, but now I declined. I no longer wanted to live with him. Since he had left me in Thailand aged eight years old, our relationship had suffered a steady erosion. He was not the fun, caring father I remembered. More than ever he seemed a stranger to me. I felt safe where I was with my family, and I loved Senegal.

But Dad persisted. He said they had received prophecies that "the team for Uganda had been personally handpicked by the Lord" and my name was called to join them. I could not ignore the summons.

By this time, prophecy was fast becoming the new method of dictatorship. It could be used to badger people into doing things they did not want to do. No one dared risk stepping out of God's bubble of protection by not obeying a prophecy.

All my family in Senegal received "prophecies" saying I should go to Uganda, so I could no longer refuse my father. Mum thought as long as I stayed, I would always be living under Mariana's shadow. I needed to carve out my own life. *They wanted me to go.* The old feelings of rejection broke over me. I was gutted. I went up to the roof of the house and cried for hours. Just when it seemed I had found a family and a place I belonged to, I was being kicked out. It was the age-old question—if they loved me, why were they sending me away?

Heartbroken, I flew to Uganda.

I identified each of the many countries I lived in by their individual smell. Uganda smelt of vegetation before rain and the rich red dirt. It is known as the Pearl of Africa. I loved the sudden cloudbursts between sunny skies, when I could run out into the rain and feel it pounding into my skin. It seemed both powerful and sorrowful at the same time. It released something in me. Other times, I would climb up on to the roof of the house and lie watching the stars for hours. I wanted to fade into the blackness and disappear into a tiny twinkling star, watching the world from a distance.

The Home consisted of my dad and Sunshine, an elderly woman called Kathleen, who had come to be Dad's secretary, a young man named Sims, who was a studio technician, and the kids. Dad and Sunshine had had a third child by now, a boy named Rory. It was obvious to me Sunshine had not wanted a third child. She wanted a ministry and a life, not to be tied down with masses of children, which was the ministry Dad wanted her to accept. Dad thought a woman's place was to bear babies and take care of her man. Dad was actually proud of his reproductive record, boasting that he had fathered fourteen children of seven different nationalities.

The day I arrived, Dad asked me how I felt about taking care of Rory. It was more of a strong suggestion than a request. I had come believing I was going to help start a radio show. Dad had misled me to get me there. I felt betrayed. I had left a place I loved to come and baby-sit Dad's growing family, cook and keep house for him.

Although I was upset by Dad's deception, I felt for my baby brother. The whole move from Japan to Africa, coupled with his mother's rejection, had turned Rory into a fussy, insecure child. He very quickly grew attached to me to the point where I could not even take him out of my arms, much less leave the room, or he would start to scream and shake with terror. He clung to me constantly like a frightened little monkey. It always took me a long time to calm him down when he fell into one of his fits.

Dad's solution to Rory's crying was to spank him. This surprised me. I had never seen my father spank a child in anger till now. He used to be fair and rarely resorted to beatings.

I often took Rory for long walks along the red dirt roads in his rickety little pram. We would spend the morning with my African mama. Mary was a tiny, wiry old neighbour who was tough as nails and unofficially adopted me. She would be out digging her vegetable garden with a hoe every morning, hacking at any elephant grass that dared sprout on her little plot of land. She was always trying to fatten me up and taught me how to cook grasshoppers and termites, the local delicacy. Rory was always very calm around her and she loved our company.

Not long after we opened the Radio Home, Dad's friend from Japan joined us with his large family, and a single girl, followed shortly by another young couple. We were now a noisy, bustling commune again—a situation I dreaded. I had to move out of my room, as I refused to share, so I made a space for myself in the garage with some straw mats pinned up around a mosquito net. It was not much to look at, but it was privacy and I could be alone.

Sometimes we went over to another nearby home for fellowship. During one party, I met a couple that were visiting from Kenya. He was an elderly Australian man, married to a young Eastern European girl. When I walked into the room, I saw Dad chatting animatedly with him. Dad waved me over.

"Julie, this is Michael! He's an old friend of mine from way back in the day!"

"Oh really? From where?" I had heard a great deal about all of Dad's old friends, but I did not recall hearing of a Michael.

"Well, we knew each other from back in India! You know who he is!"

"Yeah, we both married the same woman!" Michael offered in his Australian accent, and the two of them laughed together. I did not get it.

"He married Celeste's mother after me." Dad clued me in.

I had no idea that this "Michael" was formerly Joshua— my half sister Kristina's abuser. If I had, I would have punched him, or would have expected Dad to. Instead, they acted like best mates. To Dad, anyone who was a Family member was a brother.

Towards Christmas 2000, we heard from Celeste. She had left World Services, and wanted to come and visit us in Uganda. Dad was ecstatic. It was his dream to have her work with him. She arrived looking much thinner than the last time I had seen her in France. I knew she had been living in Queen Maria's Home and I was eager to milk information out of her about what it was like. She was pretty tight lipped and uncomfortable talking about it, but she did describe the difficulties of her pregnancy and childbirth. She saw I was unhappy and I could sense she was too, but we never got much opportunity to talk about things together. We had not managed to break through the intangible barrier that had grown between us from the time she left me in Thailand. Our lives had split off in very different directions.

Three months later, much to Dad's disappointment, Celeste decided to leave Uganda. Although I was sorry to see her go, I could understand why. Living with Dad was no longer "living the dream." It was living the nightmare of a broken dream.

CHAPTER TWENTY-FOUR

A Dream Come True

Kristina

Dad called out of the blue to say he was in town visiting his parents and would like to come over to see Jordan and me. He told me Celeste had given birth to a daughter. I had been an auntie for over a year and nobody had told me!

"Why didn't she tell me, Dad? She has my address," I said.

"Don't worry, honey—I have only just found out myself," he said, chuckling. He sounded so happy that I decided not to make his visit confrontational. We had a nice time while he played with Jordan and chatted about many things. I think we had mentally decided that he had his way of life and I had mine.

A year later, Celeste phoned asking if she and her two-and-a-half-year-old daughter, Cherie, could come and stay with us for a week. I had room at my house and told her she was welcome. It had been four years since we had seen her last and I had mixed feelings. On the one hand, I was overjoyed. On the other, I was nervous wondering how we would get on.

I needn't have worried. Celeste had changed drastically. She was no longer the scared, guarded person I remembered. She opened up and told me more about her life and her recent visit to Uganda to see Dad and Juliana. For the first time, she criticized Dad and the way he was bringing up his new family.

She also told me we had a Greek sister named Davida. My joy turned to sorrow when she said Davida was deeply depressed and on heroin with a violent and controlling boyfriend. She told me that Dad and Julie planned to visit her. I asked for Davida's address, but Celeste did not have it.

The week flew by. We talked for hours, cooked together and enjoyed being with our children. Though we did not speak much about the cult, I left informative books strategically placed around the house in the hope she would pick them up.

The last night of Celeste's visit, David and I took her out to a club to "get her drunk" and let our hair down. We drank, we chatted, we laughed; we had fun! The three of us were the last on the dance floor. When the DJ dropped Sister Sledge's "We Are Family" on the turntable, we all joined in, singing at the top of our voices. We were jumping around to the beat, arms locked together and at the end of the tune we collapsed on the floor in hysterics. We did not want the night to end.

The next day, Celeste left for Hungary to work as a secretary in a Family home. We were sad to see her go, but she gave me her email address and promised to stay in touch. I started corresponding regularly with her and she would send pictures and cute stories about Cherie.

It was only a year later when Celeste called us to say she was leaving the Family. Mum, David and I could not believe the news! I had waited for so long, and had almost given up hope.

We picked her up at Victoria Station in London and brought her to the Midlands. Our first night together as a "free family" was wonderful. We talked a mile a minute—but I knew there would be plenty of time for us to recover those lost years and catch up. It was a luxurious feeling. Celeste decided to stay with us and I looked after Cherie full time for the first year while Celeste worked as a secretary for Office Angels. Cherie looked so much like her mother at that age that spending time with her felt almost like I was making up for our years apart as children.

I knew Dad would naturally hold me and Mum responsible for Celeste leaving the cult. It was inconceivable to him why anyone would want to leave and he wrote saying we "had got to her," which frustrated and pained me. As we filled in the missing parts of our lives with each other, I realized my childhood image of my father as a knight in shining armour was only a fantasy.

Dad was still under the impression that Celeste would soon repent and go crawling back to the Family. So I wasn't surprised when after a year he came for Christmas. It was important that he saw first hand how comfortable Celeste was with her family and the tight bond that had formed between us. We arranged to take him out for a medieval banquet on the last night, something we knew he would enjoy. I danced with my father for the first time and he told me I had his eyes.

When we said our goodbyes he told me he would keep in touch more often via email. And that he loved me. I could not believe it! I thought that maybe his perspective was finally shifting. I will always hold out that hope.

CHAPTER TWENTY-FIVE

Is Justice a Dream?

Celeste

I hope I've made the right decision, I thought, as I arrived at the Budapest commune with Cherie in a pushchair and two suitcases. I was no longer a believer, but I was afraid of leaving the only life I knew. I was afraid of being cut off from my friends and, more importantly, I wasn't ready to face my dad's disappointment and rejection.

I had just come from visiting my mother and Kristina and David and a part of me wanted to stay and get to know them better. I had lived with so much fear for so long, but I began to realize it was all smoke and mirrors. After living with Queen Maria, I questioned everything I had been told—this opened up my mind to new possibilities and I was no longer afraid to push the boundaries. I stopped censoring myself and let down my guard. My mother and my sister weren't "my enemy" or out to hurt me. They were my family—my flesh and blood—and I enjoyed their company. I took with me Kristina's email address and promised to stay in touch. I had no idea what I wanted to do with my life if I left the Family. With a young daughter to care for, I had to have a plan.

The view from the balcony of the house in Budapest was amazing. It overlooked the city and the Danube winding through the heart of it. At night the lights of the city flickered below, sparkling like little jewels in the darkness.

Joy greeted me. She was the Childcare Central Reporting Officer for Eastern Europe. She was also a second-generation adult—one of the first born into the Family—in her early thirties, with light hair and striking blue eyes.

"Here's your room." She showed me to a small box-room near the communal living room. My bed was built on stilts, like a loft, and underneath was a desk with a computer where I would work. A small couch bed was in the corner where Cherie would sleep.

The next morning Joy explained to me her unusual circumstances with her husband Ben.

"Ben's no longer in the Family," she said, "but we received special permission for him to stay in the Home."

Ben and Joy's youngest daughter had died of cancer the year before, and it had affected Ben deeply. He refused to be parted from his remaining three children. They were the world to him.

Maybe the Family's being more flexible, I thought, as such an arrangement had been previously unheard of. I knew Ben from the Heavenly City School in Japan when we were teenagers. He had drunk all the alcohol for the School's Christmas party once, and was found in the pantry inebriated—of course he got into big trouble. This incident imprinted him on my memory.

"Well, I'm not so sure of the Family myself at the moment." I wanted to be upfront with Joy about where I stood from the beginning. "The reason I'm here is to help change things for the children. I want them to have a better education, more socialization, and access to schooling materials."

Joy agreed with me. Joy had not received adequate education in even the basic 3Rs. Although she was intelligent with good organizational skills, she could not spell or write structured sentences; so I was there to be her secretary.

Ben was an amazing father and his children adored him. Despite his differences, Ben worked hard to raise money for not just his own family, but for the commune. He was a selfless person and I admired him. He was the only person I could talk to freely without fear of reprisal. We became friends, and I started to voice my feelings that I had kept bottled up inside for so long. By this time it was clear to me that Queen Maria was no more a prophetess than any other cult leader who claimed a title they did not deserve.

My mind was opened even further when two visitors passed through the Home. The first was Amana, who had known me as a child in India and Dubai.

"How's your mum?" she asked. "I used to live with her in India. Where is she?" She had been living on far-flung mission fields and had not heard that my mum had left the group so many years ago. I told her she was no longer in the Family.

"I have such fond memories of your mother. She was so ill in her pregnancies and I remember she struggled with all her kids, but she was very cheerful. Your dad was such an airhead—he was never around to help her."

A week later an Italian man visited who had known my mother in India. He, too, had no idea she was no longer in the group. He raved about what a good woman my mother was. "But that horrible man, Joshua," he told me, "he was always angry and so harsh on the children. I never liked him."

This was the first time I was hearing the other side of the story. I had always known deep down that the stories told about my mum were slanderous lies, but this was the confirmation I needed. I had also found out that Joshua was living as a full-time member in a commune in Kenya and had got a young Romanian woman pregnant. Her best friend, a Bulgarian national, was in our Home—they had only been in the Family a few years—and I told her that I knew who Joshua was, my sister Kristina's abuser. At the very least, her friend had a right to know this man's past history.

I was livid. I felt betrayed. His excommunication during the court case had just been for show. I wrote two letters to Dad telling him that Kristina and David longed for a relationship with their father and how much it hurt them that he appeared not to care. "It's not right that you abandoned them all those years," I told him. Dad did not seem that bothered. I decided I would try to bridge the gap that had stood between us all those years. We were family and we deserved to be together.

The final straw came when the Home was directed by World Services to uphold the rules—non-members could not live in Family houses. Ben had to move out and get a flat in town. He was heartbroken and his children were devastated. I was not going to be a part of something I did not agree with any longer. I realised that I could never fully care for and protect my daughter or make decisions that were in her best interests as long as I was bound to obey a self-appointed Queen and a set of arbitrary rules decided for me. I told Joy I was leaving and I wrote Kristina an email saying I wanted to leave the Family. She gave me their phone number and I called a couple of days later. Mum answered the phone.

"I am so happy!" she said. "Can I ask you why you want to leave the Family?"

"Well, I no longer agree with it any more. The Family has done nothing but split up families. I have been unhappy for a long time and my daughter deserves a better life than I had."

It took me three months to raise the money for my coach fare to England. Joy slipped me $300 and although I appreciated the gesture, the sum was hardly enough to get me on my feet.

When at last I arrived with Cherie at Victoria Station, Dad's last words in an email to me still rang in my ears. "I pity you. What are you going to do as a single mother with a daughter? You'll end up on the streets with nothing." His heartless words left me enraged. "After you've wallowed in the mire of the System, you'll see how good you had it in the Family." He did not offer help or support; it was almost as if he hoped to see me fail. Dad's condescending attitude made me all the more determined to prove him wrong. Where once those words would have crushed me, I no longer looked for or needed Dad's approval anymore. I was a parent responsible for my own child now.

Dad was pushed from my mind completely when I saw Kristina, David and Mum waiting at the station to greet me.

It was the strangest feeling being reunited with them. Although we hardly knew each other, we hugged and kissed like long-lost friends. The final piece of the puzzle that was missing in my heart had finally been put into place. For the first time I knew I was going in the right direction, and the feeling was incomparable. It was the best decision I ever made.

Mum did not have much—she had a small three-bedroom house in the Midlands, but she let me have her spare room until I got a place of my own. It may not have been much of a start, but I had my freedom and I was on top of the world!

Two and a half years later, on January 11, 2005, I logged on to a website (www.movingon.org) where second-generation ex-Family can share memories and experiences of their childhoods in the Family. I had reconnected with friends I thought I had lost contact with forever via the site. But this time I read the shocking bulletin—Davidito had committed murder-suicide. I was stunned. I had just spoken to him for an hour on the phone the previous Friday. My hands started shaking and I burst into tears.

The last time I had seen him was in Portugal, at Mama Maria's Home, with his girlfriend, Elixcia. Apart from a few emails back and forth the call that Friday was our first conversation since that time.

At first, we caught up. I told him I was studying Psychology and Education at university, a subject I found helpful in understanding cult dynamics.

"I found the module on social psychology very interesting in explaining the powerful influence of group conformity and pressure to alter behaviour," I said.

I told him I had my own flat—my first—with my daughter, and that she was enjoying school. "It's strange living on my own, but I love just being able to shop for myself and decide how to decorate my home."

He was glad to hear I was doing well. He told me that since he left he had worked on a fishing trawler and then as an electrician. He wanted to go to college but it was too expensive. He went on to say that no matter how hard he tried to fit in, he could not forget his past.

"If I make friends, they ask about my family and who my parents are. What do I say?"

I understood what he meant. I faced the same difficult questions.

As our conversation continued, it was clear to me that Davidito was in anguish. He talked about the abuse he had witnessed with Mene when he was only ten. "I would go down to the basement and see her there tied up spread-eagled on a bed. She would beg me for help, but there was nothing I could do. Berg would come down and molest her right there." The anger rose in his voice.

"You know, I feel so bad for Techi," I told him. "When I was there in Mama's Home she lacked any desire or ambition. She didn't take care of her appearance, her room was in an appalling state, and she always seemed so depressed."

Davidito choked up. "But you should have seen her before they broke her. She was so full of life and was a completely different person."

He talked about the Techi Series and blamed his mother for destroying her mind. He also told me something even more shocking. The father of Techi's son was unknown and she had said officially that it was between two older teen boys, but Davidito told me he believed that the father was most likely Frank, an older man in his late thirties. I had met Frank in Mama's Home when I first arrived, but he left shortly after.

"What makes me the most angry is that it was our own mother who tried to entrap and control her. Techi wanted to leave the Home because there were no other young people, so our mother arranged for Frank to have dates with her. She was barely sixteen. And you know what the hardest thing about it is? Frank was my friend. It's just so fucked up."

"Well, people were pushed into doing things that they would have never done otherwise," I said.

Davidito agreed. He wanted to help Techi and her son get out from under the control of his mother—but all communication between them had been severed when he left the Family. He was not a helpless child anymore and he felt it was his responsibility to right the wrongs, and avenge the physical and mental abuse that thousands of children had suffered because of his parents' insanity.

I told him how I had written affidavits, which had been submitted to the FBI and the police in the UK. I gave explicit accounts of the violence and abuse I had seen and suffered in person. I wanted to support the effort for justice. He was despondent. The difficulties we faced bringing abusers to court and getting convictions seemed insurmountable.

Cult members used Bible names, making it difficult to identify them.

Many crimes took place in countries like the Philippines, India, and Thailand, where the police have few resources to pursue complicated abuse cases. We moved often, and rarely knew the addresses of the homes we lived in. In many countries, like the USA, there is a statute of limitations for sexual crimes, and the cult had destroyed almost all incriminating evidence—we were made to burn our photographs and personal letters during the court cases.

Despite these obstacles, I told him, I remained optimistic that if we stood together and told the truth, our voices would be heard. Davidito wasn't convinced.

"Really? Do you think so?" He sighed. "I just don't have the strength in me. I can't make it another day. I've tried, I've tried so hard but I can't…I just want to end it."

I struggled with what to say; I was desperate to help him see that life was worth living, and I wasn't sure how serious his intentions were to kill himself.

But he did make one thing clear—he was looking for his mother. She was just as guilty as Mo; he had seen her bring in girls to his bedroom. She had masterminded the Detention Teen programs, including Mene's torture. He wanted to confront her. If the justice system was not going to do anything about her, then he would.

"But it would take so long, and I just don't have the energy to live another day," he added.

"But your testimony and what you know is vital to getting justice. Would you write it down?" I asked him. "I'm sure that we'll find a way and that the authorities will take notice."

He hesitated. "I don't know. What about a video? I'll make a video, okay?"

"Please," I begged him. "Will you think about speaking to the police? Please call me again, will you?"

"Okay, I'll think about it. I'll call you again. It's been good to talk to you. Bye," he said, and hung up the phone.

I was sure I would speak to him again, but it never happened. That night, he met with Angela Smith, aka Sue who was pictured with Davidito naked as a toddler in the Davidito Book. She was his mother's secretary and confidante for many years. Before the night was over, he had stabbed her, and put a bullet to his head.

I cried—cried for the loss of a friend, for the needless waste of life, and the despair he must have felt to go to such lengths to show his anger towards his mother, whom he could not reach. His was not the only suicide. There have been others of our generation, friends I knew and lived with, who could not live with the pain. A month after Davidito's death, Juliana wrote telling me that our sister Davida in Greece had died. I was heartbroken. I had been trying to get her phone number to contact her and invite her to England to get to know her family. I wanted her to know we cared about her and now it was too late.

These deaths spurred me on. In mid-January, I went to California to speak on ABC News about Davidito. I wanted to speak the truth and tell what had happened to him—to me, to our generation. It was an emotional and difficult time, but something I never expected happened. As I walked into the hotel room where the ABC News crew were, I was greeted by Armi, my childhood friend. We hugged and talked together for the first time in fifteen years! That evening I also met Elixcia. She had flown from Washington to San Diego to be interviewed by ABC News. She was still fragile and devastated at the tragic loss of her husband, often bursting into tears.

I watched Davidito's home video he made the night before his death. All the anger and emotion he had suppressed for so long came flooding out. I could hear the anguish in his voice as he spoke of the lack of justice. He confessed that he had wanted to commit suicide for a long time, ever since Teen Training, and wished he had never been born.

"The goal is to bring down those sick fuckers, Mama and Peter. My own mother! That evil little cunt. God damn! How can you do that to kids? How can you do that to kids and sleep at night? I don't fucking know."

He sat on a table in his little kitchen, waving the gun that would kill him as he spoke.

By the end of it I was in tears. It was so unlike him, the timid boy I knew. I understood better his anger towards his mother when Davida, Sarah's daughter, spoke up and told her story. She claimed she lay in bed with Mo while Maria had sex with her own son. I understood why Davidito could not speak of this himself directly. It would have been too humiliating, too painful. His anger towards her was clear. She was not just an innocent bystander. She herself was guilty of child abuse.

I talked with Elixcia about what Davidito had said about Techi and Frank, and she confirmed that she knew about it. I got Frank's email address and wrote to him, asking him to come clean and to answer these charges. He never replied. Instead, Elixcia got a frantic call from Frank, who now lived in Switzerland. He had a new life now outside the cult, a good job as a businessman and admitting his past would be devastating. He could not do it.

What a coward, I thought.

There are many who try and hide from their past, but wounds cannot be healed unless they are exposed and treated. I found the courage to confront my father on the issues that have separated us and tell him what I believed he needed to hear. In an email I wrote:

> This is not a discussion about your motives, it's about your actions and the effect it had on your children. For years I tried to share with you how I felt, how I knew the other children were feeling, and you always dismissed it and made light of it. This is what eventually led me to parting ways with you. The person who has sown the most division in our family is you. You tried to divide me against my mother, David and Kristina, then Julie against me, and now are you going to continue with your other children?

Dad had had previously denied to my mother that *any* untoward sexual encounters had occurred in the Family. I challenged him on my memory of walking in on him with Armi.

I said, "You were by far not the only one with Armi, but you were a part of it, a collective abuse of an innocent child and because of that, don't you think she deserves an apology from you?—And maybe more?"

In my father's reply he finally admitted it:

> I truly am sorry that you suffered some gross encounters at MWM [*Music with Meaning*] that continue to haunt you. I honestly had no idea that you had been forced to do these

things by Paul and others. Nevertheless, as your parent, I was responsible for your protection and care, and so I take the blame for not knowing about these goings-on. What sexual encounters there were between adults and children, I believed were very mild, and more along the lines of cuddling, not what you have described, which is so gross I don't even want to type it here. Yes, it was absolutely wrong, and thank God the Family put down strict rules many years ago to put a stop to it. What I, and no doubt many others, haven't fully realized, is that those who were unfortunate enough to be children in a Home where such excesses were practised are still hurting from it, even though it is so many years ago. So all I can say is, yes, I am truly very sorry and I am asking for your forgiveness, not for what I did, but what I didn't do, to protect you at that time and be aware of what was happening to you.

Yes, you are right. I did have an encounter with Armi. I had forgotten all about it until recently. I don't remember the incident you described, but I do remember another one in the studio. I do remember that we didn't do much, and like she said, I didn't push myself on her. It may even have been her idea, I can't remember. But I do know that I never had any inclination to want to do those things. And that time with Armi was the only time I ever did, except after that Mene wanted to have a date, but from what I recall, we just lay together fully clothed and talked, as I really didn't want to do anything…I honestly do find the idea of adults having sex with children repulsive, and because of that I do empathize with you that your childhood memories are tainted by those things, and I am truly sorry for allowing that to happen.

I accept that my father feels remorse, however, I do not believe his apology has gone far enough. He still does not accept that David Berg was a pedophile, responsible for destroying so many lives of our generation. He suggests that an eleven-year-old child asked *him* for sex—as if that justifies his actions—when he was the responsible adult who should have reported any sexual contact between adults and children to the police—not turned a blind eye to it.

What he wrote in this letter was more than he has ever admitted in the past, but the apology has come thirty years too late and too little. I do not believe my father is or was a pedophile, but he still supports with his money and protects the very leaders who instigated the sexual abuse we suffered. He mistakenly credits the Family with stopping the sexual abuse—denying his own daughter, Kristina, the credit and bravery she showed in speaking up and exposing to the world the terror we all suffered, which forced the hand of Queen Maria and Peter to conform. But pedophiles still remain protected by the Family, while the victims—their children—have been threatened and slandered.

CHAPTER TWENTY-SIX

Pearl of Africa

Juliana

I was startled awake by a knock on my bedroom door.

"Yes?" I answered, groggily glancing at my clock. It was 3 a.m. and a violent storm was raging outside. Through the peals of thunder, I faintly heard my friend Tina asking me to open the door. I had a habit of locking my door at night, just in case. I got up to open it for her. What could she want at this time of night?

There was an apologetic look on her face. Two masked men stood behind her brandishing an AK47 and a machete. As soon as I opened the door, the muzzle of the gun rose to my face.

"You! Come now!" one of them ordered. I was in a skimpy T-shirt and shorts but I didn't have time to throw a robe over myself. The intruders herded the two of us into the master bedroom where Dad and the kids slept.

They demanded money, and Dad pointed them to the briefcase under the bed where he kept his savings of $1000. They prised it open with the machete and found the envelope with the money, but grew enraged when they pulled out the notes inside. The Ugandan currency averages 1800 Uganda Shillings to the dollar. This means stacks of notes. To their minds, a few crisp bills meant nothing.

"Where is your money?" they shouted furiously.

"That is all the money there is. Anything more I keep in the bank. Nobody keeps much money in their houses," Dad tried explaining to them.

They didn't believe him. The head burglar threatened to rape us women if we didn't tell them where the money was hidden. We pretended we didn't understand and they turned on Dad. One of the men held him down while the other raised the machete high in the air. They were going to hack his leg off unless we told them where the money was.

As the robber's arm lifted for the first blow, Dad cried out desperately, "Jesus, help me!"

I shouted, "Stop! I have money!" Perhaps the combination of our voices startled the robber, because he froze for an instant and then slowly lowered his arm and turned to me. "What did you say?"

"There's no need to do that. I have some Uganda Shillings in my room."

The promise of Ugandan money was something he understood. He jabbered with his accomplice quickly, and they split up. One of them stood guard over the room with the gun, while the leader escorted me to my room for the money. I gave him all my shillings, which amounted to no more than $10, but the amount of notes seemed to appease him. He then tore through my entire room searching for anything else of value.

Inspired by their success, they took the other two women one at a time to their rooms to rifle through their things.

They had been in the house for two hours and dawn would soon break. It was time to go. They told us all to go to our rooms and lie down on our beds. None of us left our rooms for another half-hour, waiting and listening, unsure whether they were truly gone.

Finally, we ventured out to look around. They had taken the video machine, mobile phones and stereo system. None of us could believe the ordeal we had just passed through. It seemed almost surreal. They did not find our music studio where the most expensive equipment was and they did not find the two young men sleeping in the house, which could have proved dangerous. But most amazing of all, none of us had been hurt. There were numerous stories of people we knew who were beaten to within an inch of their lives, raped, or even killed during robberies. We had come out shaken, but otherwise unscathed.

Our story was reported in one of the Family news publications. Family members would be sure to question why God had allowed it to happen. Wasn't He supposed to protect His missionaries? A prophecy came out saying that we had been out of the Spirit and disunited, and that was why the enemy had been allowed to break through.

This scathing article stung when I read it. We were putting life and limb on the line to spread the Family gospel, yet the moment anything went wrong, we would be hung out as the dandy bad examples. We were on our own on this one. If we did well, it was all thanks to Jesus through the Family, but if anything went wrong, or we struggled in any way, we were the ones to blame.

*　　*　　*

Around this time, an email came saying my sister Davida was taking so much heroin, it was likely she could die any day. In a final act of desperation, her mother, Sotiria, had attempted to contact Dad through Family members in Greece. Davida needed urgent help, they said, and Dad reluctantly decided it was his duty to go and see if there was anything he could do. I was resolved to go with him. Somehow, I knew I could help her more than our father ever could. He was useless, from my point of view. He had not been a father to her thus far—he didn't even know her—what did he expect he was able to do? Rescue her from the clutches of heroin by preaching Jesus' saving love to her? Pretend to be a father to her now that it was too late? It was obvious to me, by the state she had deteriorated to, that it was far too late for all that.

The money I had raised for a ticket was stolen in the burglary. If I wanted to go, I had to use my emergency money—the money all Family members are required to have in case they have "flee." This was to be used only in emergencies. I was determined to go, so I promised the Home I would work to pay this money back.

Davida was the lost sister I had dreamed of meeting. I knew in an odd way, there was a connection between us, and that I had to help her. From the moment we met, we were inseparable; as if we had grown up together our whole lives. We roamed Athens together by day, and shared a bed at night as comfortably as a pair of Siamese twins.

Dad may as well have been part of the furniture; he was irrelevant. They were civil, friendly even, but the closeness of a father with his daughter was starkly lacking. That missing affection she bestowed on me; and for a brief period of time we both experienced what it would have been like to grow up with a close sibling.

Sotiria gave me the money for us to spend out, since she did not trust Davida not to use it on her next fix. Everything of value had been stripped from the tiny apartment and sold for instant cash. Davida was encouraged in these endeavours by her no-good boyfriend, Stavros, and their interminable condition. Her mother had to hide any cash she had, yet somehow, the two of them found it anyway. Money had been a struggle for Sotiria; everything she brought home from working long hours in the hospital had been eaten up by heroin.

Two weeks into the visit, Dad decided he was ready to return home. The visit had accomplished little. He had failed to make a connection or form any bond with his daughter. But I was not ready to leave and my sister begged me to stay, so I remained for a couple of months longer.

One day we went out into the center of Athens. I decided to get a tattoo as a remembrance of Greece and my sister. She left me at the tattoo parlour, saying she'd go for coffee and return after two hours. I nodded distractedly, studying the book of designs before me.

The artist took three hours to complete the tattoo of an ancient ornamental dagger that appeared embedded through my flesh. I put it on a place that usually remained covered. The Family did not endorse tattoos, but there was no official rule against it. It was my secret rebellion.

When I emerged from the parlour, my sister was nowhere in sight. I waited about for over an hour. Night was falling when she finally returned, stoned out of her head. I was furious that she had lied to me and she saw I was upset.

"Julie, *agape mor*, I'm so sorry. I couldn't help it. I met some of my friends, and they wouldn't let me go till I had some." She clung to me, begging forgiveness. "But it wasn't heroin, I promise. It was only coke. Please don't tell my mum."

I didn't tell because it wouldn't have helped anything. She was shivering, and I took off my wrap and put it around her. As long as she stayed there in Athens, the drug environment would always surround her and she was not strong enough to resist it. I begged her to come with me to Africa. I would set her up in an apartment, I'd raise the money for her to live till she could get better and get a job.

There was a time limit of three months in which Family members could be out of their commune. Dad wrote reminding me my time limit was almost up. Sotiria and Davida begged me to stay and I begged Davida to come with me. They wanted me to leave the group, but at the time, this did not even feature in my mind as an option. I wanted to stay with my sister, but because of the rules, I had to go. A tug-of-war went on in my heart. In the end, I flew out, leaving my last $200 with Sotiria to go towards Davida's ticket, if she ever decided to join me.

After returning back to the grind of Family life, Dad broke the unexpected news. "Honey, Celeste has written to say she's decided to leave the Family." Dad looked distraught. Celeste had always been his favourite child, the one he doted on. The news rattled him to his foundations.

I was surprised. "Did she say why? It seems odd that after coming straight from Queen Maria's Home, she should almost immediately decide to leave the Family. Maybe all is not as it seems in World Services."

"Yes, I do wonder." I could see the doubt wavering in Dad's eyes. Celeste could never do any wrong, and perhaps his daughter had seen something while she was there that contributed to this decision.

Celeste wrote me a personal letter a couple of days later, detailing her decision and vaguely explaining she could no longer agree with some of the Family's beliefs, nor did she want to raise her child in it. I wanted to know details. I wanted to know exactly what had brought my sister to this decision. I was twenty-one years old, and I felt I deserved to know. In my letter I wrote to her I said:

> Basically I'm asking all this, cuz I've been evaluating my life of late, and what I'm really doing or accomplishing here, and yes, in the Family in general. But when I read your letter, and the whole "being fully persuaded in your own mind" thing, I realized, I wasn't. And haven't been for quite some time. And what I meant by you being the "strongest" of all of us was you being the most "sold" on the Family, seeing as you were in WS and everything, but if you found it didn't crack up to be all that, then that really got me wondering whether I'm the "dumb sheep" being led around by the nose.
>
> Basically, if I've been sad for this long, I should look at the bigger picture and start to wonder, why? So I have been, and I find that the way I've been living has been one long attempt at convincing myself that I'm living for a noble cause. But I've been lying to myself, hence the disillusionment, the discouragement and lack of challenge.
>
> I want to do something with my life…which I am proud of…I have absolutely no clue what to do…I don't know of any

situation to start in, or how to even start, and suddenly I feel helpless, and it's frustrating. It's like a fog I'm sitting in right now, and I'll sit a little longer till it clears and I can see my path ahead. I only hope it can be soon, as it's almost worse to be sitting here when it's the last place I want to be anymore.

Celeste was busy trying to start her new life and our contact became sporadic after this. Dad's initial doubt was replaced with doubled fervour for the Family's cause. He told me that it was inevitable that there would be a falling away of those who were not completely dedicated to the cause. "We just have to keep praying for Celeste," he said. "She'll come back once she sees how much worse it is out there!" I, on the other hand, knew my sister would not have left without good reason. I struggled in my mind, thinking one day to leave, but then the fear of not knowing anything out there, or how I would survive, kept me there. I pushed my doubts to the back of my mind and survived in auto-mode.

One day, Kingdom broke into tears and wouldn't stop crying. His mother was worried, but he wouldn't talk to anyone except Dad. Eventually Dad was able to coax the whole terrible story out. King had been awake during the night of the robbery and witnessed the whole ordeal. It had scared him. He wondered why Jesus almost let his Daddy get hacked up with a machete. My little brother was intensely unhappy. He was confined to the house all day and his life revolved around school, cleaning and Word Time. He didn't feel he was good for anything, and more than anything else, he felt unloved, unappreciated and unchallenged. In his mind this translated to mean there was nothing to live for. He had seen a machete in the garden and had been overwhelmed with the idea of using it on himself. He was just ten years old.

When Dad described the situation at Home Council, Sunshine was crying and everyone was shocked. It hit me in the gut. I understood those same emotions, but I was amazed that King was already experiencing them so young. I realized that my little brother silently bore his sorrows and never vocalized his thoughts. Both he and his sister Shirley were quiet, withdrawn and suppressed children. They had learned early on that raising their voices only attracted trouble. I never knew what was going through their minds, and this was the first time I caught a glimpse of the desperation they must be experiencing.

It had never been the same since the robbery, and that house gave everyone the jitters, so we moved again. Raising the money to live was always a struggle. Our company, RadioActive Productions, produced music and radio shows for free. It was part of our "witness," spreading the Words of David, but where it should have been financially supportive, it failed to pay the bills. Dad was trying to re-establish himself as a radio star, but we couldn't even sell the shows. In a poor African country, nobody would broadcast our programs unless they were free.

Usually we made ends meet by going around to local businesses to ask for donations. I was not proud to be a beggar for Christ. The Family called it "provisioning," but in reality it was just another form of begging. We, the privileged white man, begging for help when we were meant to be the ones helping. It seemed terribly wrong to have to ask for food and clothes in Africa, where the average local lives on an income of less than $20 a month. With our TV, our nice furniture and our spacious two-storey house, we would be considered wealthy by the average mud-hut dweller. I was keenly aware of this when we had people over to our Home for Bible Studies. Who wouldn't want to join the Family when they could live richly and all they had to do was accept a few odd beliefs?

Every so often, a supermarket or business had a surplus of outdated or damaged goods, which they contributed to us for charity. We were supposed to be a distribution center, though usually we kept most of the donated items for ourselves, and whatever was not good enough for our own use was distributed to various orphanages and poor neighbourhoods. This was called CTP—"Consider The Poor." During these CTP distributions, one person would follow the rest of us with a camera as we doled out the goods. We would pose with the African people receiving outdated goods from our benevolent hands. These pictures would be used to make up the monthly newsletter that we distributed to raise support for ourselves.

I despised the whole concept of posing for a picture. It seemed so fake and demeaning to the poor locals and I wondered what they thought of it. But beggars can't be choosers, and by the impoverished state they were in, they couldn't care less; they were just grateful to be receiving anything at all. This bothered me all the more. We were using their poverty to our own ends—to receive more goods from charitable companies that would go to us, and only the last bit of rubbish would trickle down to them.

Audaciously, we called ourselves missionaries.

But what else could we do? Most missionaries are supported by their Home Base. In the Family, it was the opposite way around. We, the missionaries, were supporting our Home Base. So we survived the best way we could, raising funds through posing for pictures. We couldn't sell the Family magazines, books and videos because most people were too poor to afford them, and the small amount we did sell was a drop in the bucket.

A mandatory 17 per cent of our income went to World Services. We ate a lot of beans, lentils, rice and cheap meat. Food was portioned out sparingly. We always struggled to pay our bills. Housing is not cheap in Uganda. We usually just made our budget, with nothing to spare. Then, Queen Maria released a letter called "Gifts," saying God was not happy with the Family contributing the absolute minimum to World Services, and that they could not expect His financial blessings if they did not graciously give above and beyond the set quota. Also, if any Home were not following all the "New Moves of the Spirit" or harbored sin in the camp, God would be obliged to toss them on to the scrap heap.

After this letter, everybody obediently voted in our Home Council meeting that week to raise the percentage to 25 per cent. I was seething when it was brought to a vote and mine was the only hand raised against the motion. A fourth of our Home's income was going to World Services in the hopes that this would ingratiate us with the Almighty. Then we looked deep into our souls to make sure there was no hidden sin the All Seeing Eye was focusing on, and lastly we sucked our spiritual Husband's golden seeds with increased fervour.

Maybe the combination or timing was not quite right, or maybe it was my failure to fuck our Savior, because that windfall we always hoped for never came.

A few months later I went on a trip to the States with Tina. We ended up visiting the Family Care Foundation Home in California, the family's charity where tithes and donations are funnelled through for tax exemption purposes. I was shocked when I arrived at a mansion. They owned a huge property. They ate good food, lived richly and had enough money to take vacations in their holiday house in Mexico. In stark contrast to the struggling homes in Africa who ate lentils and beans and could barely make the rent.

I returned from the trip slightly disillusioned. And while it was fun seeing other Family young people, some experiences from my travels did not sit well with me and gave me food for thought. The Family had changed drastically since my childhood. Instead of training the next generation through harsh discipline and boot camps, the modern Family of the new millennium was a cool place to be. The young people dressed cool, went to Family music concerts called "Wordstock" and big meetings, all in an effort to instil the Family doctrines in a cool way.

I realized the second generation of today were all young kids and that very few from my age group and above were left. Of the entire Heavenly City School of over one hundred young people, there were only about five I knew of who remained in the Family. I calculated that there were only about 2000 second-generation young people remaining. Of that, at least half were under twenty years old, meaning they would be too young to remember anything from the past. So, 1000 members of my age and older remained. Over 36,000 members have passed through the group. If even a third of them were second generation, then by the laws of averages, less than one tenth remained in the Family.

All the incriminating letters had been purged during the court cases, and no evidence of the Family's dark history remained except in the memories of those who lived through it. Most of the young people writing testimonials on the Family's websites were under twenty and had no recollection of the hard times. I wondered how they could claim the Family was the best place in the world when they knew nothing else.

Queen Maria started releasing letters saying anyone who left could be influenced by the Devil and tell exaggerated stories. A smear campaign began against any ex-member young people speaking out about their harmful experiences, or asking for explanations and apologies. Any abuse, Maria said, that may have occurred in the past had been apologized for, and it was only a handful of bitter vocal apostates, who were bent on destroying the Family and stopping our good work, who were spreading lies. This angered me because I knew these things had happened on a larger scale than Maria was saying. I lived through four Family Training Schools around the world and witnessed the widescale abuse practised on all us children. It was not the fault of the younger generation that they believed Maria. They had no memories of that time. They were too young, or not yet born. I said as much one day, as we read one of these letters in devotions.

"But it did happen!" I persisted stubbornly. I knew I would get in trouble for dissension, but I had reached a point where I didn't care anymore. They could do their worst, but I was tired of being silent. "I remember well. It happened to me. It happened to my sisters, my family, my friends! History has been rewritten!"

After Celeste left Uganda, Tina's mother Keda joined the home. She had been a top leader for many years and was still on the payroll of World Services receiving a monthly stipend. She took it upon herself to shepherd the home and Dad buckled under her influence like a little lamb. Keda had the uncanny ability to sniff out potential rebels. She corrected me for my outburst and said I needed to have a prayer of deliverance against bitterness. I went through the motions, but could not deny my memories.

I started a more regular correspondence with Celeste. Now, more than ever, I was interested to see not just the one-sided picture I was being fed in the group. The doubts I was voicing set off alarm bells with Dad. He approached me and asked whether I was writing to Celeste.

"Once in awhile, she'll write to me with her news," I answered.

"I think you should limit all contact with her," Dad said.

"What? Why?" I knew perfectly well why.

Celeste had been featured in a magazine article about her time in the group. She was now possessed by a Vandari—a blood-sucking parasite demon. She had gone over to the dark side.

Dad was having nothing more to do with her, and neither should I. I was shocked at Dad's cold-hearted dismissal of his own child now that she no longer adhered to the Family's beliefs.

"I'm not going to stop writing to my sister, Dad. Don't worry, I'll keep it positive, tell her our witnessing testimonies."

I knew that would reassure Dad enough to drop the subject for the time being, though he continued to check up on me from time to time. I realized anything I said would be twisted and used against Celeste. This upset me. I had my own thinking mind. Why couldn't I take responsibility for my own doubts without Dad throwing the blame on my sister?

CHAPTER TWENTY-SEVEN

Breaking Free

Juliana

Something in me finally snapped. The folly of it all smacked me in the face like a gust of refreshing wind. After that, there was no going back.

I began to feel the confines of my cage, stunted like a claustrophobic imprisoned in a tiny world. It was a prison with invisible bars. A prison of the mind. At times I was seized with a desperate panic, when I felt sure I would either go mad or explode.

Despite the endless attempts to try and turn me into that perfect little Family girl, they had never been able to get into my head, the place I frequently retreated to, the hiding place I had stumbled upon as a child where no one could touch me. I secreted away the innocent child in me and kept her hidden indefinitely, safe from the beatings, the humiliation, and lone-liness.

After some time, I forgot her existence entirely. Time and years grew over the lock, until it was hard to tell there had even been a door. Eventually, she grew tired of the confines of her "safe," and began to knock on the door. I heard the pounding every so often like a frantic beat in my pulse. A familiar voice called out to me begging for release, but I could not remember where the voice was coming from.

Finally one fateful day the child broke through the door. I recognized a little piece of my identity, but it was an emaciated creature who emerged from that inner chamber.

"Why did you leave me?" her haunting eyes asked me in the mirror.

"I wanted to protect you."

"From what?"

"From pain."

"Then leave it." Her answer was so simple I wondered why I hadn't thought of it before.

"I will." And I did.

It started with a trip to Europe for a family reunion, with relatives and grandparents on my mum's side meeting up in Portugal. On the way, I decided to visit Celeste and my brothers and sisters in England whom I hardly knew. My father argued against my visit, saying my sisters would turn me to the dark side. The visit was a turning point, but to what "side" was a question of perspective.

In July 2004 I found myself in Celeste's cosy flat in the Midlands. I gave her the news from Africa and Dad. Then we decided to go and see the sister I had never met before. Kristina greeted me with a massive hug as I entered her house. I found my bitter, vengeful, Vandari sister to be a beautiful person inside and out. I understood the saying "blood is thicker than water" then. No amount of dehumanizing and demonising of my ex-Family family could lessen my affection for them, or keep me away. Deep down, I knew it could not be true, and it wasn't.

Yet, the side of me that had been so brainwashed to think the way I was told to tried to surface one last time. Celeste, Kristina and I went out to a nightclub and began talking over the loud music. The conversation turned, inevitably, to the Family. Kristina began to speak of the evils done, expressly by Maria and Mo.

Suddenly a voice out of nowhere screamed, *Vandari, Vandari, Vandari! Don't listen!* And a picture came into my mind of that creature dripping blood from every opening in its face. It scared me. Had I been so conditioned that I was imagining my own sister to be a blood-sucking demon of the Netherworld? In a flash of disgust I understood the true evil. Any group that could divide a family like that was the real monster, not the other way round.

This was my point of no return. I went to the family reunion in Portugal, my mind made up. I would not return to Dad … to the Family.

In the south of Portugal, I saw my brother Victor and my sisters Mariana and Lily again. Victor had left the Family, and I wanted to talk with him about it. He had been through a serious car accident in Senegal and nearly died. When he awoke from his coma, he began to seriously think about his life and what he wanted to achieve, realizing how short life is. "During the time I was comatose," he told me, "there was nothing. No alternative reality, no spirit world, like we have been told. Just blackness. That was when I realized that there is no God."

Every day I strolled down to the deserted end of the beach, and sat for hours, thinking. The foaming waves crashing on the shore and the wind whipping through my hair had a calming effect that contrasted with the turmoil inside my head. My mind grew weary trying to process the barrage of foreign ideas, which I had refused to entertain until now. I had opened Pandora's Box, and could no longer shut it. So I let my mind run in dizzying circles until it was thoroughly exhausted; I thought I would go mad.

It's difficult to wake up and realize your entire life has been spent living someone else's lie; that you've been kept from living your own dreams in order to keep the manic delusions of one man alive. It's like believing you were born blind because you have spent your whole life blindfolded. Then when you suddenly do see, you cannot understand what it is you're seeing.

In Portugal I told my mum that I had decided to leave the Family. She begged me to try for just six more months and if things did not get better, then she'd accept my choice. After thinking about it further, I decided I would return to Uganda and promised Mum I would stay for six more months. If I were going to leave, I would not do it the cowardly way. I was also worried about leaving my little brothers and sister behind. I wanted to keep an eye on them and help maintain contact between their flesh family and the outside world.

During the months that followed, I did everything by the book, but my heart was no longer in it. I went through every fundamental Family belief and researched every letter written by Mo on the biggest doctrinal controversies, and went through the entire Bible on the very same subjects. I discovered some shocking truths. Anybody can twist Scripture to their own ends. For every single verse the Family used to justify one of their doctrines, there were four that argued against them.

I realized that I had grown up looking through the wrong side of the glass. Like Alice in Wonderland, I lived the distorted reality of a bizarre upside-down world that made no sense. I was a seeker of truth, embarking on my quest for enlightenment. I started with an open mind, and ended with a closed one. It was shut tight against those beliefs I had been told were God's truth, Mo's truth.

My life had been a sequence of barred gates, and this journey opened them one after the other, until a horizon of infinite possibility stretched before me. I stood on the brink of freedom, but I was terrified of jumping. I needed a push to take the plunge.

Davidito pushed me off.

The morning we were gathered for an urgent all-homes notice, we all sensed something was seriously wrong. The message was read saying that Davidito had killed Angela Smith before shooting himself in the head. He had recorded a videotape the night before his death, though none of us knew what was on it.

The entire room fell into a hushed shock. The message said that Davidito had allowed Satan into his mind and had gone over to the dark side, but that there were encouraging prophecies. Now Davidito had passed over he saw how wrong he had been, and was truly sorry. He had betrayed his birthright in the Family. He had cried tears of repentance in

Heaven's halfway house and he had been forgiven not just by Jesus but even by Angela.

Nobody moved. Davidito had been glorified as the little prince from the day he was born into the Royal Household. We all grew up looking up to him as a shining star. This tragedy sent shock waves through the Family.

It was so unexpected and unnerving that everyone started talking to release their agitation. I kept quiet because it seemed irreverent to speak at such a time, and I felt no inclination to do so. The "prophecies" had knotted my stomach and I wanted to puke.

"This is heavy stuff! The war in the spirit is intensifying. The Enemy's starting to pull out his big guns."

"It just goes to show how even someone as close to Grandpa as Davidito could fall so far to the point of possession."

"If it could happen to him, how much more to any of us."

I was amazed and angry. It felt like they were spitting on his grave. After ten minutes I could stand it no longer and spoke up. "Don't you guys think there had to have been something terribly wrong for someone to be driven to this extreme?" Everyone turned to look at me. "I mean, honestly, you have to be pretty desperate to reach the point where you feel the only choice left is death! Davidito was a very normal, very kind person. People don't just snap for no reason."

"No, Julie! You're right, they don't," Keda interrupted. "This is a perfect example of how letting Satan in can turn a perfectly normal person into a murderer."

I left the room before my anger overwhelmed me. Anger at the Family's self-righteous presumption that Davidito had now repented in Jesus' arms, and at everyone's blindness in failing to see why the event had occurred at all.

Davidito was just one of many ex-members to kill themselves. Nobody was asking why. His own mother, Queen Maria, did not appear the least bit heartbroken; her son was apparently better off dead than in the Devil's clutches.

The next day I packed my bags and walked out of the house. I went to stay with a friend, but I needed to get away completely. I decided to help out in the Tsunami relief work, and so a friend and I went to Sri Lanka.

The devastation was incredible. Two-thirds of the island's shoreline had been hit. With the money we raised, we were able to send five hundred displaced children back to school, buying schoolbooks, pencils, backpacks and uniforms. We went through the tents of the displaced and brought each family a gas cooker. And we spent time listening to their stories of loss. Lost loved ones, lost homes, lost possessions, but mostly, lost hope. I read a quote on a wall:

Never lose sight of your dreams.
For to be without dreams is to be without hope
And to be without hope is to be without purpose.

I had stopped allowing myself to dream, because "hope deferred makes the heart sick." But I was finally free, in charge of my own life. And I could dare to dream. I felt alive like never before, knowing that whatever came my way, I could deal with it. I was not without hope. It was on this thought that I flew back to Uganda.

Less than an hour back in Kampala, Dad asked me to go somewhere private. "There are little ears around."

After making sure there were no children in earshot, he turned to me. "Well, during the time you were away, Davida passed on."

My mind drew a complete blank. I wasn't sure who he was speaking about.

"Who?"

"Davida, your sister."

"My sister Davida, what?"

"Well, she's...she's dead."

I laughed then. "Yeah, very funny, Dad. Is this your idea of a good joke? She's not dead!"

But the look in his eyes said otherwise. "Honey, she's dead. I was contacted by the Family in Greece."

"I...I don't understand. When? How?" I could not believe this; it had to be some misunderstanding.

"About a week after you left for Sri Lanka, I got an email. The details are unclear, but there was a phone call from Sotiria. She was blubbering incoherently, crying and saying over and over, 'He's killed her. He's killed her.'"

"Who? Who killed her?" It hadn't sunk in yet.

"Her boyfriend, Stavros."

"So you're not joking?"

He shook his head. "I didn't want to tell you till you got back, so it wouldn't distract you from the work you were doing there."

While I was helping the survivors in Sri Lanka, my own sister was dying. I was still in shock too much to feel anything. I looked at Dad's face. I expected to see signs of grief a normal father would show, but Dad showed nothing. Instead he had a kind of, *Oops, that's too bad, but such is life*, attitude.

"You don't look too cut up about it," I said. "Aren't you even sad?"

"Honey, of course! We may not have been close, but she was still my daughter. It's not exactly fresh news to me now. It took me a few days, but I got over it," he said rather flippantly.

I could feel my blood begin to boil. "Really? A few days!"

"Julie, sweetheart, you know your sister was a drug addict. She's much better off now. If anything, it's a comfort to know she is happy in a better place."

"Yes, it must be comforting." I sneered. "Especially as her death was your fault!"

"What? What do you mean her death was my fault?"

"Why do you think she became a drug addict in the first place? If you had been a proper father, she would never have turned to drugs, she would never have met Stavros and she would not be dead today!"

Dad looked stunned. "Honey, you're just upset. You know that's not true. I know you need someone to blame right now, but my being her father or not had nothing to do with her death."

"It had everything to do with it, Dad!"

"Julie, you're being irrational!"

"I don't care if I am! My sister, your daughter, is dead! I think I have a right to be irrational. Have you called Sotiria? Did you speak to her?"

"No. I assumed if she wanted to contact me, she would. I don't think she wants to speak to me."

"I wonder why that is! Have you told anyone else in our family? Do Kristina and Celeste know?"

"Uh, no actually."

"Give me Sotiria's number, please. I'm going to call her and find out what really happened. I'm only surprised you haven't."

"Well, I thought maybe you'd be better to do that."

I could no longer speak. I would only say something rash. Breathing slowly, I steadied my voice. "Find it for me now, please. I'll wait downstairs."

I ran down the stairs. I could no longer look at Dad. I just wanted to leave. Leave his presence. Leave this house where death righted all wrongs. How long might Dad mourn for me if I died, I wondered, if at all?

He came down and handed me a paper with the number written on it. "Keep me updated," he said.

The next few days I moved about in a daze of remorse. I felt I had deserted my sister. I had not been back to see her. I had not called her in almost two years. And now she was dead, and she probably died thinking I'd abandoned her just like everyone else. I knew the pain of abandonment is one of the worst of all and what did I do? I abandoned someone I loved for a cult that did not love me.

Why? Had the pressure to leave her been that strong? I knew it came back to my father. He always used to mock that he could play me like a violin and I knew it was true. I wanted his love and approval. Dad could give love and withhold it as it suited him. He withheld it from Davida because she was not part of his bigger Family. Not only was she an outsider, a Systemite, but more embarrassing still, she was a drug addict!

With Davida's death, my ties with the Family and my father died too.

I learned more about life and death in those three months than in my whole life up until then. There was no bearded man in the sky judging who deserved to live and die. Death makes no distinction. Death is a great leveller; it reaches everyone. All you have is time. Through my sister's death, I experienced my own rebirth. She had died, and I lived. Well then, I'd do a bloody good job of my time! For Davida, I thought. Do it for two and live twice as hard!

For the first time, I allowed myself to look into the future. I realized I could accomplish anything I set my mind to, and the only person who could hold me back was myself. I was determined then to prove to Dad and the Family that I could thrive without their help. I left with $300 of my hard-earned savings, which I promptly handed over to a friend from Congo to assist his orphanage there. Then I went into battle, as it were.

My first purpose was clear to me—helping the plight of the child soldiers in Congo and the north of Uganda. They were children who had been kidnapped by the rebel factions and made to kill, and sometimes even eat, their own families. The rebels used this unbelievably cruel method to turn children into little killing machines. I had been exposed to different and less lethal violence but I knew what it was like to be robbed of one's childhood.

I drove to Gulu in northern Uganda with Kirsten, a Scottish woman who became one of my closest friends. We took all kinds of supplies, and we agreed to help raise money to send the brightest of these children to school in Kampala. The hope was to educate them to come back and work towards reconciliation and peace. I organized an art exhibition with a number of local and international artists on the topic of "Children in Conflict" and found sponsors for the event.

The cocktail opening of the exhibition was held at the Sheraton Hotel and featured in the two largest English newspapers and aired on the local TV station. Predictably, the entire Family Home showed up for the event and took pictures, which they later used in their monthly newsletter, flaunting the fundraiser as one of their own.

Within three months, I had my own apartment, a car and a job as manager of one of the largest nightclubs in Kampala. I received news that Mariana and Lily had left the Family. We were all out of the cult now, except the youngest siblings.

Dad was speechless with amazement. He had not expected me to succeed, let alone so quickly.

I kept myself busy, so that I would not have time to think, but I could not keep up the pace forever. Now at last on the other side, I understood the reality. You may be able to forgive, but you cannot just "forget," nor erase a lifetime of memories. Unlike a computer memory, the mind has no "delete" button.

Most of the time I pushed it to the back of my mind, but the smallest incident would bring it all flooding back. I had been four months out of the cult, and two months into my job, when I started to shut down. It was the same feeling I had when I was dragged down by anorexia—a deep, suffocating sadness. The only place I felt at peace was on the roof of the four-storey apartment building where I lived. I would stand balanced on one foot at the edge of the pinnacle, not because I thought of jumping, but because it put all the madness back into perspective.

I knew I could not carry on the way I was going for much longer, but when I was sexually assaulted in my own office, I reached the peak of my endurance. My job at the nightclub had become unbearable. I was sick of having to reason with unreasonable drunks. Sick of breaking up fights, locking up guns. Sick of watching young kids dealing coke under my nose. Sick of seeing perverted old men escorting home underage girls who were too drunk to realize how their night would end. Sick of being hit on by nearly every man in the club simply because I was the manager. Sick of catering to rich tycoons who indulged their every whim while elsewhere in the country children were starving to death. Sick of being powerless to do anything about it.

It had been a monumental year and I needed time out to think and heal, to resolve the past and move on. I had promised Sotiria that I would go and see her. I knew she suffered greatly over my sister's death and it was nagging at me like unfinished business, so I dropped my job and flew out to Greece.

Sotiria met me at the airport and that evening we talked as we sat outside a small pizzeria in Athens. I told her about my trip to Sri Lanka and the Tsunami relief.

"Ah yes! Terrible thing. So many children die this year. Davida cry when she watch that on the news. And soon after? She die herself." Her eyes grew sad.

"The day I returned home, Dad asked to speak to me," I continued. "He said my sister had passed away. I was so mad,

I could not even cry. I told him if he kept in contact she would never have got depressed and started taking drugs, and so she would never have died."

"And what did he say?"

"He said I was just upset, and needed someone to blame it on and not to be ridiculous."

"Sweetie." She put out her cigarette. "I have been wanting to write your dad for a long time, but always I decided against it. Now Davida is dead … I want to tell him all the truth. I did not want to say when you came with him to visit, but Davida, she start drugs because of him. She did not understand why her father did not want to keep contact with her. She was a very sensitive child. She was very hurt."

"It was not just her. It was all his kids. Even me."

She grew quiet and we withdrew into our thoughts. She lit another cigarette, took another drag. Finally she spoke again. "You have suffered even more than Davida. She told me this. She said to me one day after you had left, 'Mum, at least I have you my whole life. Julie has no one. What kind of father is he? He is just using her. I don't want to see him again. He is no father. I only want to see Julie.'"

"She said that?"

"Yes. After that time, she want nothing more with your dad. She was very angry. But she always love you. You must remember that. She love you very much," she said.

"Yes. I know. I loved her too." It was strange we were so close, as we had met only once.

My phone rang and I fumbled through my bag till I found it. It was Nikos, Davida's uncle. My sister and Nikos had been very close; he loved her like his own child, and she was his best friend and confidant. Maybe he could offer me a little more insight into the life of my sister. We arranged to meet the next day and go to the beach for a coffee.

The next day Nikos and I went to a pretty seaside cafe that I vaguely recognized and found a secluded spot with an undisturbed view of the ocean.

"Sotiria tells me Davida used to write some diaries."

"Yes. She wrote many things. I am planning to write a book telling her story with these diaries. I have it here." He pointed to his head. "I will do it one day. But not yet. Not now. It is too soon."

"I wish I could read them. I want to know all about her. Was she happy after she got off drugs?"

"At times. At times she was happy, but most of the time very depressed."

"Why? What was she depressed about?"

He poured coffee from the pot into his cup. "Well ... for Davida ... she live in two worlds. One was this material world around us, the other..." his voice trailed off as he tried to find the words in English, "...the other, the spiritual. She could never adjust to this one. It was very difficult for her. She tell me, she could not feel. She feel dead."

"Because of drugs?"

"Maybe, yes. At times she was fine. She would be with friends, and go out. Other times, she just shut off her phone and not speak to anyone for a week, two weeks. She like to be alone. She don't like people. She could not hold any relationship. She tell me once she would like a man, and be with him maybe a week, and then, ah!" He wiped his hands. "She don't want to see them again. They bored her. She would not see them again. So, she prefer to be alone."

If only I had been here, I thought to myself. *I understood. She would not have felt so alone.*

Nikos continued: "And she was so beautiful! She tell me her beauty was like a curse. Men always follow her down the street, call to her, all the men fall in love with her. She don't want any of them. She could not love anybody. She expect them to leave her in the end. So anybody she start to feel something for, she push away and never see again."

I understood then. "It started with our father."

"Yes. She expect all men to be like her father. Even friends. She could not accept love from anybody."

"Sotiria thinks Stavros killed Davida. Do you think so?"

"Uuh … yes, Sotiria likes to believe this, but I don't know. He would not kill her I think. She told me one day, maybe a month before she die, that she fight very hard not to take drugs, every day she must fight. And she say she is tired to try. One day she will take again, and that day she will die."

"She told you this?"

"Yes. She did not feel any will to live. She tired of life. I don't know what is truth, but maybe because she meet Stavros again one week before she die."

"She met him again?"

"Yes, he find her at her work and she talk to him. I don't know. Maybe he gave her drugs and she not strong enough to fight him … ah! Yassus Sotiria!"

I had been concentrating so much on what he was saying I did not notice Sotiria approach. She kissed her brother, pulled up a chair and sat down between us. I told them about Davidito's tragic death.

Sotiria crossed herself and muttered, "God's mercy. I pray every day for these children, for their souls. Poor children! Poor, poor children." She pulled out a cigarette and lit up. "You know, I never lie to Davida. Always I tell her, her father is busy with his life, and we have ours. But if she want, when she turn eighteen, she can go to see him. But then, this woman who live with your father calls one day when Davida is fifteen. She tells her many things about her father, and so she writes to him and her father sends her a letter."

I cleared my throat. "I ... I remember that letter."

Celeste and I were horrified when he showed us his letter. We told him that we thought it was insensitive; he emphasized that he had a new family now. We had asked him to write another one apologizing for abandoning her. We added a letter of our own and gifts, but a year later Dad told us that they never received the package. Then we heard that she had started taking drugs.

"After his first letter," Sotiria continued, "she never hears anything again. So she becomes very depressed. This is when she begin to drink and take drugs. When you visit I say nothing to him about this. But now I understand, he did not come because he want to know her. He come for himself. Just to make peace with his own conscience. I think I am going to call now that she is gone, and tell him what I think. You think it will do any good? He will even listen?"

"Maybe. I think if he hears it from enough people, he may wake up to the fact that he has been a negligent father to many of his children."

"You know after you leave, she very angry with him. She say, 'He is no father. Not to me, not to Julie. I never want to see him again. What he want me to come to Uganda for? What I do there? Only to work for him like Julie. No, I don't want to go. I will only fight with him.'"

By this time night had fallen and a cold wind blew around us. Nikos looked at his watch.

"Come on, let's go get dinner," Sotiria offered. "Tomorrow, we will visit Davida's grave."

The next day, a gray morning saw us make our way through the cemetery towards Davida's grave. Row after endless row of crosses stretched into the distance. It was a full five minutes before we reached the area where Davida's grave lay. Even from afar, it stood out from the rest.

"I did not like the idea of marble," Sotiria explained.

Instead of marble, the entire plot had been turned into a luscious garden. Bright purple and orange gardenia and chrysanthemums bloomed amidst roses of every size and color. A huge red rose, the size of three ordinary roses, leaned against a tall ornate cross at the head of the grave with a statue of an angel on one side, and a dancer posed gracefully on the other. There was a heart with a picture of Davida dancing and a short epitaph inside written by her mother.

"Do you think I could have just a couple minutes alone to talk to Davida?" I asked.

"Yes, of course. Take as much time you like. I just go for a smoke, okay?"

I watched her walk away, waiting till she was a good distance. When she was out of sight, I found myself still waiting. For what, I was not sure. Maybe for the words to come:

I wanted so badly to say something, but what it was eluded me. The cemetery seemed unnaturally still, as if it was holding its breath … or me.

"Davida … I came to tell you something, and now that I'm here, I don't know what to say. I guess, I just had to see you again."

And though I had fought it hard the whole visit, I finally cried. "I'm so sorry. I'm sorry I did not come to see you again. I'm sorry I left you and you felt so alone. I'm sorry your life was such a difficult struggle and you had such a rough go of it. But mostly I'm sorry I was not there to help you. I know it's too late now to say it, but I want you to know how much you meant to me. How much I loved you … love you still and always. I want you to know that I will live my life the best I can, for both of us, okay? Goodbye, sister."

I kissed my hand, put it against her picture, and walked away without looking back.

As I left Greece, I thought of the last entry in Davida's diary:

I am looking at the sky, the trees, the lights and the people. All leaving their smells on this world. I wish to forget all the times of pain and loneliness. I wish that time would stop and I could go back to the center of Athens to see again the people who have broken my heart; to see my fears, inside their sad faces.

They looked into my blue eyes and not the pain that is in my heart. I cry, I sing, and I wait for someone to embrace me.

CHAPTER TWENTY-EIGHT

The Chained Eagle

Juliana

I drove into the commune to pick Dad up for a drink. We had not spoken more than a couple sentences since my return from Greece, and I felt it was time to break the stalemate. I had a letter to deliver from Sotiria, and I could not keep putting it off.

Going back to the commune house always made me edgy. Everyone inside wore a fake veneer that reminded me of the passage in the Bible calling false believers "whitened sepulchres full of dead men's bones." The Family loved to use this verse against church Christians, but I thought this passage applied to them. I knew the same lips now stretched in welcoming smiles were more often exercised in prayers against those like my sisters and I, who were speaking the truth.

I drove with Dad to a nearby wine bar.

Naturally, I was paying.

We sat at a light wood table; two glasses of cheap white wine before us, and waded through the usual small talk. Then I produced the letter.

Dad made a show of opening the grubby envelope, pulled out the sheets of smudged notebook paper and settled down to read. He skimmed over the broken handwriting far too quickly and folded the pages back into the envelope.

There was an unsettling silence, as he contemplated what to say. I let him squirm, in no mood to start the dialog.

"What can I say?" he looked up at me, but I remained silent.

"What can I say?" He repeated again, as if I should give him a cue; he was starting to sound like a broken record— annoying.

"If I could do it all over again, I'd do it differently." The large gulp of wine he swallowed seemed to suddenly lubricate his tongue.

"Would you?" My voice had a sarcastic edge that surprised me. I did not plan to get into any kind of argument. Arguing with Dad is a tiring pastime I did not have the energy for. I was perfectly content to deliver the letter and let it speak for itself, but his calculated response set me off.

"Of course I would, honey," he replied.

"How? How do you think you would have done it differently?"

"Well, I wouldn't have left you guys."

"Yes, you would!" I snapped back a bit too quickly.

"Honey, of course not!"

This childish back and forth was getting us nowhere. I counted to ten before responding, this time in an attempt to reason.

"Dad, you would never have even considered the idea of leaving your wives and children if you had not been told to."

"*No!* I gave you up because God asked me to."

"Was that before or after 'leadership' approached you and asked you to 'pray' about leaving us for God's Work? The idea would never even have crossed your mind if someone hadn't put it there."

"No! I prayed about it, and I felt that was God's will for me. Besides, I left you in the best care."

This drove me over the edge. "The best care! How do you know that?"

"Because. They sent me reports. I got letters from you. You always sounded very happy and well-cared for."

"And so you blindly took their word for it." I was smiling now, but it was the furious smile that involuntarily crosses my face when I am about to explode. "Did you never think your children might have been abused? Anyone can take a snapshot of your kids smiling and say they're happy. There was not a word we wrote to you that wasn't censored. They took pictures of us all dressed up, after which we were promptly undressed, and never saw those nice clothes again!"

I was seething now. "If you hadn't pursued your famous career, we would have had a father. How could you put such blind trust in people you didn't even know?"

"I trusted the Lord for you," he replied, "and you were left in the best hands. Just look at you! You've turned into a fine young woman."

"No thanks to the Family or you! I was a sad, scared little girl, a depressed suicidal teenager and an unfulfilled adult. You knew this. Did you never ask why?"

"Sweetheart, there are thousands of kids abused all over the world, and in comparison, you were very well off."

"Oh please! Don't try to minimize our experiences by comparing it with someone else's. One of your children is dead; all of us except the youngest have left the Family. Did you never once stop to think that maybe the Family is not all you imagine it to be?"

"The Family is a very unique place; the best in the world, of course; but it's not for everyone. It's a high calling."

"More like a never-ending struggle! Don't you get tired of constantly trying to attain this illusive state of perfection that's always just out of reach? I sure did!"

"Well, all I know is when the Endtime rolls around, it will be the best place to be!" he answered confidently.

"When the Endtime rolls around? And what if it doesn't? I never expected to live past twelve years old. You've been living your entire life on tenterhooks thinking 'it's just around the corner.' And when you're on your death bed, and Jesus still hasn't come back, will you still be saying, 'you'll see'?"

"You can believe what you want, sweetheart, but when it happens, you'll all come crawling back to the Family with your tails between your legs."

"Still believe you're going to be the leaders of the Christians and save the world? Do you really think the world respects the Family? Your past has soiled you forever in their eyes. Do you actually believe that you're going to be shooting lightning rods out of your fingers, blasting Antichrist helicopters out of the sky? Come on, Dad! Life is not a science-fiction movie!"

"Yes, of course I believe it. I don't know how it's going to happen, all I know is, the Lord said it. And it's happening already! Just look at our radio show here listened to by thousands of Ugandan Christians."

"Actually, Dad, you've been stuck out here in Africa so long, you can't see the big picture." His naivety was infuriating and yet I found I also pitied him.

"The Family is in the headlines, but not in a good way," I explained, "especially since Davidito's death. Just how much does your Christian audience know about the Family's beliefs? Do you think you'd still have any kind of following if they knew about your 'Law of Love' beliefs? If they knew about your sexual beliefs? About your 'Loving Jesus' beliefs?"

He was silent, but finally, he replied like a programed zombie. "Well, we'll see! All I know is, if the Lord said it, it's going to happen."

"Over two thirds of our generation have left the Family. Thousands of them have horrific stories to tell. Many suffer depression; some have committed suicide. Doesn't the Bible say, 'By their fruits you shall know them'? Isn't that a pretty good indication that something is seriously wrong with the fruit of the Family's doctrines?"

"No," he was quick to respond. "If they leave the Family, then they are no longer under God's protection, so the enemy can get them. The Bible also says, 'Many are called, but few are chosen.'"

"That's a nice line you've been fed so you'll feel better about your rapidly dwindling ranks. I know the Bible as well as you. Jesus said, 'If one of you shall offend one of these little ones in My name, it were better for him that a millstone be hung about his neck and he were cast into the sea.' I wonder what he would have thought of the hundreds of little ones the Family abused in 'His' name?"

"I don't understand. Why have you become so bitter? Why can't you just leave it alone and move on? I don't judge you for living a Systemite lifestyle; why do you have to judge us for ours?"

The old "Us-versus-Them" syndrome the cult created was clearly showing.

"I'm not judging you, Dad. I'm trying to get you to understand that some terrible things happened and you want to close your eyes and pretend they don't exist."

"I'm not denying they existed in the occasional rare circumstance, but this has all been apologized for numerous times."

"No, they made large sweeping statements saying that they're sorry if some members took things to the extreme and mistakes were made. Well, it was a lot more widespread than anyone is willing to admit. It's not in the past when many of our generation are still suffering psychological damage. 'Mistake' is a nice sounding word for it. 'Crimes' is much closer to the truth."

"Now you sound just like a bitter apostate."

"How clichéd, Dad. Now you just sound brainwashed."

I paused to take a drink, expecting some half-baked retort, but Dad just sat there staring blankly, so I continued. "I thought God doesn't make mistakes."

"He doesn't. It was people who made them."

"But these 'revelations' were supposed to have come from God. These 'revelations' condoning free love—with children. So the theory wasn't wrong, just the practice...since they have since admitted the practice was wrong?"

"The practice wasn't wrong. It was the System who made it wrong." This was the reason he had never believed any of his children were hurt. He never thought of it as abuse.

"Wake up, Dad! The 'System' as you call it is the law! And it is illegal to have sexual relations with children. It is illegal to practise incest! You can be thrown in jail for it. It is wrong, no matter what. And don't tell me you would let an old man have sex with little Shirley!"

"No, of course not! And no one was practising incest!"

"Actually, that's not true! Your very own leaders—Zerby—Maria—having sex with her own son. Berg—with his daughters, and his granddaughter Mene!"

Dad's face went red with rage. "How dare you speak like that about God's prophet!"

"God's prophet? Says who? I know he said it, so that makes him right? Anybody can prophesy, but you know a true prophet by the accuracy of his prophecies. Show me one prediction Berg made that came true!"

He did not have an answer, so he had to change the subject. "Zerby! Berg! Why do you call them that?"

"That's their names, Dad! What's wrong with using their names? Why does it bother you?"

"Would I call you Buhring? Would you call me by my last name?"

"I'm your daughter. Obviously, that's not the same." His arguments were becoming more ridiculous by the minute. He was no match and he knew it. "I would call Keda 'Yamaguchi'—who I happen to know helped to kidnap a little boy from his mother, and forged illegal documents and passports for the leaders. I have no doubt she's here in Africa because it's the safest place to bunker down outside the law."

"So what do you want to do—throw her in jail?" Was it just my imagination, or was his hand shaking as he raised his drink.

"I think there comes a time when everyone must pay for the crimes they've committed whether in or out of the Family. What goes around comes around. That's all any of the abused parties want—justice. All secrets have a way of coming to light. What was that verse? 'There is nothing hidden that shall not be revealed. What was whispered in the closet shall be shouted from the rooftops.'"

"Look at that! Justice. Revenge. You've turned to the dark side just like the rest of them."

"Turned to the 'dark side'?"

"Yes. You've let your bitterness take you over. You've listened to your sisters."

"And now I'm possessed by Vandari demons?"

"I didn't say that."

"But if I've turned to the 'dark side' I would have to be under demonic influence. That's what the Family believes, isn't it? Honestly, Dad! Look into my eyes and tell me I'm influenced by demons!"

He did, briefly, before turning back to stare into his own murky reflection in the glass.

"I don't know," he quivered weakly. "It's possible."

"You don't know? Can you honestly look at your daughter who you've lived with the last five years and consider the idea that she may be possessed by demons?"

"I do know by the way you're carrying on you've become a foe of my household."

"A foe of your household?"

"Yes, you are, if you're attacking the people I love like my own family."

"Dad, we aren't foes of your household. We are your household! We are your family!"

"Jesus said, 'Those who do the will of My Father the same are my mother, my sisters and my brothers.' You left your birthright and your highest calling to become a Systemite. The people in the Family are my true family."

"So you were lying when you told me you were proud of me and what I was doing? How do you know the Family was my highest calling?"

"It's the highest calling in the world."

"What's right for one may not be right for another. How can you claim to know the mind of God? Dad, if Kristina and other kids like her hadn't spoken out about what was happening, the Family would still be the same today. It could very well be that they were being used of God to do His will."

"You're just consumed with bitterness!" This was the best rebuttal he could give, and he used it for everything.

"Bitterness? Against who?" I almost choked.

"Against me."

"Bitter against you? No, Dad, I feel nothing but pity for you."

And I realized that I really did pity him. He stubbornly stuck to Berg's beliefs and it cost him his loves, his children, his life and his youth. Had it been worth it? When his last children left him in the end, would he finally give up, I wondered? He was staking all his hopes in these last kids, like he had once put in Celeste, and when she had disappointed, in me.

"Well, since you've made it very obvious you're no longer on the side of the Family, you realize I can no longer trust you."

"What do you mean?"

"Trust you to take the kids. I don't know what garbage you're going to put in their heads."

"That's crazy, Dad! I've never said a negative word to them all this time, and I could have. You know that. If they decide to leave the Family, it'll be of their own accord, because they'll realize pretty quickly, just as the rest of us did, the ridiculousness of it all."

"If I ever hear you've said anything to them at all against the Family, it'll be the last time I let you take them out."

"Of course, Dad. I promise I will not say anything to them; you have my word. Then when they do decide to leave, you will know they made the decision entirely on their own."

"They'll never leave. It'll be different with them."

"Really? What makes you so sure?"

"Because I'm giving them extra attention and personal training, and I'm being a father to them."

"So you're saying we wouldn't have left if you had been a father to us?"

"Maybe not."

"You're still taking this all personally, Dad. At the end of the day, us leaving had nothing to do with you; it had to do with the abusive doctrines Zerby and Berg were instigating. They are the ones responsible for the crimes committed, and pain inflicted. They are the ones who must be held accountable."

He visibly flinched when I mentioned their names, and I wondered, as I had countless times before, how people could allow themselves to be more loyal to a personality than to their own family, their own heart. Berg had made an idol of himself equal to God, and his word was taken as God's own. To Dad, he was the mouthpiece of God, and disrespecting him was the same as disrespecting God.

In the end, I realized, all this debating was pointless. It was best to just shake hands as friends, agreeing to disagree.

I had once desired Dad's love so desperately I would have done anything for him. Today, I feel absolutely nothing but indifference. All respect for the man he was has vanished. Today, he is a faint shadow of the man he might have been.

He still tries to tell me he loves me, but that statement is difficult to digest. He preaches love, but if his own life is anything to go by, he doesn't know what love means. If it is turning your back on your children and a blind eye to their pain; if it is letting them die over caring for their welfare; if it is calling the abuser "family" while demonizing the abused who are your own flesh and blood; if it is refusing to accept their personal choices in life and take pride in their accomplishments—then Dad is indeed full of love.

Love like a fire without heat, just ashes and smoke. A whitened sepulchre full of dead men's bones.

CHAPTER TWENTY-NINE

The Power of Love

Kristina

Once, on the bus with my five-year-old son Jordan, a stranger sitting next to me asked if I would go out with him. I politely declined, but my son quickly piped up. "Oh yes, she would love to! She needs a boyfriend."

Though this was embarrassing, I knew what my son really wanted most was a father. My brothers lived with me during the holidays and Jordan had plenty of good male role models, but it was not the same as a father. Jordan had brought me so much joy in my life, and it was hard for me to hear him ask, "When will you find me a dad?"

Though I had a number of relationships after Bryan, none of them ever turned into anything more serious. I refused to settle for anyone less than the best. The one thing I had learned and come to rely on was my determination and patience.

By the time I met Karl I had almost given up the hope of finding a soul mate and stepfather for my son. I simply did not trust myself to make the correct choices anymore after being let down and hurt so many times. Trust was a loose concept I kept trying to get right and I was used to being on my own.

It was a snowy Christmas Eve when, laden down with last-minute shopping, I stumbled into a pub for a drink with Kiron before he went traveling. He had grown up so fast and was no longer just my kid brother. He was sitting with Karl when I arrived. I knew Karl through friends from work, but we never had a real conversation.

When Kiron had to rush off, Karl invited me to stay for a drink with him. We ended up chatting for hours and found that we had many things in common. He had moved to Nottingham at nineteen to study mathematics around the same time that I arrived there with my family. After graduating, he decided to follow his dream of becoming a music producer. We knew the same people and frequented the same places. It was surprising how many times we could have met, but did not. The time had not yet been right. Our meeting that night felt like fate. There was an immediate attraction between us.

Looking after others had been my coping mechanism for so long, it was hard to stop. It made me forget about my own sadness and anxieties, but it also meant that I was not letting "little Nina" rest. Some of the decisions I made let her down, causing her to feel abandoned and frightened all over again. Karl showed me how to find the balance and put myself first sometimes. He taught me that I was allowed to be angry myself, and how to release the bottled up emotions. I needed to learn how to be able to express my feelings without fearing that love would be withdrawn from me. He created the safe environment I needed to grow as a confident adult.

There was no doubt from the start that we were meant to be. Karl called me his "moonbeam," although he told me later that he did not want to ask me out until he was confident that he could first be a good father to Jordan.

One evening he announced, "We're going to Krakow for a week over Valentine's Day."

I hugged and kissed him. I loved how romantic and thoughtful he was.

Poland was a chilling 15 degrees and crisp snow blanketed the ground. The countryside dotted with quaint little villages looked even more beautiful cloaked in white. The Hotel Retro was a cosy guesthouse overlooking the river, only a short walk from the largest "main square" in Europe. Krakow is the ancient spiritual capital of the Polish people and one of the only cities to survive the Second World War. It was amazing to finally be in the homeland of the grandmother I'd been named after.

That evening we strolled in the square and I suggested one of the many restaurants around to have a romantic dinner. I noticed Karl had been acting strangely and indecisive for the past hour. It seemed we were aimlessly wandering around the square, and I was cold and hungry.

"I'm just going over there for a minute—" he said, and wandered off with his camera.

As I stood waiting for him, the snow began to fall. All the city lights were coming on and I gazed about me at the magical scene. That was when I spotted Karl striding purposefully towards me.

"Take your hat off," he said. "I've found someone to take a picture of us together."

I slipped my woolly hat off and stuffed it in my pocket, turning to pose with him. But Karl pulled away and got down on bended knee.

"Will you marry me?" He held out the ring.

I was stunned speechless, smiling from ear to ear.

"Is that a yes then?" Karl had to ask me while he waited on a wet knee.

I looked up from him, and realized that quite a crowd had gathered, expectantly watching the scene.

"Yes!" I shouted and Karl put the ring on my finger. The crowd clapped and whistled as he picked me up and swung me around in his arms. Both of us were delirious with happiness and as we walked away from the square, the street band struck up with "All You Need is Love."

We agreed.

We entered the first café we saw, called "The Moon Bar," where we toasted our engagement. Then we phoned our friends and family with the news.

As I stared and fiddled with the ring on my finger, I noticed it was inscribed with the initials "KJ."

"That ring was given to my mother, Kathleen, by my father," Karl explained. "When my father died a few years ago, she gave it to me as a remembrance. My mother, my father and I all carry the same initials, "KJ." When I decided to propose to you, I remembered the ring—it is also inscribed with your initials—Kristina Jones."

I felt that my life had come full circle and I couldn't get any happier.

Epilogue

Over two-thirds of the second generation have broken free from the "Family" and are rebuilding their lives. David Berg's successors, Karen Zerby ('Maria') and Steven Kelly ('Peter Amsterdam'), continue to live in hiding, even from their own members. They have failed to make amends or restitution. Instead they call us liars and bitter apostates, dismiss our claims as exaggerations and portray us as blood-dripping demons.

Karen Zerby has never accepted responsibility, shown true remorse or extended compensation to those who were hurt by the doctrines and policies she and David Berg instituted. They may claim the Family no longer practises brutal physical punishment or adult/child sex, but how does that rectify the crimes that were committed or erase a whole generation of children whose innocence was stolen from them? The Family tries to hide behind a humanitarian image, but while they say they are trying to "help the world" they refuse to help their own children. Most of those guilty of crimes have not been brought to justice and many remain protected within the Family, who to this day continue to operate around the world without any firm child-protection policies in place. They have so far refused to report crimes committed by their members to the proper authorities. In England, any adult with access to children must first pass a criminal-background check. But in Family communes, members have full access to children without proper safeguards in place, increasing the risk of abuse.

Our younger brothers and sisters are still isolated and denied free access to information and appropriate education, and not told their basic human rights. They are still being indoctrinated and groomed to be God's Endtime soldiers, believing the world will end soon.

We were thrown into adulthood unprepared for life outside the cult's confines. We had no identity, no bank account, National Insurance number or medical histories. It took time to sort out what we believed and who we were. We were never taught to reason, think, analyze, or evaluate for ourselves. We had to define our personal boundaries and discover our own self-worth. There are a substantial number of children growing up in cults or high-demand organizations, and there is little current provision to help them to adjust to a new culture when they leave. Many have no support structures and feelings of embarrassment, alienation, and gaps in knowledge can make it difficult to integrate into society.

As outlined in the UN Rights of the Child, we believe that children have an equal right to "freedom of expression" and "the freedom to seek receive and impart information and ideas of all kind," and to education that allows them to develop their personality and talents to their fullest potential, and prepares them for "responsible life in free society in the spirit of understanding, peace, tolerance, equality of sexes, and friendship among all peoples" (UN Rights of the Child Article 13). A balance must be found between protecting the right to religious freedom, and protecting children from damaging or criminal behaviour justified under the guise of "religion."

Though time was lost that can never be returned to us, we are thankful for each day we have together building new memories and friendships. We feel the story of our family is a tribute to the strength of the human spirit. When we look at our accomplishments, we realize we have much to celebrate. Our brother David graduated from Oxford with a degree in Mathematics. Jonathan has a degree in Philosophy from Durham University and is a chartered accountant. Mariana lives in Senegal with her boyfriend and works in the import/export industry. Victor is reading Law at university. Lily is studying art restoration in the south of France. Rosemarie finished a college course in music and is a talented singer. Christopher finished his A-levels and is training to be a nurse. We look forward to Kiron returning from his world travels for Kristina and Karl's wedding, set for the summer of 2008.

Kristina supports and works with Safe Passage Foundation with her sisters. Celeste has worked as a volunteer for Parentline Plus, and graduated from Nottingham Trent University in 2006 with a degree in Psychology and Education. She now lives with her daughter in Somerset. Celeste is currently a family support worker and hopes to become a clinical psychologist. Juliana is pursuing her dream as a writer and is studying for a BA in Philosophy with Psychological Studies.

Together, the sisters have founded an organisation called RISE International (Resources Information Socialisation Education), which works to protect children from all forms of abuse in isolated and/or extremist cults.

We are thankful for those who supported us during difficult times and who we can count on. Despite the obstacles that were put in our path, we are living our lives free to make our own decisions and look forward to a better future, a future we thought we would never have.